THE SACRAMENTS

Readings in Contemporary

Sacramental Theology

Edited by
Michael J. Taylor, S.J.

ALBA · HOUSE   NEW · YORK

SOCIETY OF ST. PAUL, 2187 VICTORY BLVD., STATEN ISLAND, NEW YORK 10314

Library of Congress Cataloging in Publication Data

The Sacraments: readings in contemporary sacramental
theology.

Includes bibliographical references.
1. Sacraments—Catholic Church—Addresses,
essays, lectures. 2. Catholic Church—Doctrinal
and controversial works—Catholic authors—
Addresses, essays, lectures. I. Taylor, Michael J.
BX2200.S24 1981 234'.16 80-39534
ISBN 0-8189-0406-2

Designed, printed and bound in the United States of
America by the Fathers and Brothers of the
Society of St. Paul, 2187 Victory Boulevard,
Staten Island, New York 10314, as part of their
communications apostolate.

1 2 3 4 5 6 7 8 9 (Current Printing: first digit).

ACKNOWLEDGMENTS

"Do We Still Need the Sacraments?" by Joseph T. Nolan. Reprinted from *U.S. Catholic*, Vol. 38, No. 6, with permission of the publisher. *U.S. Catholic* is published by Claretian Publications, 221 W. Madison, Chicago, Illinois 60606.

"The Sacraments: A Catechism for Today" by Jared Wicks, S.J. Reprinted from *An American Catholic Catechism*, edited by George J. Dyer, copyright © 1975 by The Seabury Press, Inc. Used by permission.

"The Sacraments and Human Life" by J.D. Crichton. From *Christian Celebration: The Sacraments*, copyright © J.D. Crichton, printed by permission of Geoffrey Chapman, a division of Cassell, Ltd., London.

"Methodology and Christian Sacraments" by Kenan B. Osborne, O.F.M. Reprinted from *Worship*, Vol. 48, No. 9, pp. 536-549. Copyright © 1974 by the Order of Saint Benedict, Collegeville, Minnesota. All rights reserved.

"Models for a Liturgical Theology" by James L. Empereur, S.J. Reprinted from *Chicago Studies*, Vol. 16, No. 1 (Spring, 1977), pp. 45-62, under the title: "The Theological Experience." Reprinted with permission of the publisher.

"How to Receive a Sacrament and Mean it" by Karl Rahner, S.J. Reprinted from *Theology Digest*, Vol. 19, No. 3, pp. 227-234, with permission of the publisher.

"Initiation: Baptism and Confirmation" by Aidan Kavanagh, O.S.B. Reprinted from *Worship*, Vol. 46, No. 5, pp. 262-276. Copyright © 1972 by the Order of Saint Benedict, Collegeville, Minnesota. All rights reserved.

"Still a Case for Infant Baptism?" by Eugene Maly. Appeared under the title: "Why Baptize Babies?" in *St. Anthony Messenger*, September, 1978. Copyright © Franciscan Friars of St. John Baptist Province. Reprinted with permission of the publisher and the author.

"The Theology of Confirmation" by Thomas Marsh. Reprinted from *The Furrow*, St. Patrick's College, Maynooth, Ireland, Vol. 27 (November, 1976), pp. 606-616, with permission of the publisher.

"Eucharist, Mystery of Faith and Love" by Joseph M. Powers, S.J., appeared in *Bread From Heaven*, Paul J. Bernier, S.S.S., ed., copyright © 1977 by the Missionary Society of St. Paul the Apostle in the State of New York. Reprinted by permission of Paulist Press.

"The Unfolding Presence of Christ in the Celebration of the Mass" by Everett A. Diederich, S.J. Reprinted from *Communio*, Vol. 5, No. 4 (Winter, 1978), pp. 326-343, with permission of *Communio* and the author.

71328

CONTENTS

INTRODUCTION

Going back some thirty-five years or more and continuing up to the early seventies, sacramental theology was in the forefront of theological investigation and renewal. It is well known that one of the first major reform documents to come from the second Vatican Council was the *Constitution on the Sacred Liturgy*. This was clear evidence of the solid historical, liturgical and theological work that had been done on the sacraments prior to the council. But since the early seventies it seems sacramental theology has only rarely or passingly been discussed by the theologians. After a period of remarkable progress and development, the movement toward a deeper understanding of the sacraments seems stalled. What happened?

For one thing several theologies emerged that had a great influence on our thinking about the nature of grace and the supernatural (theology of the secular, process and liberation theologies to mention a few). Without the usual readjustment struggle many believers came to accept grace more as the mystery that capacitates us to be truly human than the mystery that elevates us to some supernatural level of being. And this has had its effects on the sacraments. We recall that they were and are regarded as grace-giving encounters, moments of special and unique access to Christ and the supernatural.

But for some years now we have been wondering if access to Christ and his grace need be so narrowly associated with these special, symbolic encounters. Could we not for instance meet Christ in a grace-giving way in the important but ordinary circumstances of life as formerly we met him at the eucharist or in confession? Earlier we knew that we could indeed, but rarely with seriousness thought through the implications of this belief. Now it is becoming more clear to many that the eucharistic, reconciling, healing Christ is also at the heart of the specifically human and secular activities that predominate our lives. Grace is not only or mainly effected in the sacraments; grace "happens" wherever human life is lived and celebrated authentically. This is not to say authenticity is endemic to the nature we inherit from Adam. No, our humanity needs redemption, it needs grace. We must be born again of the second Adam where grace abounds. But human nature *has been redeemed* and grace in

Christ *is* always available to it.

But it would seem that such an understanding of grace might render the more specific, sacred encounters with Christ we know as the sacraments less significant or important. But herein lies a problem that would be too simply solved by assuming Christ to be present only or mainly in the authentically human moments of life and not also in an imperative way in the special actions we call the sacraments. Even with a new understanding of grace the question remains, just what is the authentically human that Christ wishes and helps us to be? The only one who surely knows this, Christians believe, is God, and he has given his answer in Jesus. Jesus manifested human authenticity through his dealings with those he shared the human condition with. He revealed the truly human to us as he reacted to situations and as he lived out relationships. In the actions and reactions of his life we saw what humanity was meant to be. For us to be authentic like Christ we must know in an explicit way his authenticness. And though we now say that the one truly authentic human being meets us outside the sanctuary, it was in the sanctuary of his personal history that the mystery of grace or human authenticity was experienced in a memorable and convincing way. So those who look at sacraments as no longer valuable or important should take another look. Dealing with a mystery of authenticity we should be mindful that this mystery, like all the mysteries of life, is known not in some intuitive way but is known and understood especially as we express and celebrate it in a meaningful, symbolic way with Christ and the brethren.

Jesus reveals to us the mystery of grace with great directness in those special moments of symbolic celebration we call the sacraments. We all agree that sacraments must speak more convincingly than they have in the past to the needs, desires and hopes of human persons where they live, but they nonetheless do show what Christ specifically brings to the human condition and what the Father specifically wants for the human person. Authenticity needs Christ's presence, his example, his specific involvement, as much as it needs a consistency of effort on our part to be human in the important situations of life. In fact, we cannot be human without him. And in the sacraments we have the vision and celebrate with clarity and explicitness the mystery that Christ is with us in specific ways to facilitate our becoming human. The person who never expresses or celebrates love symbolically can wonder if he or she loves or is loved at all; one who never symbolically expresses repentance or celebrates reconciliation with the brethren can never fully know forgiveness. We who are beginning to see a mystery of grace at the heart of human life must see and celebrate it together in a formal and explicit way with Christ, else in time that mystery could escape us altogether.

The Father, his Christ and Spirit seek our love in every important circumstance of life and attach their love and presence to every important aspect of life. The sacraments must help us to see this; they must convince us that this is so. Certainly there is much work to be done to recast sacramental theology and sacramental celebration to help bring this about. Work toward this end has barely begun, but it has begun. Unfortunately, however, no systematic synthesis along these lines has been successfully undertaken. Still, in this time of transition one can discover some movement, much re-thinking, some steps being taken toward a new synthesis. And the editor has tried to assemble essays that reflect to one degree or another this movement, this new, more life-oriented, pastoral understanding of sacraments.

The essays selected for this reader are written by theologians and liturgists who obviously have a sensitive feel for where we have been these last two millenia, with an appreciation of the more permanent values we have picked up along the way. They are also clearly open to the insights coming from contemporary theologians, modern philosophers, social scientists, anthropologists, etc. Their essays are submitted to the reader not as examples of the new synthesis arrived at, so much as essays for a time of transition toward that awaited day. We may be in the process of searching for new understanding, a new synthesis, but we still need some interim food, some contemporary wisdom to nourish us along the way.

Michael J. Taylor, S.J.

CONTRIBUTORS

JOSEPH T. NOLAN, theologian, liturgist, editor of *Good News*, a professional resource publication for ministry.

JARED WICKS, S.J., author, theologian, Professor of Historical Theology, The Jesuit School of Theology, Chicago, Illinois.

J.D. CRICHTON, author, liturgist, lecturer in the field of Sacraments and Liturgy.

KENAN B. OSBORNE, O.F.M., author, theologian, Professor of Systematic Theology, The Graduate Theological Union, Berkeley, California.

JAMES B. EMPEREUR, S.J., author, theologian, Professor of Theology and Director of the Institute of Spirituality and Worship, the Jesuit School of Theology, Berkeley, California.

KARL RAHNER, S.J., internationally renowned theologian in the field of Christian Dogma and its historical development, Munich, West Germany.

AIDAN KAVANAGH, O.S.B., author, theologian, Professor of Liturgics, The Divinity School, Yale University, New Haven, Connecticut.

EUGENE MALY, biblical theologian, chairman, editorial board, *The Bible Today*, Professor of Scripture, Mount St. Mary's Seminary, Cincinnati, Ohio.

THOMAS MARSH, author, theologian, Lecturer in Theology, St. Patrick's College, Maynooth, Ireland.

JOSEPH M. POWERS, S.J., author, theologian, Professor of Systematic Theology, The Jesuit School of Theology, Berkeley, California.

EVERETT A. DIEDERICH, S.J., writer, theologian, Professor of Theology, Weston School of Theology, Cambridge, Massachusetts.

PAUL QUENON, O.C.S.O., theologian, monk, The Trappist Abbey of Gethsemani, Kentucky.

WALTER J. BURGHARDT, S.J., author, theologian in residence, Georgetown University, Washington, D.C., editor, *Theological Studies*.

GEORGE McCAULEY, S.J., author, theologian, Professor of Sacramental Theology, The Graduate Institute of Religious Education, Fordham University, New York City, New York.

LEONARDO BOFF, O.F.M., author, theologian, Professor of Systematic Theology, Institute for Philosophy and Theology, Petrópolis, Brazil.

TAD W. GUZIE, author, theologian, Professor of Religious and Moral Education, Faculty of Education, the University of Calgary, Calgary, Alberta, Canada.

ZOLTÁN ALSZEGHY, S.J., author, theologian, Professor of Dogmatic Theology, The Gregorian University, Rome, Italy.

CHARLES GUSMER, author, theologian, Professor of Sacramental Theology and Liturgy, Immaculate Conception Seminary, Darlington, New Jersey.

THOMAS TALLEY, author, theologian, Professor of Liturgics, The General Theological Seminary, New York City, New York.

DONALD J. KEEFE, S.J., writer, theologian, Professor of Dogmatic and Systematic Theology, Marquette University, Milwaukee, Wisconsin.

Readings in Contemporary

Sacramental Theology

DO WE STILL NEED THE SACRAMENTS?

Joseph T. Nolan

There is a famous story by Archbishop William Temple about his own specialty, theology. He said: "Many people think a theologian is someone who sits around with other theologians saying, 'What can we cook up for Jones to swallow?' But actually, the theologian is Jones, asking, 'What is there to eat?' "

I have felt this way after reading books on the sacraments. We don't lack for definitions; we are quite sure, at least, that we are dealing with signs and rituals. But even if we call them sacred signs, a great many people are asking: *"What is there?"* "Grace," is the shortest answer, but what is grace? The old answers were: Supernatural life. A participation in God's life. Divine life. These are still valid answers, but they do not seem as helpful today, for several reasons.

What is in the Sacraments?

It is difficult or impossible for man today to believe that he has a higher life that is "super" or superior to his fellowman simply because he is baptized and the other is not. He knows much more about his neighbor and the world than formerly: he knows there are Hindu saints and Jewish mystics who never heard of baptism or received a single Christian sacrament. If baptism is a sign that his life is open to great enrichment—a sign of potentiality—O.K. The *possibility* of expanding life to the infinite comes *from* the infinite, or God. But we have often acted with sacraments as if they were an achievement, not an invitation; as if they were grace itself and not a means to grace or goodness; as if communion received were already communion fully achieved; as if the new life given in baptism were a guaranteed Christian life; as if all life were not pilgrimage, struggle, incompletion, a journey towards the totality and unity we call God.

I said we acted in the past as if we had a finished fact. This is how a modern theologian wrote of sacrament:

> When an individual is baptized, he passes symbolically through the death and resurrection of Jesus, through the waters of chaos to new life. . . . In fact, he passes from being an individual in a chaotic and unjust world to being a member of a community that lives differently and makes it possible for him to live differently.

Part of that is sadly not true. The community in which he is baptized, (for example the parish, or the church of New York City or Sioux Falls) is not particularly distinguishable from its neighbor, is not caught up with the passion of the prophets about injustice or the concern of the Quakers for peace. Many of its members spend the same supine hours watching pro football as anyone else. They are no more honest in public life, no more trustworthy in repairing an automobile, than their unbelieving neighbors. Some signs of difference have been recorded, such as a less frequent rate of suicide in the past at Catholic colleges, and a lower rate of divorce (until recently) in Catholic marriages. This does something, but not enough, to render the world less chaotic and unjust. What does it *mean* to say the baptized "passes symbolically through the death and resurrection of Jesus?" (More about that later.)

A second reason for the turn-off from sacraments and religious language is that great numbers of people are anti-institutional today. Statements are common such as, "I love Jesus but not the church;" and, "I don't need the church." Youth demands sincerity and talks angrily about the hypocrisy of form. To reject the institutional frames of life as so many have (family, church, school, job, and society) also means they reject, or feel no need for the rituals or symbols involved (shirt and tie, white shirt, church weddings, "services," punctuality, respect for age, money in the bank, big parish, head of the firm, success). They drift, the anti-institutional people. Mary Douglas, in an intricate study called *Natural Symbols*, points out that they turn to inner experience and will not turn up with an allegiance to new symbols until they are newly integrated in some group process. All this means that right now they do not like or feel the need of the old "clubs." They do not join, do not even mock, but just ignore the conventional or ritual things to do.

The church has always taught that there are extraordinary means of grace when the sacraments are not available. Thus, to use the old language, a man achieves baptism of desire through a good life, or a return to grace and forgiveness by true repentance (the act of contrition based on love), or salvation (even dying without the priest) if his life was correctly oriented and his heart well disposed to God. Before the believer wonders "why bother with sacraments at all?" he remembers that he has been taught that they make this process of salvation easier. He may suspect now that sacraments have made it something else: not easier, but magical, removed from true faith. Some might angrily protest they never thought of sacraments as magic. But some who protest might have thought it was unlucky for the mother to go to a baptism, or that the child was in the grip of the devil until he was baptized, or that you could do what you wanted ethically or morally provided you got to confession. You might have thought that going to holy communion would help you win the ball game, and that anointing was a sure ticket to heaven. All this is magic or superstition, the kind the church had in mind when the Vatican Council said it must be uprooted and replaced by genuine faith.

These reasons, then: the failure to produce a qualitative difference, the present lack of credibility by church and institutions, and the decline of rituals to magic, all these explain a lack of interest in sacraments. But many who still use them, or have a lingering feeling that they or their children should use them, are wondering, "What is there?"

A New Viewpoint

The fall-off from confession implies that nothing essential is there, at least for many who still worship at Mass and receive communion. In the case of confirmation the experts are so divided as to what is there that the acceptable time for receiving the sacrament now ranges from infancy (in the Orthodox tradition), to the first grade, to young adulthood.

What is there in the sacrament of marriage has always been an uneasy question for pastors who struggled to put the transcendent there over against the florists and the style show. With many marriages the church itself may not be there if the trend to "do it yourself" continues. If the church and the ex-believer cannot rediscover the authentic power of their sacraments, he will remain an ex-believer, and marriage will decline for many into an ex-sacrament. When a girl says that "a piece of paper does not make us married," she is right. But a marriage without any *signs*—words, ring, gift, touch, embrace—would have to be angelic, dispensing even with the body, which is the medium of all signs. A few basic signs (including pieces of paper) have been assembled for the marriage ritual, to say that life is a gift, love is a mystery and part of freedom, and life is sustained by friendship *and* community.

There are some indications that sacraments are making a new stand and taking on a new look. Let us consider them. First, baptism. The new rite ends such anomalies as "churching the mother." An evening of preparation by parents before the baptism of their children is now the pattern in some dioceses. You can also choose total immersion and become as wet as any Baptist or your fellow Eastern Christian. The idea of a welcoming community, perhaps even at a Sunday Mass, is in.

Marriage—people plan the service even more than the official options expected; i.e., by writing their own vows. Recently I saw couples give the vows personally, *ex tempore*, speaking without a script about "what John means to me and how I intend to be his wife and love him until I die." The Catholic wedding is no longer conducted by the "professional holy man" with the people standing numbly by. They read, pray, and in many places make their own music, design their own cards and programs and signs of love.

Holy Orders—it is streamlined, sometimes done with éclat, with wide, multicolored stoles, bells and banners and jubilant trumpets. In the good old days the people used to sit through Latin speeches asking their approval of this candidate. Now they hear them in English and they break out in applause for the answer. The Offertory is never more meaningful than at the ordination Mass when the priest's family, who brought *him* up, bring up the gifts of new life.

Last anointing—it is slowly beginning to escape the association with the undertaker. Many parishes and institutions have a communal service for the anointing of the sick, using the procedure or formula from Lourdes. It is a moving experience. The community becomes a sign of love and concern, but it is a sign of *Christ's* love and concern of Him who alone has the power to go into the aloneness of death.

And much change and newer understanding surround the sacraments of reconciliation and confirmation.

But still we come back to the question, *what is there?* Before we answer further, a capsule history of the sacraments might help. There was no *definition* until Augustine, no *doctrine* until the scholastics, no *definitive number* of seven until the Council of Trent. St. Augustine's famous reply to Januarius said, "Christ bound the community of his new people together by means of sacraments that were very few in number, easy to administer and clear in meaning, such as baptism with its invocation of the Trinity and the communion of his body and blood and some other ones insofar as there is mention of them in the canonical Scripture." Since Jesus himself never baptized, Augustine is stating here a doctrine of ministry, an extension of Christ through others.

The word "sacrament" does not occur in the New Testament. The reality certainly does, because a sacrament is a sign. And Jesus Christ is a sign, *the* sign of the Father's love for us. Many see John's gospel as in part a reflection on the sacraments, baptism and the eucharist especially. He does not give the words of institution in his description of the Last Supper; rather, he gives a commentary, an exegesis of these words in his sixth chapter. His many comments on passing from death to life underscore his understanding of Eucharistic worship. He does not give the scene of Jesus' baptism or the familiar command, "Go and baptize," but the story of the man born blind is, many believe, a baptismal instruction (catechesis). Even the story of Lazarus is perhaps a sign of what is implied in baptism; that we are invited to begin a new life and leave behind the old bondage. ("Untie him and let him go," says Jesus of the man now living who had been dead.) *"Untie him"*—it is not a self-generated force that sets us free. It is the power of the Word that does this, but a Word made flesh in Jesus, communicating the Spirit of the living God.

This still happens. "Lazarus, come forth," Jesus says to the newly baptized, "come out into the world with all its demons and its darkness, because it is still my world and your homeland. Come and join me in our common life." It is the baptismal invitation.

Sacraments as Mystery

The New Testament speaks of mystery, and what mystery connotes was eventually transferred to the Latin word, sacrament. Leo the Great's famous sentence is, "All that was visible in the work of our redemption has passed over into sacred signs." His words seem strange to us because we have not fully appreciated that all of life is a complexus of signs. We communicate this way, we sustain each other by the interchange of meaning through words and sounds, but also through our visibility; our very bodies are a sign, a "body English."

When a man dies, his memory is continued, perhaps in his word (as in Lincoln's Gettysburg Address), but also through pictures and monuments and word-of-mouth or tradition. His spirit lives, we say, and what we mean is that it takes new form in order to *in*-form us of what originally "*trans*-spired." In Jesus' life this has happened to an extraordinary degree. Men believed He was still living even after the cross, that his love and power were present in their lives. To say what He meant for them they used rituals, told stories, retold his stories, developed what we now call the gospels and the "breaking of the bread," or Mass, and continued an ancient rite of death to life or transition like washing or baptism. All this is not play-acting (like most passion plays and "biblical" movies); it is not an attempt to reproduce the *details* of an historical event but to *re-enter the original power*.

The followers of Jesus also showed signs of his healing power and of his authority by placing hands on the head or body of another. Most of all, they themselves in their bodies, in their manner of living, in their deeds of goodness and of faithfulness even to death, were the sign that he was still living in them. In St. Leo's words paraphrased, the work of redemption goes on in the deeds of men who manifest his Spirit. *They* are the sacred signs. Men do not always speak to communicate meaning; they engage in gestures, actions, and symbols. The most famous and the most central of these is sharing food, and the central sign of Christian faith is expressed around a table.

So far, we have caught, perhaps, some insight into sacraments (sacred signs, Christ's saving presence, his healing love continuing) through the teaching of John and the minds of the early Church Fathers (Augustine and Leo). Now a medieval scholastic formula can be of help. It is the famous *sacramentum et res* phrase. Don't back off right away. It means "sign and reality." And it is said of any sacrament that it begins simply as a "sacramentum" or something visible, tangible, audible: like words of prayer, the community gathering, bread and wine upon the table of offering, etc. Words, bread, wine, water, crowds could mean many things. It could be an assembly of people intent upon evil.

So a *reality* has to enter here which, on the one hand, is God's gift, his wish to communicate Himself; that is, a power of loving, a sense of belonging, a feeling for life and for each other, a place and pride in creation.

And on the other hand, there is the contribution of faith—or in the beginning perhaps it is just openness and goodwill on the part of the recipient. So around the bread and wine placed on the table, people gather. And within them is the mental-spiritual attitude of expectancy and openness. And above them and within them, we hypothesize, there is a deeper reality waiting to be revealed, to instill itself in us, to grow into our very consciousness, into the fibre of our being and the quality of our loving.

Then what happens? The sign is carried out. Water is not made merely to look at, but to pour, to drink, to wash and to bathe in. Bread is not something to admire from a distance. Wine is the cup that cheers. Hands touch in friendship and in power. Bodies meet, love is expressed, and life is communicated. In other words, an action takes place, and the sign is used up, so to speak. The water flows over me, the bread is in me, the hands joined in the marriage vows are parted, the gesture of comfort or power to the sick or the ordinand or the confirmed is ended, and I am alone. Apparently unchanged. But the reality is in me. There is no longer the original sign (*sacramentum*), there is the reality (*res*). I *feel* changed, and my feelings are a clue. Something more than the emotional has taken place. Faith has invited me to perceive a new reality, a small part of a new creation.

What is it? In baptism I sense my own importance. In penance, my belonging again, my need for reassurance in the face of falling down. In marriage, that I have entered upon a mystery so great I can enjoy but never exhaust it in one lifetime. In confirmation, holy orders, and marriage, too, I feel called, stirred to a sense of importance, filled, perhaps, with an elation that there is something I can do. I can help to create: a world, a community, a child. In sickness, in suffering, and in dying I feel that I am not alone. Aloneness is an accurate definition of hell. I am saved from this loneness by a presence, more than a presence of the priest or the praying community, though they are the welcome signs.

And so we say the "sacramentum" or the outward sign is withdrawn, and although the baptized, confirmed, ordained, married, anointed, loved, united, and forgiven person seems the same, a new reality has laid hold of him to some degree. The outward sign now will not be a washing with water, or a partaking of bread or sharing of a special cup. It will be love, peace, gentleness, forbearance, patience, passion at injustice, concern for others—everything St. Paul calls the gifts of the Spirit, which is another name for the reality which has been enlarged within me. There will indeed be washings of my body and of bodies of the sick and of babies and of clothes; there will indeed be sharings of bread around many tables; there will be many new gatherings of comfort, acts of love, words of forgiveness, work with my hands of building and making. And these actions, too, will be holy, just as much as the rituals of the sacraments. They will be signs that the redemptive love and service of Christ to another is continuing in the world.

Are we still ill-defined or ill at ease about "what sacraments do," "what is really there?" Chesterton defines a bored person as one condemned to listen to the endless repetition of a story he has never really heard. All of us have heard endless repetitions of phrases about sacraments, such as "they give grace;" "to become a soldier of Christ;" "inserted into the paschal mystery;" "three degrees of the priesthood;" "married in Christ;" "anointed unto glory," etc. Could we now try to hear the story for the first time? I will not use traditional or "churchy" terms; but when we find the meaning behind them, we may use them once again.

We are often told that doctrines in our church were developed in reaction to controversies or heresies. Some were; but even more fundamentally the teaching is an attempt to answer a fundamental question of existence. Who am I? What am I for? Is the universe friendly? I must die, is that *it*? Does anyone love me? How can I be happy? Doctrines summarize what the teacher or prophet has said about these questions. Sacraments try to say it with actions, or communicate it with traditional symbols (like water, the flood waters, the waters of death and life, the meal, the friendship meal, the covenant meal). Once we tried to explain sacraments by drawing a parallel between natural and supernatural life. Now we would be more inclined to talk about *human* life, expanding it to "that more abundant life" that Jesus promised.

There is a film about baptism, called "Baptism," which does not show the ritual at all, yet takes the approach we mean. It is the story of a Mexican boy, living in poverty, whose family was lost in a fire in which his own features were hideously scarred. He is barred from food and shelter, and lives completely alone.

At last he comes upon a community of children like himself. We would call it an orphanage, but that is not a happy term. It is a real-life community, more like a brotherhood, and the youngster wishes with all his heart to be a part of them—their games, their living, their sharing. The priest is kindly, he leads the way, but he also explains the situation to the community and awaits their action. There is a tense moment when he leads in the scarred youngster. And a deadly serious Mexican child breaks the silence by going over to the stranger, taking his hand, and saying: "You are my brother."

The next scene is the fiesta in the community, and here are some real baptismal signs: celebration, clothing, rejoicing, and new life. But still no ritual. The boy is wearing a serape. Everyone is, for that matter; it is their colorful, festive garb. There is light in the darkness—fireworks, jubilation, and a blissful air of happiness on his scarred face. He belongs. There is love for him; he can dare to trust, and hope, and give love in return. Is he not "graced" or gifted? Is not this what we mean by the supernatural gifts? For him a new life has begun.

The film is not a complete doctrinal statement. But many have found it a most effective way to teach some of the most important truths about baptism. And yet there will be angry comments, like one who said, "It doesn't show anything of the sacrament at all. No water, no oil, no priest or godparents, nothing!"

Nothing, except the way the sacrament really works. I don't mean that it's just a matter of joining and being welcomed. Behind this is desire, and answering this is love. The desire (to belong, to be, to be one) is rooted in our being; the love that responds is greater than our invention. Both the desire and love are part of the "given;" they transcend us, and are signs of the Infinite who is God.

The body did nothing to deserve the burden he carried. His scars, of course, are an image of original sin, a doctrine which attempts to say that there is not only evil in life, but much of it comes our way unbidden through the genes, through the home, through the society, through enormous, complex factors over which we seem to have little control. Think how easily we inherit the prejudice of race, the attitudes of our parents toward sex or money, toward food and drink, and pleasure and work. We may feel cheated or helpless before an evil that often enmeshes us and leaves us warped or deformed in trying to cope with life. A lack of training in adult responsibility, or preparation for sexuality and marriage, or a social misery which leads to alcoholic or drug abuse, would be examples. And yet it is still possible to find a redeeming love in human life. The boy's story is only one example. If the community of Christians into which we are baptized has any meaning at all, it is to give this sustaining power.

Sacraments: For Human Needs

Here is another approach to an easier understanding of "what is there" in giving or receiving a sacrament.

You are an individual starting off as an infant with two hugely fundamental needs: one is love, and the other is meaning. We know that we die or wither without love (the "TLC" that doctors now even find necessary to prescribe). But we don't fully understand the importance of meaning—meaning to life, or truth. Truth means a relationship to reality. If we are not in touch with reality, we lose the center or core of being; we "*dis*integrate." Think of a child who cannot or does not know such fundamental things as "my father," "my name," "my house"—he is destroyed. Neither love nor meaning (truth) can come without people; so you need to belong (and that *longing to belong* is part of your very *longing to be*). A baptism surrounds you with signs of acceptance, meaning to life, and direction. What we call "eternal life" is a "spiritual" or religious way of saying that you are of great value, and have infinite possibilities. (Don't worry! if they are truly infinite, life *is* eternal). You may not become president, but you are called to the role of man, the process of being human so beautifully set forth in *Genesis*—to be a brother, lover, maker, artist, scientist (the one who gives names), and creator.

Suppose these external signs of love and meaning seem lacking: that the child being baptized was not wanted or loved but a "mistake," and has no natural family to claim it. But already love is entering the picture, perhaps through adoptive parents, creating a bond stronger than biologic life. And the ceremony is saying that there is still a creative power that begot you, that touched the flesh of two humans and claims you for itself. The baptismal ritual and the last anointing, or the anointing of the sick and the feeble, are always signs of what the poet meant with his words: "Gather us, O Lord; we are the sons of your desire."

These are some statements of *fulfillment* that we think can be linked with and accomplished by the sacramental action. "My life is significant. I am an original production, not a Xerox or facsimile of anyone else. I belong. I am not doomed to chaos or darkness or drift." This is baptism.

"I am needed. My talents are real. Something of me, my gifts, can be part of a larger work that helps to humanize and save the world, to bear witness that it began and is completed in love, not in senseless power; and in light, not in darkness." This in part is confirmation and holy orders.

"My love is part of a love that made God make man, a mystery of unity, a two-in-oneness that begets new life, that is creative." This is marriage.

"My sin is overwhelmed in a love that forgives." This is reconciliation.

"My pain and my fear of death are part of a larger pain called the ,Passion, and of another man's fear of death, both of which—fear and death—he overcame." This is the anointing.

"I am not alone. I am in touch with a greater reality which is part of me as much as the food and drink I share. My neighbor is a presence. To serve, and love, and be loved, is a possibility. God is not remote, but somehow present in this mystery of giving and receiving, eating and drinking, sharing and loving." This is Eucharist.

All religious philosophies say that we are part of Another. The sacraments say we are part of the One who is God, or Spirit, all in all. (In our tradition our name for the One is Christ.) We are part of his life (baptism, Eucharist); we are part of his energy, his creativeness, his thrust into matter and its transformation (this can be confirmation, holy orders, Eucharist); we are part of his love (this is marriage and Eucharist); and part of his healing and wholeness (this is reconciliation and anointing).

These are clumsy words saying that every sacrament, particularly the Eucharist, is a sign of a larger reality that includes and embraces us, that has to come through simple human events like eating and drinking and dying and working and making a friend or falling in love. All of these human activities enlarge the sense of presence or of the mystery or of the oneness in which we partake.

We have no guaranteed ways to prove this. We can appeal to our own experience, and also try the following suggestions.

The first is the insight into matter that the physicist and biologist, with tools such as the microscope, have given us in our time. They have discovered so many worlds within worlds, such a core of infinite energy and design, that we have had to use the words of poets to express what they have found. "There's more mystery in mud than stars" is not great poetry, but a great truth. And Teilhard de Chardin said:

> Never, if you live to work and grow, never will you be able to say to matter, "I have seen enough of you, I have surveyed your mysteries and have taken from them enough food for my thought to last me forever."

He continues:

> I tell you even though like the sage of sages you carried in your memory the image of all the beings that people the earth or swim in the sea, still all that knowledge would be as nothing for your soul, for all abstract knowledge is only a faded reality: this is because to understand the world knowledge is not enough, you must see it, touch it, live in its presence, and drink the vital heat of existence in the very heart of reality.

This may fly too high for many seekers. Consider the mystery of matter in more humble ways. When you look at water, let it run over your hands, splash on your face, needle you in a shower, wash over you in a pool, lift you up and bear you along, cresting, exuberant, in the ocean. When you see it descend from the skies, rise up in the misty fingers of the earth, tumble down a thousand streams, and come to you on a hot, hot day, surely there is mystery and delight here, and enough to engage us. Remember the story of the Arabs visiting France, who waited for the waterfall to cease. One of them said, "The God of the French is generous." Or the African youngster who knelt on one knee as he drank the cup of precious liquid because, he said, "It is thanksgiving."

Teilhard's statement is much more significant if we reflect on the meaning of the incarnation. The human life of Jesus keeps "abstract knowledge" from becoming "a faded reality." He was so much the Spirit enfleshed that He gives matter its ultimate meaning. Because He shared "simple human events like eating and drinking and dying and working and making a friend or falling in love," they have a new exhilaration or potential for us. They knew Him in the breaking of the bread, the New Testament says. "Did not your fathers eat and drink, and do righteousness and justice—is not this to know me?" says the Lord.

Signs and Symbols

A second approach to understanding might be a consideration of human psychology, the need for signs. Some years ago Gerard Sherry gave an account of a trip to Russia and his encounter with a Lithuanian family who had just shared worship with him at the Church of St. Louis of France, still the only Roman Catholic church that functions as a parish in all of Moscow. The Lithuanian couple were old and exiled; that is, they had been transplanted to a remote area of Siberia as part of a farm colony. They were cut off from the visible signs of religion, and had used their savings to come on a tourist bus trip to Moscow. Their real aim was to find the church of their faith, confess their sins, receive communion, share the Mass. They had done so, and they could hardly contain their joy.

"We are going back now," they said; "we know it will never happen again. But it *has* happened, and we will remember in the years ahead."

One might well ask, why did they come, for God loves them without a ritual, their sins are forgiven in his mercy, there can be a presence of God by what we have always called, clumsily, spiritual communion; prayer does not need mediation, and God is everywhere. All true—but they came because they are human. Christ was human. His body became a sign. Those signs continue through the body called humanity, or particularly that section of humanity called the church.

The third insight into the significance of our religious rituals might come from considering symbol. There has been a vast reclaiming of this word in our time; what scholars call "cognitive reduction and symbolic reassertion." Don't be put off by their language. What they mean is that ordinary words, even when they come from the mind of Immanuel Kant or Thomas Aquinas, are not enough to organize and explain very much of being, or reality, or truth, or love. They fall short. Every thinker and writer knows this, including the ones we named, and yet the discovery has been dramatic in our time that we must develop approaches to reality which earlier men took for granted: the making of poetry, songs, myth, art, dance, ritual.

Symbol, to sum up many, many arguments and explorations, can be fairly put as *containing a reality to which it still points*. Man himself is a symbol. We call him the image of God, broken off from the whole, and we call him the symbol maker because he is forever trying to enlarge that reality which is already seeded within him. The image needs to be complete, the design to be fulfilled. A man symbolizes experience through words, gestures and actions because he lays hold of, or grasps, more of the experience thereby. We used to see symbol as something exterior to reality, on the fringe of man's real work, which was thinking. Now we know that words themselves are symbols. We used to say that it was wrong to refer to the Eucharist as symbolic. Now we would use that word the same way we use "sacramental sign."

To speak of something as "only symbolic" is inaccurate. "Symbol" does not mean everything, but it does mean a thing on its way to becoming much more. For instance, in the communion of the Mass there is certainly a reality of God present. There is an enlarging of myself with brother, with life, and with mystery that my tradition tells me is the "locus," or place, of finding God.

I am in communion with what *is* (truth, love, the eternal One). But who thinks this is a complete communion? The very body that puts me in contact also slows me down, robs me of the conscious moment. The sin I have rejected reasserts itself and divides me from this unity, so briefly, fleetingly, felt and achieved. To receive communion is to achieve it, but only partially; and the whole of life becomes an effort to become one, even as Jesus prayed, "That they all may be one, Father, as you are in me and I am in you." The holy communion, then, is indeed a symbol containing the most profound reality and leading us on, impelling us to its completion. Because sacraments are actions, because they are related to the real world, we should be impelled to complete that reality: to love, to forgive, to serve, to trust, to make human life possible, to reverence and join with all creation until, in Augustine's words, "There is one Christ giving praise and glory."

THE SACRAMENTS: A Catechism for Today

Jared Wicks, S.J.

Where did the word "sacrament" originate?

In the ancient world, the Latin word *sacramentum* was the term for the oath of allegiance by which a soldier pledged his services upon induction into a legion of the Roman Empire. With this in mind, the Christian writer Tertullian called Christian baptism a "sacrament" in the early third century.

In introducing this usage, Tertullian was underscoring the importance of the renunciation of Satan and the commitment to Christian discipleship made by a person receiving baptism. The ancient term *sacramentum* is a constant reminder of the new lifestyle and allegiance to which we dedicate ourselves in receiving the sacraments—a point St. Paul developed at length in treating baptism (Rm 6:3-11) and the Eucharist (1 Cor 10:14-21; 11:17-34).

Does the word "sacrament" occur in the Bible?

In the Latin Bible *sacramentum* translates the Greek word *mysterion* (mystery), the term which Paul used in referring to the hidden plan according to which God in his eternal good-pleasure intended to save, renew, and unite all things in Christ (Ep 1:9; 3:3-9). Thus, God's great "sacrament" is now revealed in the Gospel which proclaims the outpouring of his blessings as we are called to freedom from self-seeking and death. Climactically, this "sacrament" leads to our incorporation into God's Son now risen and glorified. The old divisions that scar our humanity are overcome and a new life and spirit is offered us (Ep 2). This is the unfolding of God's plan or "sacrament" of salvation.

How were the sacraments understood in the ancient Church?

The early teachers who wrote in Greek spoke often of the Christian "mysteries" as they referred to many of the prayers, rites, and practices that were growing up in the Church. A privileged place among these Christian mysteries was held by the complex series of acts making up one's initiation into Christianity: Lenten instructions, exorcisms, anointing, profession of faith, and the solemn rite of baptism which led to one's first full sharing in the Eucharist on Easter Sunday.

In the Latin world, Tertullian expressed the awareness that a spiritual effect is linked in the sacraments to a bodily action. "Indeed, the flesh is the hinge of salvation . . . The flesh is washed, so that the soul may be made clean. The flesh is anointed, so that the soul may be dedicated to holiness . . . The flesh is shaded by the imposition of hands, so that the soul may be illuminated by the Spirit. The flesh feeds on the body and blood of Christ, so that the soul too may fatten on God."

The most influential early Christian teacher was St. Augustine, the bishop of Hippo in North Africa (d. 430 A.D.). Augustine formulated four important principles that have entered into Christian consciousness as fundamental to understanding the sacraments. (1) A sacrament is a holy sign (image, symbol, expression) through which we both perceive and receive an invisible grace. (2) In its rite, the sacrament or sign is made up of two essential parts, a material component or element and a spoken word of consecration and conferral. "The word is joined to the element and the result is a sacrament, which becomes in a sense a visible word." (3) Some sacraments, including baptism and ordination, are never repeated. Their lifelong effect is like the military brand, or "character," by which a soldier was marked for life as a member of a Roman legion. These sacraments are therefore once-for-all enlistments for service amid God's people. (4) Because it is Christ who ultimately confers a sacrament, the gift of grace and holiness is not prevented or impeded by the possible moral failings of the priest administering the sacrament.

In spite of these initial precisions, writers and teachers continued long after Augustine to speak of a considerable number of rites as Chrstian sacraments, including the sign of the cross, the conferral of ashes on Ash Wednesday, and Christian burial. About 1150, St. Bernard of Clairvaux even used the word in the more ancient sense as he reverently referred to the mysterious oneness of the three divine persons as "a great sacrament to be worshipped rather than investigated.''

How were the sacraments understood in the medieval Church?

Between 1100 and 1300 the sacraments were vigorously discussed in the schools and universities of Western Europe. Church teaching on the sacraments soon came to be marked by the orderliness and careful precision of academic theology.

There was early agreement that ''sacrament'' should be used in the strict sense for only those seven rites instituted by Christ in which God is offering us grace and life *through the rite itself*, whereas other prayers and actions are principally occasions for our personal devotion and prayer for God's grace. Thus, there are seven ecclesial sacraments, but many other ''sacramentals.''

One of the chief contributions of St. Thomas Aquinas (d. 1274) was the explanation that the indelible sacramental ''character'' given in the unrepeatable sacraments is in fact a spiritual reality on the order of a commission or appointment. Persons baptized, confirmed or ordained are singled out to share in the priestly calling of Christ and thenceforth to live lives of worship and service in the likeness of Christ.

Aquinas dared to use the ideas of the ancient Greek philosopher Aristotle in building his theology. Thus Aquinas spoke of the sacraments as the *instruments* God uses in causing in us or communicating to us the graces of salvation. To show the overall harmony of God's plan, Aquinas compared the sacraments to the human nature of Jesus Christ, for in being assumed into union with the Eternal Word, this human nature was God's primary instrument in working out his plan of reconciliation and salvation.

How were the sacraments understood in the era of the Reformation?

The Protestant Reformers were greatly concerned to simplify the sacramental rites so as to give the people a deep personal experience of God's forgiving grace as they received the sacraments. Martin Luther (d. 1546) and John Calvin (d. 1564) argued that according to the strict word of Scripture only two sacraments, baptism and the Lord's Supper, were instituted and ordained by Christ as trustworthy signs and means of grace.

Early in the Reformation, Ulrich Zwingli (d. 1532) and others began teaching that the sacraments were to be seen as expressions of *our* remembrance of Christ and of *our* devotion stirred by the Holy Spirit. Luther responded sharply that the sacraments are "the bridge, the path, the way, the ladder . . . by which the Spirit might come to you." Thus, for the main Reformers, the preached word and the biblical sacraments are the divinely instituted "means of grace."

John Calvin urged people to understand baptism and the Lord's Supper by way of analogy with the seal stamped or embossed on a charter or document to give it official standing. Calvin taught that sacraments are the actions that confirm and corroborate the word of the Gospel in which God promises us forgiveness of sins. Therefore, one received the sacraments by trustfully casting oneself upon God's word as the only basis of assurance and not by seeking to influence God by offering him good works to gain his mercy.

In responding to the Reformers, the Council of Trent (1545-62), impressed on Catholic consciousness the conviction that there are in fact seven sacraments in the Christian dispensation, even though Scripture's witness to each of these is not of the same clarity. The Council also reaffirmed that sacraments are not simply stimulants to our weak faith, but are the means or instruments by which God confers upon the devout recipient his gift of grace and new life.

Trent also formulated a number of answers to particular questions about the sacraments raised by the Reformers, for instance, the real presence of the body and blood of Christ in the Eucharist, the effectiveness of baptism in really removing original sin, and the necessity of telling all serious sins in receiving the sacrament of penance. But most of all, the Catholic response to the Reformation was a strong affirmation of the importance of the sacraments over against the eventual Protestant tendency to greatly subordinate them to the preached sermon.

How are the sacraments being understood in the Church today?

The word "sacrament" is again being applied more widely than to just the seven principal rites of sanctification and worship in the Church.

Christ himself, both as the Incarnate Word of God and as the man so totally "for others" that he gave his life, is seen as the *primordial sacrament* of our encounter with God. In Christ, God's loving kindness becomes visible in a great sign and God's saving mercy becomes effective in the world of men and women needing salvation.

Also, the church, as the community of believers in Christ, is grasped as the *fundamental sacrament* by which God both reveals in sign and effects in action the unity of all mankind. The people of God show forth already that ultimate unity of mankind toward which all of God's works are tending. In her mission of witness and service, the church is actively engaged in promoting this reconciliation that anticipates the final Kingdom. Thus the church is both sign and cause (as instrument) of what is to be God's ultimate gift to mankind.

This wider use of the term "sacrament" is but one indication of a many-sided movement of *integration* by which the ecclesial sacraments are being understood less as detached "events of grace" between God and man and more as meaningful moments within God's universal dispensation of salvation. Because Scripture reveals this dispensation as a many-splendored reality, we must look at it from a series of different viewpoints or perspectives. The following five questions will indicate the place of the sacraments within five different perspectives or frameworks of understanding which emerge from Scripture and the tradition of Christian teaching.

What is the role of the sacraments in the renewal of creation?

Scripture affirms that the ultimate intent of God's saving work is the creation of "new heavens and a new earth in which righteousness dwells" (2 P 3:13). The end of our world will signal the beginning of a new *world*, and not simply an ethereal dwelling-place of ghostly spirits. It is in this vein that our creed confesses, "We look for the resurrection of the dead."

But this new creation is not simply way off in a distant future. The risen Christ is "the beginning, the first-born from the dead, that in everything he might be pre-eminent" (Col 1:18). And through his Spirit, Christ, the firstborn, is now preparing mankind to pass into the coming new creation. His primary work is of course the conversion of men and women, as he renews human hearts and effects reconciliation. But the earth is to be renewed as well. "Creation itself will be set free from its bondage to decay and obtain the glorious liberty of the children of God" (Rm 8:21).

Therefore, by Christ's use of water, oil, bread, and wine in his present work of sanctification and renewal, the sacraments introduce a profound truth into our religious lives. Already, Christ incorporates the *things* of this world into his encounters with human persons, and this expresses that his pre-eminence extends through the whole of creation. As a teacher of the Kingdom, Jesus referred to sowing seed, finding pearls, and catching fish to make his point. Today, we meet him, not by escaping from the earth, but through acts of dialogue and exchange that includes earthly elements expressing his saving work and bringing it to bear on our lives.

The sacraments are thus expressive of Christ's lordship over creation; they point to the day on which all things are to be subject to the Son (1 Cor 15:27f). His is not the domination of abject elements by one with power, but a sovereignty that confers righteousness, holiness, and new being. Our earth too is to share in this renewal.

What is the role of the sacraments in the course of personal living?

Each of the seven sacraments responds to a deep personal need we have of God's redemptive presence at the *critical moments* in our individual life-histories. In the sacraments, God works to place our major life-decisions in a meaningful context of graced service of him and of others. God recalls us from rootless wandering and the morass of isolated choices in the face of life's central problems. We need not seek in darkness for the meaning of life, growth, guilt, illness, sex, vocation, death, and relating to other people.

Baptism envelops the beginning of life in God's loving kindness and stamps it with the irrevocable concern of Christ and his assembled people. As a person approaches maturity, confirmation renews the gift of God's Spirit as the source of strength and support in a life of discipleship and service. In ecclesial penance, we can deal with the cancer of sin and the wounds of guilt and infidelity by approaching the Lord, "a God merciful and gracious, slow to anger, . . . forgiving iniquity and transgression and sin" (Ex 34:6f). When serious illness threatens to engulf us in self-concern, sacramental anointing brings God's presence and assimilates us to Christ who suffered on behalf of many. Ordination and marriage are sacramental dedications of mature Christians to the lifelong vocations of loving service to which God calls them.

Our basic problem, however, the one that accompanies us for a lifetime, is the way we relate to other people. Can we overcome the stifling effect of self-seeking so as to live in peace with others? Can we grow in prompt readiness to help and serve the Christ who calls to us through people in need? Thus, God would have us return constantly to the eucharistic meal where we and those near to us are made one body in Christ and where we are inserted into Christ's selfless giving of himself on behalf of every human person.

Through the sacraments, therefore, the course of our personal lives is repeatedly punctuated by God's loving presence at just the moments of our greatest need of him.

How do sacraments serve as signs of the single mystery of God's saving love?

When we speak of the single mystery of God's saving love, we mean to express the deep Catholic conviction that in truth "God our Savior . . . desires all men to be saved and to come to the knowledge of the truth" (1 Tm 2:3f). In this view, God does in fact make a genuine approach to every human person to offer each one the gift of transforming intimacy with himself through grace.

Thus, the life of every man is in fact enveloped by God's Spirit, whose incognitos are more varied than we can imagine. The Spirit's intent and purpose is solely to open hearts and transform them in loving submission to the Father. Consequently we do not see the church or even the whole of Christianity as the exclusive area in which God's love unfolds itself in human lives. Christians are not those selected out of humanity to live in communion with God. Christians, rather, make up the elect people who give witness to God's one mystery of love and who by their service seek to facilitate the universal reconciling work of God's Spirit.

Therefore, the life of God's people is shaped by those expressions or articulations of the one mystery that repeatedly raise it to a heightened level of memory and consciousness, that engage a person in receptive response to God's love, and that unfold the implications of this mystery for the lives of individuals and communities.

In the community of God's people, the sacraments explicitate and celebrate the many facets of the loving kindness with which God already embraces the life of every human person. This one mystery of love aims at our birth into new life (baptism). This love is strengthening and supportive (confirmation), cleansing and forgiving (penance), healing and faithful unto death (anointing). God's love conforms us to Christ's selfless service of others (orders and marriage), and it repeatedly breaks the barriers of selfishness that divide and alienate us from one another (Eucharist).

In the sacraments we celebrate the many-splendored mystery of God's saving love as it works continually in the lives of all men and women.

What is the role of the sacraments in the saving history of God's covenant people?

It is a truism that God does not deal with us as isolated individuals independently of our families, our work-situation, and our community of faith and worship. But there is another kind of context for our moments of conversion, growth, and worship of God. Scripture inserts the lives of both individuals and communities into the vast panorama of "the history of salvation."

In very ancient times, God spoke and worked in manners that repeatedly promised a new and fuller presence of his love. The old covenant with Israel became pregnant with hope and expectation of a new more intimate covenant (Jr 31:31-34). In the death and exaltation of Christ, this promise reached a fulfillment in which we now share, "because God's love has been poured into our hearts through the Holy Spirit given us" (Rm 5:5). But the ultimate stage, the consummation, has not yet come. We still look forward to that fullness of time when all things will be united in Christ (Ep 1:10) and creation will no longer groan in futility (Rm 8:21f).

The Christian sacraments are the events in which the climactic moments of this salvation history are brought to bear on our lives. The phases of God's plan become contemporaneous with moments in the lives of individuals and communities. The liturgy of baptism, in the Easter vigil celebration, involves each of us in God's creation of the world, his liberation of Noah's family from the flood, and the passage of God's people out of Egypt to a land of promise. Our baptism is our insertion into the death and rising of Christ (Rm 6:3-11), a fact made vividly clear when the sacrament is given by completely immersing the person in water and then bringing him out in the likeness of a resurrection.

In the Eucharist, Christ is present in a living memorial of his death on our behalf and we are called to dedicate ourselves to the Father with him in a sacrifice of praise. In the eucharistic meal, we anticipate the final union God intends to grant, a communion of intimate nearness which Scripture often presents as a banquet. Confirmation, ordination, and marriage celebrate anew the sending of God's Spirit to consecrate his people in their individual vocations.

Thus, as we share in the sacraments we come to be inserted more fully into the history of salvation. Our memories are stamped more deeply with God's purpose; we are conformed to the central event of Christ's obedient death on behalf of men; and we are emboldened by hope as our future is bathed in the light of the coming triumph of God's peace over our hostilities and hardness of heart.

What is the role of the sacraments in the life of God's priestly people?

The sacraments are key events both for expressing and for further developing the self-understanding of the people God has gathered and made a priestly body. This people does indeed acknowledge the presence of God's Spirit touching the life of every man and woman. God's saving work, under whatever guise, is coterminous with the complete span of human existence. Still, we who are in the church sense that God has chosen and marked us out for a special role.

We are not the sole recipients of his grace, but are rather a people called to a special service within the unfolding of God's saving work. In the image of Christ, the church is anointed for messianic and priestly service in the midst of the world. As a priestly people, the members of the church are called to witness to the world about what God is accomplishing, to become a focal point of unity in the service of human reconciliation, and to approach God in prayerful worship in place of and on behalf of all men.

In the sacraments, therefore, this priestly people strives to become more and more possessed by the self-understanding of Jesus as he lived and died on behalf of the many and for the benefit of all. Baptism incorporates new members into the priestly community. Penance reconciles repentant sinners to the community of worship. Anointing heals the inner wounds which prevent illness from becoming an act of witness and redemptive suffering. Marriage and ordination dedicate couples and individuals to their special roles of service in building up the priestly people. In the Eucharist Christ gathers his people about himself, incorporates them as his body and leads their worshipful approach to the Father.

Thus, in the sacraments, God's people is fitted to pursue its role and vocation to be a priestly and messianic people. Ever aware of its unworthiness, the church seeks to deepen its sense of being called out to extend into our world the mission of Christ, the Lord's Servant and High Priest.

What, then, is a sacrament?

The definition of a sacrament will differ according to the specific perspective one adopts. Using as a framework the life of God's priestly people, as developed in the preceding response, we can both insert the sacraments into the larger dispensation of the Spirit in the world beyond the church and also highlight the communal dimensions of Christ's sacramental work of forming and preparing his priestly people.

Accordingly, the sacraments are *rites of incorporation* in which Christ is drawing men and women more fully under the influence of his redeeming grace and his saving mission. Sacraments are *events of grace*, in which the Spirit of God is imparted by the Lord who is ever sending his Spirit into the world. In the sacraments, incorporation and grace are extended through *symbolic* or *ritual* acts of human communication and human worship in the church, such as initiation, reconciliation, a festive meal, or a marriage commitment.

In receiving a sacrament, a person is both *receptive* of God's loving nearness and responsive *in worship*. Receptivity to grace, or "faith," is basic to a life near to God. In sacraments both the community and individuals give expression to their faith and under the influence of the Holy Spirit develop and deepen this fundamental receptivity to God's presence and influence. In sacramental events, we are not, however, exclusively passive or receptive. Sacraments entail worship and in every sacrament we respond to God in acts such as confession and thanksgiving, sorrow for sin and dedication to a new life, heartfelt petition, self-forgetting praise, and yearning for ultimate union and intimacy with God. Of such strands is woven the worship of God's priestly people.

Sacraments are not performed to benefit an individual or the Church.

As in the Gospel, so in the life of his people now, Christ *gathers* his followers so that he might *send them out* as heralds of God's loving design for the world. God has deemed it right to use our services in his approach to men, and in the sacraments he is gathering, forming, strengthening, and commissioning his people for their mission in the world on which he sheds his loving kindness.

Thus, sacraments are the symbolic or ritual acts of incorporation into the sphere of Christ's grace and mission; in sacraments we demonstrate our receptivity to the Spirit and responsive readiness to worship and serve the Lord, who is both gathering and sending his priestly people into the world.

THE SACRAMENTS AND HUMAN LIFE
J.D. Crichton

If you ask the question: why seven sacraments? you can, as a recent author has remarked, look at the question from two sides, from the point of view of revelation (what Christ willed) and from the point of view of man.[1] Setting aside the first for the moment, the author suggests that the material principle of the diversity of the sacraments (which convey the power of the paschal mystery in different ways) must appeal to the anthropological constituents of man:

> The seven sacraments do not come from arbitrary decisions of Christ (and much less from a church which would dominate Christ). This diversity comes from the fact that the actions of Christ lay hold of or take up fundamental human situations to make them Christian situations.[2] The sacramental organism is an adapted organism. To be born, to pass to adult life, to review one's life with a view to a new start, to marry, to fall ill, are so many situations taken up by the sacraments and thus shown to be and established as divine-human situations. This constituent principle of the seven sacraments shows that the Christian life is the opposite of a life that is simply juxtaposed to human life. It is in fact the life of God penetrating to the anthropological roots of human existence. There are no sacraments that are not sacraments of Christ living his paschal mystery in man. But also, there are no sacraments that do not draw from the world and from man the "materiality" of their sign. The seven sacraments can be thought of as the great and fundamental lines or the strong points or even the great axes by which the Lord Jesus reaches into the depths of our human nature and transfigures it.

There are two points here worth pondering. The first is that by the sacraments Christ reaches down to the deepest level of human life, not merely and superficially, as might be concluded from the above statement, to acquire the right kind of material signs (water, bread, wine, etc.). That is not the whole meaning of the writer. Christ who 'knows what is in man,' reaches down to human nature, to the very 'materiality' of human nature (e.g. sexual love) because man is like this and because it is only in this way that he can grasp existentially the divine reality Christ wishes to convey. This is why 'the sacramental organism is an adapted organism.' One could say that it is a conditioned organism, an organism that is conditioned by the exigencies of human nature. Sacraments are, then, profoundly human and not just something 'stuck on' to ordinary human living. They touch the deepest springs of human existence and, to use the terminology of Karl Rahner, they make it possible for man in Christ to live out the human tragedy of birth and life and death and suffering.

But the sacraments do not just go down to the roots of the human condition. They transform it. They are not to be thought of as actions, even actions of Christ, that reach our human condition and leave it where it is and as it is. The materiality of the human condition is the very stuff of the Christian life. It is not merely a means, sanctified by grace, by which we go to God. It is *in this* that we go to God. It is in the wholeness of our human personality that we need to go to God and in the sacraments Christ takes over these human situations and makes them specifically Christian 'grace-ful' situations, directing them and us to God. Here is an interpenetration of the divine and the human that at least in principle makes it possible for us to live in God. All is now taken up into him and through the enrichment he gives, we are able to carry these riches, which are both his and ours, to the world.

If redemption is to be thought of as something more than an abstract noun, as something deeper than a legalistic 'substitution' of Christ for ourselves, it is here in the sacraments that we can see what it really is: the penetration by Christ into human situations from which he removes, if we will, *self*-centeredness and gives them a Godward direction. In this way, we are able to establish or enter into the interpersonal relationship with God in which salvation ultimately consists. Certain situations are sin-situations, such as that which involves the sacrament of reconciliation, and here the redemptive, reconciling aspect of the work of salvation is to the fore. But in every human situation there is the danger of the movement towards self, e.g. marriage and sickness, and here it is precisely the *re*-direction the sacraments give that is important. Examples will make clearer what we mean.

1. The sacrament of reconciliation is the sign in the here and now of the reconciliation we read of in 2 Cor 5:19 'God was in Christ reconciling the world to himself.' This he did in principle on the cross; this he, with the Christian community, continues to do in the eucharist, for all the power that was to be found in the cross is to be found in the Mass. Indeed, the whole liturgy, including therefore the eucharist and reconciliation, is the sacrament-sign of the redeeming, reconciling work of Christ in the world and for the world. The church as a community of reconciliation and penance is in a special way the sacrament-sign of that reconciliation by which it is conveyed to the world. Men and women bring precisely their 'broken-ness' (contritition) to the sacrament and there seek encounter with the reconciling Christ. They have experienced the tragedy of (spiritual) death and alienation and now seek life and reconciliation. It is a normal human experience which in the sacramental situation is 're-deemed' and one which enables them to insert their lives into the reconciliation of Christ.

2. It may sound pompous and perhaps heartless to say that illness and suffering, which are so personal, are part of the world's tragic experience, since suffering turns us in on ourselves so that at times, and even against our will, our whole personality is shrunk to not much more than a consciousness of pain. Yet it is so and when the pain has abated we are aware that we are involved in something that exists outside us in all the suffering of whatever kind that the human race experiences. We may indeed think of illness and suffering as an assault on our personalities that is quite unaccountable and if we do, we may find a clue to an understanding of it in the Old Testament view that illness, whether mental or physical, is related to sin. Not in the crude sense that our suffering is a punishment for our wrong-doing (though we can bring disease on ourselves) but in the sense that just as sin, at least for the Christian, is a symptom of the disorientation of the world as we know it, so is illness. It throws our life out of gear and we sense a rift in the harmony of things. The good, health, is struggling with evil, disease; it is a conflict we now

experience in our own personalities and not just something 'out there.' It is this maimed condition that Christ in his church invites us to bring to him and into this condition he inserts his healing, his comfort and his peace. Here you have an encounter between something that of itself is purely secular and the healing of Christ. And it is not unimportant to realize that healing means wholeness. The broken is repaired, the forces making for the disintegration of the human personality are turned towards integration. What has fallen into dis-ease and conflict is harmonized and the personality, now made whole, can once again turn itself out to Christ and to the world of men where its true vocation lies, even if the sick person is still confined to bed. Of all this restoration the sacraments of the sick are the sign, the sacrament-sign of Christ's healing, who is thus shown to be present in the world of suffering and pain.

3. Marriage may be regarded as the archetypal case of the coinherence of the natural and the supernatural, the sacred and the profane, of the divine and the human. Here is a human love, earthy, warm and rich with every kind of fleshly association which yet reaches beyond itself to a total self-giving. It is this love that two people bring to God and in the encounter that ensues God's love meets theirs and transfuses it so that henceforth they are able to love each other with a love in which God is creatively present. None the less, their love remains fully human and yet at the same time is the sacrament-sign of their covenanted love as it is also the means by which they and their love are sanctified. Furthermore, this love is not restricted to murmured words or affectionate gestures. It is expressed in the very ordinary events of everyday life so that the very life-together-in-married-love also becomes the permanent sacrament-sign of the presence of God's love in their life. Here can be seen the involvement of God in the ordinary life of human beings, here we can see that God is not locked up in an ecclesiastical box but is to be found in human lives in all their ordinariness.

These situations are indications that the sacraments are not alien to human life. They celebrate it, they enhance it and are witnesses to the 'human-ness' of God who thus enters into it. It should not be supposed however that these situations (and others) are *proof* of the seven sacraments. First, not all the sacraments are so clearly connected with the human condition as those mentioned. If we give the impression that confirmation is the sacrament of adolescence *because* it corresponds to natural growth we are in danger of distorting its true nature. It is to be thought of as the perfecting of what is begun in baptism and this can be done at any age. We are so accustomed to think of baptism in the terms of infant baptism that it does not occur to us that a person baptized later in life has no possibility of 'growth' in the physical sense. Yet since confirmation has something to add to baptism it is perfectly right and proper that baptized adults should be confirmed. In other words, if we press the analogy between natural life and the Christian life too far we shall distort the sacramental organism. It is also difficult to find a credible analogy for the sacrament of holy orders. We no longer live in a sacral order and the notion of the 'sacralisation' of a human person is either unacceptable or meaningless. On the other hand, the dedication of a human being to a particular way of life, for instance monasticism, is covered by the rites of religious profession.

All we can show, then, by this kind of investigation is that the sacraments are congruous with the human condition. We are thus brought to the consideration which is fundamental that the sacraments are 'given,' they are part of Christ's revelation and in every sense of the word they are 'mysteries.' They are mysteries because they embody the mysterious presence of God active in human situations and are the signs of it. They are mysteries because they declare the faith of the church and that of the participants. They are mysteries because however well we think we understand them, their ultimate nature and effect lie beyond us. They are in fact part of the whole history of salvation which is a *datum*, something given, the pure gift of God, and we can only understand the sacraments as we understand the history of salvation. We look at it, we ponder on it, we 'see' that it is the divinely given way God willed to save us and that the sacraments are so many ways by which we are saved, justified and united through Christ in the Holy Spirit with the Father. Other ways would have been possible. A man could be saved by turning to God in wordless repentance or lifting up his heart in the wordless prayer of praise. But then we reflect, man himself is 'given,' he is made by God, and the way of salvation is in accordance with the nature of the radical gift. In effect, so long as we do not see the sacraments as 'emerging' from the needs of human nature and thus finding their justification, it is safe to say that they meet the needs of human nature because God has arranged the matter that way.

There remains the question of the relationship of the sacraments with the world. It will be agreed that the celebration of the sacraments is not a missionary device but it does not follow that Christians can be indifferent to what the world thinks of them or indeed of the way we celebrate them. The sacraments are not only signs of a particular intervention of God in a particular situation, for instance baptism. As the *Constitution on the Sacred Liturgy* (2) made clear, they are signs of the church, revealing its nature, and when the Christian community celebrates the sacraments, it is constructing a sign of the church which may be read by others even if for lack of faith they cannot have a full understanding of it. What the church *is*, the sacraments declare; what the church believes, that the sacraments profess in word and action. It follows, then, as the same document teaches (34), that the liturgy of the sacraments, as of the whole liturgy, must be simple and understandable to ordinary people. It is a matter of experience that the sacraments, when celebrated as they should be by a believing community, draw the non-believer towards the church and dispose him to listen or to come again. We also know that a bad celebration of the sacraments can repel people, sometimes for ever. We know too that in the new situation in which we are, the quality of the celebration depends on both clergy and people and sometimes, even when the former do all that is required of them, the people are reluctant to play the part that belongs to them. However, what is important is that it is the community that celebrates and it is the impression created by the whole community that will make an impact on others.

But the *Constitution on the Sacred Liturgy* makes clear that the celebration of the sacraments is a beginning and not an end. Members of the church, by virtue of their status as Christians, have the obligation of carrying the Good News to the world. Nor is there any need to expound at length the truth that the mission of the church belongs to all the members of the church. It is however worth repeating that, according to the *Constitution on the Church* (31, 33), the mission of the people flows directly from their baptism and confirmation: 'These faithful are by baptism made one body with Christ and are established among the people of God. They are in their own way made sharers in the priestly, prophetic and kingly functions of Christ. They carry out their own part in the mission of the whole Christian people with respect to the Church and the world.' More concretely still: 'The lay apostolate is a participation in the saving mission of the Church itself. Through their baptism and confirmation, all are commissioned to that apostolate by the Lord himself' and since the heart of mission is love, a love that urges us on (2 Cor 5:14), it is in the sacraments but especially in the eucharist that they will find manifest the source of that love.

How all this is to be carried out is a large question but the *Constitution on the Sacred Liturgy* (2), which from this point of view might seem to be a less practical document, has an interesting emphasis. It sees the liturgy as the outstanding means by which the people may *express in their lives* and manifest to others the mystery of Christ and the nature of the church. It is the daily living of Christians that manifests the great mystery of Christ which is the mystery of salvation. It is in this daily living that the non-believer will (or will not) find, as it were incarnated, the love God has shown to men. Clearly this puts a very heavy responsibility on all of us who *dare* to celebrate the liturgy and perhaps we have not always thought of it this way. But at least we can say, however unsuccessful we may be, that the notion of the liturgy as simply a ritual operation is banished. As it must be approached with a living faith, involving the whole personality, so its consequence and, in a sense, its validity must be seen in the life of Christians. The liturgy lives and moves and has its being in the flowing life of Christian people who through it, through the mystery of Christ with which they come in contact, reach out to the world around them and strive by example and word to carry Christ to it.

Footnotes

1. Henri Denis, *Les sacrements ont-ils un avenir?*, Paris, 1971, pp. 48-49.
2. Literally, "situations in Christ."

METHODOLOGY AND THE CHRISTIAN SACRAMENTS

Kenan B. Osborne, O.F.M.

To understand the religious phenomenon of the Christian sacraments, one's methodology is of the utmost importance. It would seem, however, that no one method can lead to a satisfying grasp of the issue, due to the fact that the sacraments themselves are highly complex, involving a number of dynamics from various dimensions of both human and divine life. One method of gathering and interpreting available data would surely be predominantly biblical. But a biblical procedure involves the use of the several methods commonly employed today by biblical scholars: linguistics, textual criticism, form criticism, redactor criticism and so on. Understanding the biblical data on the sacraments, utilizing as an interpretative or hermeneutical device or instrument such a variety of methods, is extremely important and should figure in any theology of the sacraments. But perhaps the biblical area is not the best starting point, in view of the complexity of sacramental theology. Another method could be predominantly historical, and here the several methods common to any solid historical research would be involved, critical editions of pertinent texts, contextual problems, linguistics and so on. Historical data on the sacraments and the hermeneutical tools of these methodologies are likewise unavoidable for a sound theology of the sacraments. But this historical approach in turn may not be the ideal starting point.

In this essay I would suggest that two methodological approaches to the sacraments are necessary as a preliminary step, the one approach christological, the other phenomenological. Like a pair of tongs or tweezers which we use to grasp an object, a method provides us with a way of getting hold of something in order to be able to study it, identify it and appreciate it. The christological and the phenomenological approaches will, we hope to show, allow us to grasp the Christian sacraments and thus begin to identify them and understand them better.

A Christological Approach

To understand to some degree the mystery of the sacraments depends on a comparable understanding of the mystery of Christ. Indeed, a study of Christology should normally precede any study of the sacraments, for in the Christian Church sacramental action is based on the life, death and resurrection of Jesus. In the Christ event something happened, and it happened to and for the world, to and for mankind. In other words in the Christ event the world and mankind have been affected, changed, transformed.

Precisely because of this, the theme of causality is important in sacramental theology. As a technical term, so far as we know today, "cause" was first introduced into the theological discussion of sacraments by Peter Lombard. But Thomas and Bonaventure, Luther and Calvin, to name only a few outstanding and divergent witnesses, have agreed that God himself is the main cause of all the power and effectiveness of the sacraments and that Christ's life, death and resurrection are but major secondary causes. To understand the sacraments, then, we must ask: What is God doing? Not, ultimately: What is the minister doing? What is the recipient doing? But quite deliberately: What is God doing? This question, however, cannot be resolved satisfactorily in the matter of sacramental theology unless we first ask and to some extent answer: What is God doing in the Christ event? This situation indicates the mutual relationship between the Christ event and the sacramental event.

The christological method is, indeed, more vertical in its approach— more supernatural, one might say, if that term does not connote a two storey system. It is an approach from above rather than from below. This "from above" trait is both its strength and its weakness: its strength because the awareness that in the sacraments God himself acts is brought strongly into focus; its weakness because we must start from above, from something that we come to know only by way of revelation and faith and that is, therefore, less immediately clear to our mind.

In the christological approach to an understanding of the sacraments, then, we must ask what God is doing in the Christ event. But God is not acting directly in the sense of not using an intermediary. Indeed, God is using the humanity of Jesus, and it is for this very reason that Christ is called the *Ursakrament*, the original sacrament. His "humanness"[1] is *the* sign, *the* symbol, *the* sacrament of God's self-communication to us; all other signs, symbols and sacraments are secondary to the humanness of Jesus. Since this humanness is the original sacrament, other sacraments will begin to make sense only after we have some grasp of why this humanness is the *original* sacrament and what it originally symbolizes. The humanness of Jesus is the context in which the sacraments find their meaning.

Contemporary theology, however, has stressed the sacramentality of the Church and has called the Church the *Grundsakrament*, the basic sacrament. This application of sacramentality to the Church has further complicated the understanding of the various sacraments, such as baptism, confirmation and the eucharist; for it confronts the theologian with the question: Why is the Church the basic sacrament? Basic to what? A sacrament of what? Here we begin to see the ecclesiological dimension of the sacraments and the christological dimension of the Church. Expressing the idea negatively, but perhaps more clearly, one might say that baptism, penance, the eucharist and the rest are to a large degree meaningless unless we first understand something of the sacramentality of the Church, in which these sacraments take place. The Church itself, however, is meaningless both theologically and spiritually unless we have some grasp of what is meant by calling Christ the original sacrament. Let us consider this question more at length.

The emphasis on Christ as the original sacrament has surely been strengthened by the Second Vatican Council. Schillebeeckx's book, *Christ the Sacrament of the Encounter with God*, has likewise aided in this understanding of Christ. When we say that Jesus Christ is the original sacrament, however, certain aspects must be kept firmly in mind. The first of these is the fact that it is his humanness which is the sacrament. If we employ the terms "human nature" and "divine nature" following the model of "nature" which the Council of Chalcedon (A.D. 451) offers us, then our focus is on the "human nature." God's nature is not a sacrament; it does not point to anything beyond itself. Nor would "Father,"

"Word" and "Spirit" be sacraments, for they too do not point beyond themselves, and if one were to say that in traditional trinitarian theology the "Word" is an image of the Father and is therefore a sacrament of the Father, unavoidable misunderstandings would occur and even the danger of subordinationism would arise. The term "sacrament" is not a theologically useful term when speaking of the divine.

The humanness of Jesus, his bodiliness, his sensitive created spirit, his human way of being in the world—all this is sacrament and does point to something else. The fathers of Chalcedon, as we know, laid heavy emphasis on the fullness of Jesus' humanity. They did not, of course, tell us very much about what it means to be human, but they did stress that whatever goes into the meaning and composition and reality of human existence must be predicated fully of Jesus Christ. He was neither subhuman nor superhuman: he was fully human, fully a man, like us in all respects except sin. Today theologians are asking with increasing inquisitiveness what it means to be human, and they are speaking more and more about the humanness of Jesus. They are not simply paying lip service to the phrase "Jesus is truly man" as they move on to consider his divinity. Rather they are talking about his human consciousness, about his human condition, about his religious ideas. Overemphasis on the divinity of Christ leaves little room to delve deeply into an understanding of Christ as the original sacrament.

Then, too, our own personal appreciation of the meaning of human existence plays a role in the insight we get into the meaning of Christ's humanness as a sacrament. When we begin to realize how deeply symbolization is involved in our communication with one other, both verbal and nonverbal, we begin to perceive our own human situation somewhat differently, and this new perception helps us understand the depth of sacramentality in the humanness of Christ as well. This aspect, however, forms part of the phenomenological method rather than the christological. But it should be kept in mind whenever the term "humanness" comes up, for Christ was *homoousios hemin*, of the very same nature as our own—"consubstantial with us," in the Chalcedonian phrase.

A third aspect that we must keep in mind is that the term "sacrament" as such is hopelessly ambiguous, for a sacrament is always a sacrament *of* something and *for* someone. If, for instance, we wish to say the humanness of Jesus is a sacrament, indeed the original sacrament, then we must make every effort to understand *of* what he is a sacrament and *for* whom he is a sacrament. Or again, if we wish to say that the Church is the basic sacrament, then we must also make fairly precise *of* what the Church is a sacrament and *for* whom it is a sacrament. Similarly in the case of baptism we must ask: *Of* what and *for* whom is baptism a sacrament?

Of what and for whom is Christ's humanness a sacrament? Schillebeeckx implies that Christ is the sacrament of the encounter with God: "The man Jesus, as the personal visible realization of divine grace of redemption, is *the* sacrament, the primordial sacrament, because this man, the Son of God himself, is intended by the Father to be in his humanity the only way to the actuality of redemption."[2] God's own self-communication, his love, his covenant, his judgment in the Johannine sense, his mercy, his revelation—of all this Jesus' humanness is a sacrament. But for whom is he sacrament? Would it be only for the "chosen"? Would it be only for Christians throughout the centuries? Would it be for all men? Our common theological heritage tells us that he is the sacrament for all men, none excepted.

All that God intends for man—that is to say, the comprehensive and ultimate meaning of creation—comprises that "of which" Christ's humanness is a sacrament. What God fully intends is, of course, the mystery of which eye has not seen nor ear heard nor has it really entered into the hearts of men. But Christian faith has insights into this mystery and certain symbols are used as pointers; for instance, the symbol "heaven" or "kingdom of God," which has been used to describe this divine intention from an eschatological or end-of-history viewpoint. Other symbols, such as "eternal life" or "unending love" or "beatific vision" might also be mentioned, as well as "justification," "grace" and "covenant." Were one to ask, and assuredly this question has been asked repeatedly throughout Christian history, "What is the central message of Jesus?" the answer would be drawn from one or other of the above symbolic words, and still none of these answers would be exclusively or exhaustively correct, since each of the symbols represents only a facet of God's intention vis-a-vis man.

In approaching the mystery of Jesus with the hermeneutical device or key of sacrament and in calling his humanness the original sacrament, Christology takes on a revelatory character, or as the Alexandrian school of Clement and Origen would say: Christ is seen as the Illuminator. The focus is on Jesus as the revelatory sacrament of God's self-communication (designated by one of the symbolic terms above) and revelatory to all men. Karl Rahner's approach to the sacramentality of Christ is similar, as the following passage indicates:

"But now in the Word of God, God's last word is uttered into the visible public history of mankind, a word of grace, reconciliation and eternal life: Jesus Christ. The grace of God no longer comes (when it does come) steeply down from on high, from a God absolutely transcending the world, and in a manner that is without history, purely episodic; it is permanently in the world in tangible historical form, established in the flesh of Christ as a part of the world, of humanity and of its history.

"That is what we mean by saying that Christ is the actual historical presence in the world of the eschatologically triumphant mercy of God. It is possible to point to a visible, historically manifest fact, located in space and time, and say, Because that is there, God is reconciled to the world. There the grace of God appears in our world of time and space. There is the spatio-temporal sign that effects what it points to. Christ in his historical existence is both reality and sign, *sacramentum* and *res sacramenti*, of the redemptive grace of God, which through him no longer (as it did before his coming) rules high over the world as the as yet hidden will of the remote, transcendent God, but in him is given and established in the world, and manifest there."[3]

In this essay our concern is to point out a basic and primordial methodology which will enable us to grasp some of the meaning found in the various sacraments. We have spent some time on the sacramentality of Christ's humanness as the *sine qua non* for such an understanding. We have argued that unless there is some clarification of how this humanness is the sacrament of God's self-communication for all men, then the very context in which the individual sacraments are possible and meaningful is removed. It is only within the horizon or framework of the sacramentality of Christ's humanness that the sacraments themselves are credible theologically as well as pastorally. Methodologically, then, Christ as sacrament is the indispensable beginning for any study or liturgical renewal of the individual sacraments.

It is likewise methodologically important to insist that only when the Church is seen as the basic sacrament do the individual sacraments become theologically and liturgically credible; for the Church as sacrament also forms a vital part in any renewal of the sacraments. Although this might appear as a theological truism, there are some issues which complicate the situation. If we ask of what Christ is a sacrament and of what the Church is a sacrament, is there any discernible difference between the two?

I would differentiate them as follows: The humanness of Christ is the sacrament of God's self-revelation, as described in the citations from Schillebeeckx and Rahner. His humanness is the original and fundamental revelation of God's reconciling relationship to our sinful world. On the other hand, the Church is a sacrament of the Christ event; it is a sacrament of a sacrament, it is the basic sacrament of an original sacrament. This maintains the primacy of Christ and the auxiliary position of the Church. The Church is the basic, historical and abiding sacrament of the original, revelatory and one salvific self-communication of a God who so loved the world that he gave it his only Son.

Again, if we ask for whom Christ is a sacrament and for whom the Church is a sacrament, the answer would seem to be: for all mankind. The Church is very much in the world and of the world. When the Qumran scrolls were discovered, scholars very carefully opened them and began to catch here and there the Hebrew words. A certain word, a certain phrase gave a clue to the meaning of the entire scroll. At times the words would indicate that the passage was from the Old Testament, and the entire scroll became meaningful. So too with the Church; for it is like a magnifying glass drawing into focus and intelligibility a certain small area on a page and thereby indicating what the entire page is about. As a basic sacrament, the Church—that is, the people of God—lifts into some sort of focus what our world, our history, our human existence is all about: a world that God loves in spite of sin, a redeemed world, a world that God himself has entered and shared in through the incarnation. In a somewhat analogous way the Church and the world are so united, for the Church is not of itself a sacrament, much less the original and primordial sacrament, but a sacrament of what creation is ultimately all about, and not just creation in the abstract but a creation that includes the God who has become part of the human situation. Only within this kind of ecclesial horizon and framework do the various sacraments begin to have meaning.

For they are the sacraments of this community called the Church. They are part of the symbol system which keeps the people of God a community. In other words, the sacramentality of both the humanness of Christ and the Church are centrifugal, outgoing, while the various other sacraments are centripetal. They are sacraments of individual aspects of the Christ event and the Church event but for the upbuilding and unifying of the Christian community. In this regard, baptism, penance, eucharist and the rest do not have a universal signification; they are not sacraments for the whole world, but rather they are sacraments for the people of God. They are intended as a means of building up the community of Christians so that it will truly be a sacrament to mankind. For instance, we celebrate the eucharist not to proclaim anything to the world at large but so that the people of God, gathered around the Lord's table, will become a more effective sacrament to the world. We celebrate the forgiveness of sins so that, being more penitent and turned from sin, the people of God will more purely radiate the revelation of God's good news to man in Christ.

In summary, the basis of a christological approach is this: only within the context of the humanness of Jesus as the original sacrament does the sacramentality of the Church take on meaning and reality, and only within the context of the twofold sacramentality of the humanness of Christ and the Church itself do the individual sacraments find their significance and function.

A Phenomenological Approach

G. van der Leeuw in his book *Sakramentstheologie* comes to an understanding of what a sacrament is in the Christian religion but not from an immediate definition of Christian belief.[4] Van der Leeuw feels that sacrament has too often been discussed as a specifically Christian phenomenon, ignoring the fact that it is connected with all sorts of human structures. In his view sacraments are not accidental, Christian phenomena—what are known as "epiphenomena." Instead they are anchored deep in man's nature, in the phenomenon of man himself. Take the eucharist as an example. This sacrament could be seen as something totally new, something that came down directly from heaven; and as such it would be epiphenomenal in character and might even be considered magical. On the other hand, one can situate the eucharist within the entire pattern of human eating and see it as basically a meal. An analysis of this everyday phenomenon of human eating leads to an insight into the meaning and intelligibility of the eucharist. In this phenomenological approach the focus is not just on any phenomenon but specifically on *human* phenomena, on a phenomenon which is intrinsically anthropological and not merely physical. To discover the humanness of a meal, one would ask why in German there are two words for eating: *essen* (to eat), used when one speaks of human beings eating, and *fressen* (to eat), used only of animals when they eat. Is human eating different from animal eating, and if so, in what way? What are the dynamics involved in human eating which do not occur in the mere animal ingestion of food? It would be questions of this nature that the phenomenologist would wish to investigate and pursue.

In this phenomenological approach each of the sacramental actions should be considered in the light of that human phenomenon which has been caught up into the sacrament itself. Schematically the two might be lined up as follows:

The Sacrament	*The Human Phenomenon*
Baptism	Initiation
Confirmation[5]	
Eucharist	The human meal
Penance (Reconciliation)	Human Forgiveness
Anointing of the sick	Human care for the sick and dying
Marriage	Human consent
Order	Service

The same kind of phenomenological approach can be applied to an understanding of the Church as a sacrament and to Christ as the original sacrament:

The Sacrament	*The Human Phenomenon*
The Church	All those interpersonal dynamics which bring about a community of men and women
Jesus Christ	The perception of what it means to be a human person

The thrust of this phenomenological approach is to focus on a wider dimension of interpersonal activity than that circumscribed by a particular sacrament. In the case of baptism, for instance, a phenomenological methodology would lead the theologian to isolate and examine all those instances of interpersonal behavior where there is some form of initiation: an initiation into a benevolent society, an initiation into a new country, a child's initiation into a family. Some initiations are, of course, perfunctory and superficial, as in the case of an unknown house guest who is introduced to the others. This may be simply a formality, and once the person takes his leave he may never see the other people again. Certain initiations are highly ritualistic, as is the case with some of the benevolent societies. Other initiations are far more complicated and involve much more of one's human depth.

This can be seen best in the case of a man and wife who already have two or three children yet want another. How will this new child be accepted (initiated) into the already ongoing familial society? The attitude of the parents is paramount, for they must really want another child if the baby is to be welcome. Economic preparations play a not inconsiderable role, and preparing the other children for a new baby is likewise part of the dynamics. Then there is the care which must be shown so that the baby grows up feeling at home with this particular family. Most of us can look back and say that as children we felt "at home" in our parental house. The phenomenologist would ask: What were the factors, the dynamics, the processes at work that made us feel "at home" in this particular place and with these specific people? Those factors, those dynamics and those processes are the components of human initiation. Somehow, in a very deep and personal way, a group of people said to us—and they said it over a long period of time, in both open and subtle ways: "We want you." In our turn we replied to them: "I want to be with you."

When we place baptism within this kind of horizon, we immediately see that it entails much more than a minister with the proper intention, water and an unbaptized human being. In its visible aspects baptism is a human event and a human action. In the baptismal process the people of God are saying: "We want you as part of our religious community," and the person to be baptized, if he or she is an adult, is saying: "I want to be part of this religious community." Now such a human action and process does not occur in an instant, for the preparation of the one to be baptized and of the people of God is vitally important and generally takes considerable time. In a phenomenological approach, the theologian studies all the dynamics and processes which bring about this mutual acceptance, this initiation, and in doing so he is "unpacking" the *visible* part of the sacrament. Or rather he is bringing into intelligibility the sacrament itself and seeing that this quite visible, not epiphenomenal but deeply rooted human dynamic is itself the sign of something that is going on in a transcendent way. When the people of God say to a person: "We want you to share our community," and the individual says to this community: "I want to be part of your community," all of the visible and human dynamics of this process are a sacrament of the fact that God is saying to the individual: "I want you to be part of my trinitarian community," and the individual in the hidden depths of his being is saying: "I want to be part of that trinitarian community." Likewise in the renewal of our baptismal liturgy, dynamics that today convey this notion of initiation and mutual acceptance are precisely the areas that deserve to be celebrated liturgically.

If we turn to the eucharist and study it from this phenomenological standpoint, locating it within the framework of a meal of people eating together, we see that human eating has a wide range of contexts. Human eating includes a quick lunch at the counter of a coffee shop among virtual strangers as well as a very meaningful Thanksgiving or Christmas dinner among friends and relatives. Particularly in the latter instances does the phenomenologist catch the truly human implications of a meal. In such meals there is much more than mere food and eating. There is a being with others, a sharing, a communication, a presence.

Martin Heidegger has expressed what this "being with" involves: "By 'Others' we do not mean everyone else but me—those over against whom the 'I' stands out. They are rather those from whom, for the most part, one does *not* distinguish oneself . . . those among whom one is too. This Being-there-too (*Auch-da-sein*) does not have the ontological character of a Being-present-at-hand-along-with them within a world. This 'with' is something of the character of *Dasein*; the 'too' means sameness of Being as circumspectively concernful Being-in-the-world. 'With' and 'too' are to be understood existentially, not categorically. By reason of this with-like-Being in the world, the world is always the one I

50   THE SACRAMENTS

share with others. The world of *Dasein* is a with-world (*Mitwelt*). Being in is Being with Others. Their Being-in-themselves-within-the-world is *Dasein*-with (*Mitdasein*)."⁶

Passages from other phenomenologists could just as easily be cited, but what Heidegger attempts to describe is existentially actualized in the human action of a meal, of people eating together. A significant meal involves many symbols, expressing this "being-there-too." It brings about a "with-world." It catches people up into a group of others from whom one does not distinguish oneself. Why does a meal do this? Is it only the presence of food and drink? Is it only the fact that people know each other? Why do human beings generally celebrate the important moments of their lives with food and drink? Is this only custom? And even were this mere custom, why does the celebration of such occasions become enriched by the presence of food and drink? To catch something of the real presence between people who eat together, to understand the intersubjectivity that is enriched and developed in the meal situation, to see the meal not as some sort of epiphenomenon on the surface of human life but as a deeply imbedded dynamic of the human phenomenon itself—all of this enables the theologian to see the eucharist in a much more meaningful and less mechanical way.

The phenomenological method involves the theologian in areas that are far from the center of the theological enterprise. He would look at and study in detail such human phenomena as initiation; the dynamics of a meal; all the psychological, sociological, existential factors present in the numerous instances of human forgiveness; the human care for the sick, the elderly, the dying and how that caring is received by the sick person himself; what dynamics enter into the human process of consent in its many forms along the entire spectrum of interhuman commerce, but especially why human sexual consent is something more than the mere instinctual "consent" of animal copulation; and finally the dynamics that enter into any real service that is offered and accepted by human beings. Each of these areas is caught up in the various sacraments of the Church and, secular as they might seem to be, these areas deserve much closer theological attention.

To understand the Church it is not enough simply to describe the selection of the apostles and the gospel mission on which they were sent; it is not enough to recount biblical passages or even to talk about the presence of the Spirit in the people of God. We must ask a further question: Why is the people of God—that is, a group of people in a religious community—a sacrament of the Christ event? What visible aspects serve as the symbol and sacrament of this unseen mystery? The phenomenology of interpersonal dynamics which bring about a community of men and women is basic to an understanding of the Church both as an institution and as the people of God.

By far the largest share of work, however, should be devoted to what it means to be a human person, so that God's becoming *man* will be theologically more intelligible. It is in this area that phenomenologists can be of the greatest service to theology, since what these men are studying is basically the human phenomenon. If we cannot come to some insight of Jesus as man, then Jesus is not a sacrament to us; he is not revelatory of the good news. The humanness of Jesus—or, more abstractly, the incarnation—is the key to the Christian understanding of both God and our world, but the humanity of Jesus remains just another phrase until we are in a position to appreciate the very phenomenon of the human, since it is only when we begin to grasp Jesus' "being there too" with us that we will for the first time see what our "being there too" with him means. This understanding of the human phenomenon leads us to appreciate the humanness of Jesus and only on that basis can Jesus become a sacrament for us. In other words, the phenomenology of man is basic for understanding the foundation of all Christian sacramentality— Christ, the *Ursakrament*.

Conclusion

The sacraments need to be approached from many standpoints and with the help of several hermeneutical methods. The two methods applied in this essay are meant only as the first ones to be used in studying the sacraments. The christological method—that is, adopting the hermeneutical process of Christology in order to understand the theology of the sacraments—is an intratheological method leading us to an initial understanding of the *Christian* sacrament. The phenomenological method, which studies human phenomena as the hermeneutical process for understanding the theology of the sacraments, is an interdisciplinary method leading us to an initial understanding of the Christian *sacrament*. Once this is done or at least begun, then the biblical, historical and liturgical approaches to the sacraments fall into place and help draw out the meaning of the sacraments even further. In the present period of theological and liturgical renewal the sacraments, both in theory and in practice, must lead us ever closer to their incarnate center, Jesus Christ, while at the same time speaking more meaningfully to their human participants of Christ and the human phenomenon—the basic framework for any theological study of the Christian sacraments.

Footnotes

1. In this essay I prefer the term "humanness" to "human nature." The Chalcedonian term is a technical one, to be understood within the context of its age, whereas the contemporary use of the word "nature" does not totally reflect the Hellenistic term *physis*. See the second paragraph below.
2. *Christ the Sacrament of the Encounter with God*, p. 15.
3. *The Church and the Sacraments*, pp. 15-16.
4. *Sakramentstheologie* (G.F. Callenback, 1949) p. 219.
5. Baptism and confirmation are here taken to represent two aspects of one and the same sacramental process.
6. *Being and Time* (Harper & Row, 1962), pp. 154-155.

MODELS FOR A LITURGICAL THEOLOGY

James L. Empereur, S.J.

Liturgy is a mystery and cannot be defined according to visible components alone. A definition of the liturgy which would proceed from clear and univocal concepts is impossible. As with everything else in the area of faith there are no categories which exhaustively express the meaning of the liturgy. It is a mystery of faith and can only be dealt with in terms of symbols, models and paradigms. But because the liturgy as mystery is a rich and complex reality, it is possible to speak about it in terms of several models.

Models by their nature are inadequate. They attempt to clarify reality in terms of our human experience. No single model can be used alone. One should not absolutize any particular model to the detriment of the others. What one model might be obscure about, another will serve to enlighten. This pluralism of models is a theological necessity today. For instance, in the last few decades there have been several operating models to describe the Church that have been popular: Mystical Body, People of God, Sacrament of Christ and Church as Servant. The models change as the Church seeks to find its identity in a changing world. There are obvious limitations to the use of models in theology but the value of this kind of approach is that it allows for conversation among the various theological outlooks at a time when theological pluralism is considered a desideratum.

Needless to say, this shift of paradigms can be very threatening for some people and they resist such change. Such a shift implies more than a change of language. It means the adoption of new values, priorities and commitments. The polarization in the Church today should come as no surprise to someone who is aware of the changing models of the Church. Tolerance of pluralism is the only solution. No benefit will result from trying to impose any one model as the last word. It is true that one model can function as a unifying focus for a particular theologian's framework of thought. And even in the same theologian, one model will be operative in one area of theology and another model in another area. But the theologian is called to go beyond these images. He/she must use the image in a reflective and critical way and when that takes place, he/she is working with the model theologically. The use of models in theology should emphasize for us that at no time do our concepts and symbols actually capture the infinite that lies behind our liturgical experiences. And since all models have their limitations, the task is to work with several models as complementary.

It is very important to realize that when the liturgy is described in terms of theological models one is talking about it in metaphorical terms. One is using images that have an evocative power. The use of models in a liturgical theology is only an attempt to speak of worship analogously in terms of life experiences. Such images and symbols are able to focus human experience in a new way because they so exceed the powers of abstract thought. These models convey a meaning which is apprehended in a nonconceptual way and which have a transformative effect on the horizons of human life.

Religious Models and Experience

While religious models can influence our attitudes and suggest courses of action their validity is dependent upon their ability to articulate our own religious experience. Certain models of the liturgy no longer are able to thematize our present experience of worship and these models are less helpful now than others. The images of the liturgy which are important today are those which can be found to be deeply rooted in the experience of the worshipping congregation. There is a kind of schizophrenia that takes place when there is such discontinuity between the models we use to talk about liturgy and the way we actually experience it. In a sense the crisis of faith is a crisis of images as Avery Dulles has so well indicated. He says: "Many traditional images have lost their former hold on people, while the new images have not yet had time to gain their full power . . . Many of us know very little from direct experience about lambs, wolves, sheep, vines, and grapes, or even about kings and patriarchs as they were in biblical times. There is need therefore to supplement these images with others that speak more directly to our contemporaries'' (*Models of the Church*, p. 19). We cannot, however, pretend to create these images on the spot. They are born and they die but they cannot be manufactured by committees or individual theologians. Yet these models are indispensable for any liturgical theology.

Some of the models of the liturgy have an exploratory or educative value in that they highlight for us elements and qualities of our worship to which we have not previously averted. Often this will have practical consequences for us which were less pressing at a former time. But there is no way in which one can prove the truth of the models used. One can say that their validity depends upon whether or not they work, whether they are more helpful than some others to articulate what is going on in the worshipping community informed by Christ and the gospel. Liturgy like any area of theology must begin in faith and with the fact that we are dealing with a community of revelation. Because certain models do not describe what is actually going on in certain parishes today does not immediately call into question the usefulness of the model. It may be that such a model is necessary to call those parishes to a ''liturgical conversion.'' The truth of a model depends upon the consequences that follow upon the use of such a model. If a model leads to distortions and abuses on the practical level, then it is judged to be a bad model.

There are more models than the five described here. But the ones I have selected appear to me to be most helpful. It is better to work with a few models in an article of this length and risk some oversimplifications than to cause confusion by multiplying the paradigms of liturgical theology. It should be obvious that what is said of each model does not apply to it exclusively. It is a matter of emphasis and predominant reference.

Liturgy as Institution

This view of the liturgy presupposes an ecclesiology which sees the Church primarily in terms of its visible structures, its officers and its required procedures. Such a view is more than the affirmation that for the Church to accomplish its task for building up the kingdom of God, it is necessary to have some kind of visibility, some leaders and some accepted methods of conducting its business. Rather it is the institutional aspect of the Church which is regarded as primary. It is *the* model for understanding the Church.

According to this model the Church is described in terms of teaching, sanctifying and governing. All three of these tasks are done for the faithful by the leaders of the Church, thus identifying these leaders with the Church itself. The liturgy in this framework would be seen as something which is primarily done by the clergy for the people. The clergy is the source of grace that flows through the ritual actions. The liturgical celebration is basically a pyramidal event, in which the ordinary worshippers find themselves in a primarily passive position. There is also a clear cut distinction between clergy and faithful in the liturgy itself.

Liturgy here becomes a legalistic consideration. The observance of liturgical regulations takes on paramount importance and the sanctifying power of the sacraments is dependent upon the proper observance of canonical rules. It is important in this model that the test of authentic liturgy be what can be juridically verified. The criteria for the liturgy of the Church must be visible as are the standards for membership in the Church itself.

This view of the liturgy is basically triumphalistic in character. Those who consider worship primarily as institutional see little need for the liturgy to change. It was perfect from the beginning and any questioning of the significance of any of the structures becomes a threat to the underlying ecclesiology. And so it is only logical that this model which is based on the presupposition that what is essential is unchanging would place a great deal of importance on the institution of the liturgy by Christ. The seven sacraments would be seen as being either directly or indirectly instituted by Christ. And the Church must have been brought into existence by Christ with the same fundamental structure that it has today. The liturgy is necessarily hierarchical because that is also of divine institution.

Since theology in this view becomes basically defending what the Church has already taught and since there can be no question in this position of any new revelation after the close of the deposit of faith, liturgical theology becomes the attempt to find in the sources of revelation the proof for what the Church is saying about the liturgy.

As in the case of the other areas of Church life, the chief beneficiaries of liturgy are the members of the Church themselves. The sacramental liturgy becomes the source of nourishing graces for those who belong to the "Catholic Church." Other liturgical forms such as the liturgy of the hours are reverenced to the degree that they approach the sacramentality of the specifically seven sacraments. And the purpose of this liturgy is to bring people to heaven, to help them to stay on the straight and narrow path and to stay within the parameters of the Catholic Church so that their salvation can be assured.

In this empirical approach to liturgy a great deal of stress is placed on what is statistically measurable. For instance, baptisms, marriages, anointings, converts and communions are counted. Remember the days when the priest sat in the confessional with his hand counter clicking away as he tallied up the number of penitents. Or how often in the old days did one hear at jubilee celebrations the recounting of how many thousands of masses Father so-and-so said in his life as a priest.

Limitations of the Institutional Model

Is this view of the liturgy still in existence? Very definitely. It has strong endorsement in official church documents and by the leaders in the Church. Certainly, it is still clearly stressed in the document on the liturgy that the Church's worship is of divine institution. Many hold on to this view of liturgy because it gives them a sense of stability in an ever-changing world. At times these people focus on relatively unimportant aspects of worship such as genuflections and incense because they want to have at least one thing in their life which does not change. The unchanging liturgy gave Catholics a strong sense of identity. The remark was often made that the wonderful thing about the Latin Mass was that one could go anywhere in the world to worship in any Catholic Church and always feel at home.

There are some serious limitations to the juridical model of liturgy. There is little if any New Testament evidence for such an approach to worship. What we find there is more flexible, pluralistic and adapted. The liturgy before the formation of the Roman Rite in the fourth and fifth centuries was a rich and variegated phenomenon. Until the freezing of the Missal by Pius V in 1570 there was considerable diversity in the Roman liturgy itself.

Another problem with this approach is that it reinforced the clericalization of the liturgy. It is no coincidence that as the institutional model of the Church gained control, the juridical model of the liturgy became paramount. The history of the liturgy becomes the gradual removing of the liturgy from the people. Fidelity to rubrics becomes more important than the quality of the celebration and attendance at mass under pain of sin looms larger than the call to authentic worship. The concern over communion in the hand has gone far beyond any regard for worshipping in spirit and in truth. Liturgy can hardly have a prophetic quality about it if the local authorities are preoccupied with the observation of minor liturgical regulations.

This juridical concept of liturgy raises problems for theology. For instance, there is little leeway for the developing of the ecumenical liturgical experience. The problem of intercommunion becomes one of fidelity to the Roman See. This view of liturgy seems to render the liturgical life of other Churches (non-Roman) as without content and life. Needless to say, in this approach anything like a charismatic liturgy would be highly suspect. Perhaps, that is the reason why the Catholic Charismatic Movement has gone out of its way to be "law-abiding" in its liturgical celebrations.

Liturgy as Mystery

Odo Casel, the author of the mystery-theology approach to liturgy, has been unjustly passed over. The fact is that despite the criticisms about his position, many of the ideas of Odo Casel have been accepted by the document on the liturgy of the Second Vatican Council. This is especially true of his notion of Christ's presence in the liturgy. It is inappropriate for a council of the Church to embrace any particular theologian's position, but the sounds of Casel ring through the *Constitution on the Sacred Liturgy*, especially in Chapter one. For instance in No. 2 the document states: "The liturgy is thus the outstanding means by which the faithful can express in their lives the mystery of Christ." It is a fact that many of Casel's ideas have become part of post-conciliar theology.

Casel defined mystery as a "sacred ritual action in which a saving deed is made present through the rite; the congregation, by performing the rite, takes part in the saving act, and thereby experiences salvation."

The content or meaning of mystery in Casel's thought (and in the framework of those who identify themselves with the mystery-theology approach to liturgy) refers first of all to God himself as he exists in himself and in the things that he has made. Secondly, it refers to Christ, not just the person of Christ but Christ performing his salvific actions, especially his death, resurrection and ascension. Thirdly, mystery means the saving activity of Christ in the Church and in the sacraments. This third sense is really the one that is most operative in this liturgical theology. As such the liturgical mystery possesses a sacramental mode of being. It means making present again by a cultic action. The content of this ritualizing is not just the power of the effect of Christ's saving deeds, but these very deeds themselves. It is the presence of historic-non-recurring actions of salvation, not of some eternal, extra-temporal salvific will nor of an event in heaven. And what is made present is the reality which lies behind the historical actions, not these actions in their historical trappings.

Christ is not separated from his mysteries but is present and active within them. The presence of the Risen Christ is not properly speaking the reality made present in the liturgy but is the preliminary condition making possible the presence of what is essential, the saving actions of Christ. It is necessary that Christ *and his saving work* be present in the liturgy because a person only becomes a Christian by participation in this saving activity. Neither the presence of the person of Christ, nor the presence of divine life in him, nor the mere presence of the body and blood are enough. The redeeming work itself must be present. Our participation in the mystery of salvation demands a real and mystical participation in the life and death of Christ which must be present in the sacramental act. The great breakthrough that Casel made was to move the focus in eucharistic theology away from the presence of Jesus' body and blood to the presence of the redemptive action itself.

Word and Sacraments

The saving action of Christ is not limited to the sacraments. It is communicated by the Word of God. Casel says that one should not make too great a distinction between the presence of Christ in the divine office and in the eucharist. He admits a difference but blames late scholasticism for seeing almost nothing in the Mass but the real presence as the effect of transubstantiation. It makes too little of Christ's saving action in the Word. For the ancient Church there was only one saving action of Christ and this was the ground for the entire liturgy, both word and sacrament.

Christ is not divided. Even blessings and consecrations participate in and show forth the mystery of Christ.

How the saving acts of Christ are rendered present is difficult to understand. We can say that the mystery of Christ is incarnated in the mystery of worship which consists of actions performed both by people and by Christ. Salvation becomes visible because the sacramental symbol is visible. The content of the cultic mystery is present as soon as the sign is set forth because there is a necessary connection between the sacramental process and the incarnation. The sacraments are images of Christ full of the reality of his being *and his activity*. The saving work of Christ is objectively present in the sacraments and it exists before the effect itself.

Past historical events can only be rendered present again through the sacramental mode of existence which can only be understood in faith. Just as the mystery of Christ's redemptive work is *sui generis* because it is both supernatural and yet accomplished in time, so the sacramental mode of existence is different from every natural way of existing. The sacramental mode of existence is not the same as the natural or historical way of existing. The exterior rites are performed in time but the content of these cultic actions does not exist in time. There is no question of a repetition of Christ's saving deeds. The act of Christ is one because it is an eternal, supernatural and transtemporal mystery. There is no before and after. Odo Casel did not attempt to explain metaphysically how the mystery of Christ is sacramentally present in the liturgy. It was for him a matter of understanding what a sacrament is and how it differs from other signs.

There is only one mystery although birth, death and resurrection are events different from each other. It is the substance of this mystery in its totality that is rendered present in the cultic acts. And the substance of the liturgical mystery is the *transitus Christi*, the paschal mystery. Since the paschal mystery is the central mystery, Easter is *the* feast. But a liturgy adequate to the whole mystery of salvation requires a liturgical year and liturgical feasts. The Christian liturgy participates in the sacramentalism inherent in the whole life of the Church in time. There will be present in every liturgical celebration the mystery of God communicated to people in Jesus Christ. Each liturgy celebrates the real presence of Jesus who came at the end of a period of preparation, the paschal mystery now reconciling people to God in the Church, and the prophecy of the kingdom inaugurated in sacramental signs and to be manifested fully in the parousia.

Liturgy as Sacrament

The sacramental model of liturgical theology is presently the one most widely used. It is basically the model that is operative in the *Constitution on the Sacred Liturgy*, although the institutional model is ever present in that document. This model is the one employed by most Catholic (Eastern and Western) liturgical theologians today. There is a considerable spread of emphasis among these liturgists and there is a variety of ways in which they utilize this method for articulating a liturgical theology. For instance, on one hand, you have Vagaggini with his highly scholastic approach to liturgy and on the other, Broccolo who makes use of the psychological model as an adjunct to the sacramental one. Theologians such as Bouyer, Verheul, Martimort and Dalmais are found somewhere in between. But to the extent that these liturgical theologians attempt to construct any real systematic approach to worship, they work within the rather wide parameters of what is called here the sacramental paradigm.

In this view the Church is the primordial sacrament and the liturgy, which at heart is sacramental in the narrow sense, is the expression of the Church and is directed toward the building up of the Church. We have the Second Vatican Council to thank for the most articulate and official expression of the sacramentality of the Church. In the *Constitution on the Church* we find this: "The Church is a kind of sacrament of intimate union with God and of unity with all mankind; that is, she is a sign and instrument of such union and unity" (art. 1). The *Constitution on the Sacred Liturgy* says: "The Liturgy is the summit toward which the activity of the Church is directed; at the same time it is the fountain from which all her power flows" (art. 10)). The same document says that the Church "reveals herself most clearly when a full complement of God's holy people, united in prayer and in a common liturgical service" join together in worship.

A contemporary understanding of sacramentality as applied to the Church and liturgy would be based upon an understanding of the human person as an incarnate reality. Avery Dulles has put the matter as well as anyone. "The structure of human life is therefore symbolic. The body with all its movements and gestures becomes the expression of the human spirit. The spirit comes to be what it is in and through the body. The symbolic expression does not simply signify what previously existed independently of it. Rather, the expression and the realization accompany and support each other. The corporeal expression gives the spiritual act the material support he needs in order to achieve itself; and the spiritual act gives shape and meaning to the corporeal expression" (p. 60, *Models of the Church*). Liturgy according to this model would be seen primarily in terms of this meaning of a sacrament: an outward sign of a spiritual reality, not in the sense that it merely points to something beyond itself, but as an efficacious sign so that it intensifies that which it is bringing to expression. Because of the incarnational structure of the human spirit, we can talk about sacraments conferring what they contain.

Sacraments as Social Symbols

Sacraments are dialogic in character. They are social symbols which allow the experience of God to break through in terms of a human interaction. Sacraments as the encounter with God are not experiences in isolation. They are communal symbols of grace coming to visibility. For this reason we do not baptize ourselves, we do not anoint ourselves and for this reason the so-called individual celebration of the Eucharist can only be described as a highly deficient sign. Thus, worship in this model is primarily participative. There is no room for spectators at the liturgy. Sacramentality by its very nature calls for participation. In participating in the sign of the liturgy, the worshippers are actually creating the Church and the sacramental sign.

To the extent that this model makes use of such images as Body of Christ and People of God it sees the liturgy in the context of the Church as community. This emphasizes that what is being brought to sacramental expression is a Spirit-filled fellowship of charity and truth. The main focus will not be on the visible institutional structures of the liturgical assembly. A liturgical theology in which these metaphors are prominent would stress the union of grace on the personal level which is made visible through the ministry and the sacraments. The union that exists among the worshippers is that of the graces of the Holy Spirit which make this community more than a purely sociological phenomenon. Worship is not seen primarily in juridical terms but according to a union which is deeper than any merely human union. The purpose of the liturgy is to establish a deep and lasting union between God and Christians. What is celebrated in the liturgy is grace as a communal gift.

The sacramental approach to liturgy then, brings together the institutional and more community oriented approaches. For liturgy to be sacramental it must be visible; it must be incarnated through outward signs. It must be structured. It is more than communal undifferentiated enthusiasm. But it is more than structure. It is event. It is the dynamism of grace realizing itself in coming to visibility. It is the community's spirituality achieving historical tangibility. There is an internal thrust in the spirituality that the liturgy articulates that demands coming to expression. In the actual liturgical celebration this spirituality is not only reflected but also constituted. And this means that something must happen in the lives of the worshippers. They must be transformed by the spirit so that they manifest the biblical gifts of that same Spirit.

This approach does not claim for liturgy a monopoly of the grace of God coming to expression. Grace and salvation are found outside of liturgy. However, it would affirm strongly that liturgy is the clearest articulation of the Christian's experience of God. Christ and the Church as sacraments of God's reconciling love for the world imply that liturgy is the unambiguous manifestation of this sacramentality of Christ and the Church. Grace is always seeking visibility, and it is most adequately articulated in the liturgical celebrations. God's working in the world outside of the areas under the sphere of influence of the Church's liturgy will tend to be more ambiguous in their witnessing character.

This liturgical theology can easily view the worship situation in a much too exalted fashion. References to the heavenly liturgy can make the theology seem too artificial or unrelated to actual liturgical experiences. With this approach liturgy can turn out to be the plaything of aesthetes and the social and ethical dimensions of the liturgical assembly can be underplayed.

There is an inbuilt tension in this model when it stresses the community aspect of worship. There can be a great deal of frustration with the liturgy when it is described in terms of a community celebration. The fact is that the experience of community at most liturgical services is quite deficient. One can so idealize this aspect of the sacramental model that it cannot be found verified any place in human living. It is necessary to be realistic about what can actually be achieved here in terms of this more interpersonal mode. The search for a perfect human community which can adequately celebrate the liturgy is illusory.

Liturgy as Proclamation

Most Protestant and some Catholic liturgical theologians are more at home with understanding the liturgy as an event of the proclamation of the Word of God. Liturgy is constituted in the proclamation of the Word. It takes place in the very act of proclamation. Proclamation is a linguistic event in which the Church is constituted. Sacraments are looked upon as "visible words."

The theology of liturgy which is articulated in terms of proclamation is based upon the fundamental understanding that the relationship of God to the world and to human beings is to be seen in terms of a dialog between the two. God has shared himself in creation and is calling it to union with himself. This dialogic relationship which describes the reality between God and persons presupposes the mutual presence of God and humans to each other.

In this dialog between God and ourselves, it is God who takes the initiative. God speaks first. The basic attitude on our part is to listen. It is necessary to listen if God is to become present to us. God becomes present in his actual speaking. If the relationship between God and ourselves is one of dialog, then this relationship can only come about through communication. When God speaks and when we listen there is that mutual presence which is so necessary for this dialogic union. The presence of God to us is a human presence; it is a personal presence. But it is a presence brought about through language.

Wherever sharing in someone's life is to take place (and this is what is meant by a dialogic relationship), it is necessary to be adequately present to that person. This is equally true of the dialog between friends, married people or between God and ourselves. This adequate presence comes about through communication. And this communication requires a form of language. In the case of God he is adequately present to us in Jesus Christ. Christ is the form of his communication. Christ is the language of God. He is thus called the Word of God. Not that he says everything about God that there is to say, but that he adequately expresses the reality of God so that this sharing of life, this mutual presence, this union or dialogical relationship can be brought about without excessive difficulty.

To understand how it is that Christ is the Word of God, how he is the one who makes it possible for the dialog between God and ourselves to take place, and why it is that it is the liturgy which becomes the common language of God and his people, it is necessary to know something of the nature of proclamation. What is the meaning of proclamation? Surely, it is more than speaking in a loud voice. It is more than mere talking. One could hardly talk about liturgy as proclamation if to proclaim meant little more than communicating information such as reading a dinner menu to someone who is blind.

The Meaning of Proclamation

Proclamation is language, but not any kind of language. It is not the language of ordinary conversation or of a business transaction. It is more than verbal communication. It is what theologians call a language-event. By that is meant that language has a broader meaning than the words we use. All forms of human communication such as smiles, laughter, music, art, dancing, making love and other non-verbal gestures can be proclamatory. Two persons embracing, kissing, or having sexual intercourse may use the words "I love you." But they need not, and real communication, real proclamation would have taken place without any words at all.

In this wider sense, language becomes the way that human beings communicate and become mutually present. In this sense human presence depends upon language. The human presence brought about through a language-event is a personal presence. For instance, if you are in a crowded subway train, there may be a number of people who are physically present to you, especially if they are pushing and shoving you. But it is only when someone speaks or smiles at you that there is a question of human personal presence. At that moment your personal reality has been constituted by language. We live in relation to others to the degree that they are present to us through a language event.

The point of all this is that language creates us because it enables us to relate with others. When this happens we have an event of proclamation. The proclamatory word (which need not be verbal) brings meaning into our lives. It challenges us to make a decision. We can accept or reject this proclamation to us, but in some sense it calls for decision. Whether it is a question of acceptance or rejection, a new relationship is constituted.

This kind of proclamation can be creative of community. The eventful word both depends on the community and is constitutive of community. A community is that group of people who share the same language, who assent to the same proclamation in their lives. The community of the Church is that group of individuals who have heard the proclamation of the Word of God and who now live according to the vision put forth by that language-event. They are people with the Christian vision and the Christian language, because what they share is Jesus Christ with a certain explicitness. This is so because Christ is for them their eventful word.

Liturgy then can be described as the dialog between God and ourselves because of the place of Christ in the liturgical celebration. When God speaks, proclaims, to us his Word who is Jesus Christ, we have liturgy in the form of the gospel and the sacraments. When we respond to God through the prayer of Christ we have the language of liturgy in terms of praise and thanksgiving. In the liturgy Christ becomes God's most perfect proclamation and at the same time he is our most adequate response. Christ is God's best answer to his own call and he is also the fullest proclamation of the community.

Christian liturgy, as the community's proclamation, is the articulation of the presence of God in Christ especially in terms of the Paschal Mystery. In the words of one liturgist: "Liturgy is the permanent proclamation of the Paschal Mystery which constitutes and reflects the Church. The liturgical assembly is the most explicit expression and manifestation of the Christian life because it lights up what is going on in the rest of Christian living."

This model of liturgical theology has some important implications for the planning process. The liturgical dynamic is one of proclamation and response. The very structure of the liturgy should be designed in terms of the rhythm of proclamations and responses. This will influence the placing of music in the celebration, the use of gestures and the celebrational style of the ministers. In all of the rites, response should follow proclamation. One should not employ several proclamations or several responses in a row. To do so would destroy the rhythm which is so necessary for an enlivened celebration which is supposed to articulate the very rhythm of our lives in a Christian perspective.

Liturgy as Process

The process model for constructing a liturgical theology is developed in the light of the principles of what is called process theology, a specifically American systematic conceptuality for understanding God and the Christian message. This theoretical framework stresses the relationship of God to the world as one of unity rather than separation. God is always at work in the world and the world is the symbol of God, the manifestation of God's presence. This world, the only one we have, is the arena of God's activity and existence.

According to this view there is no possibility that liturgy would be seen as worship of an absent God, or a God who is infinitely separated from this world. Rather it is the liturgy which is the human activity which highlights for us that God is working in and through the world to bring about a greater union with himself.

This view of reality places considerable emphasis on the interrelatedness and interdependence of all reality. Reality is highly relational. This means that the usual dichotomies between God and the world, the Church and secular society, Christ and the rest of humanity are broken down and blurred.

Another important component of a process theology is that it is the "becoming" of reality which is stressed. It is process rather than substance, becoming rather than being which are the inclusive categories of understanding reality. God who is intrinsically related to all reality is a God who changes, who is living and yet is perfect. Perfection in this framework does not demand immutability. With such a presupposition, liturgy can never be seen as a finished product. It is an event always in process. It is the constant result of creativity in life and in the actual celebration. The process mode of thinking would eschew anything like an immutable Church or an isolated and independent liturgy. The Church is a distinctive stream in the general flow of reality. Its purpose is to bring out of concealment the directionality of the total process but it is in no essential way separated from it. Thus, the language and gestures of liturgy would be the language and gestures of today's culture.

God Involved in Life

A process liturgical theology presupposes a God who is very much involved in people's lives. It rejects the God who has no feelings and emotions, who is self-contained and outside of time, a God to whom nothing in the world can really make any difference. The fact is that worship does presuppose a God who is personally concerned with the worshipper's problems and desires. Process theology says that God is so personally involved in this world and with human beings that he is actually affected by what is going on. He is diminished by our sinfulness to the degree that he cannot become that kind of God which he would become had we not sinned. God is enriched by our contributions as we become more fully human. In this sense the world is constantly changing God. He sees the direction in which he would like the world to go and he tries to lure this world to greater and greater humanization, to greater and more creative things. But he cannot coerce. This position is not pantheistic. God and the world are not reduced to each other. But God is part of the fabric of this world. God and the world are unthinkable without each other.

This view, then, helps us to overcome the kind of conflict we have had between our traditional theology and the prayers of our liturgy. Often our theology said that God could not be affected by what we did and yet our prayers and hymns presumed otherwise. Liturgy can be seen as that event in the Christian community where we have the clearest and best statement, by means of ritual, of how God is affecting the world and how the world is contributing to God. God does not enter our world through the liturgy and when we are at worship we are not addressing someone who is outside of the liturgical assembly. God is always there and because of our ritualizing he rises to visibility for the community which is gathered together, hears the gospel, shows forth its ministry and shares in the supper of the Lord.

The liturgical experience which is constantly undergoing change is open-ended. The Christ of the liturgy is evolving. There is no immutable, static Christ. He is always in the process of completion. This does not mean that there is no relation between the Christ of the liturgy and the Christ of the past. There is continuity with the death and resurrection. However, this is continuity and not mere repetition. There is always something of the past in each liturgical event, but there is always something that is novel. In this sense, the direction of the liturgy is more to the future than to the past. It follows from this that if liturgy is truly to be alive and working, then it is necessary to build change into the structure of worship itself. Christian ritual does not mean to repeat only what Christians have done before.

The liturgy does more than reiterate the past because it responds to the present community and where it is at the present time. Liturgy facilitates the growth of the Church by taking into itself what is new in present ecclesial relationships. In that sense liturgy is caused by the future. As the process theologian sees it, God, Jesus Christ, the Church, and the sacraments are in the process of becoming, and in this sense the liturgical life is lived from the future. God through Jesus Christ assumes a persuasive posture toward the Church in the direction of greater humanization and union with himself. Thus, the Chruch's sacramental life is to be in a constant process of creative advance.

Sacramental liturgy is to be viewed as the special moment in the Church where the relationality that makes us Christian, our relation to God in Christ, is highlighted and established in a deeper and more unambiguous way. Through the individual sacraments, the event of the Church in process continues to be created. Liturgy is the way that the Church is maintained in process.

This process liturgical theology can be summarized in the following points: 1) liturgy is a processive-relational event; 2) the God to whom the liturgy is directed is a changing God who so interacts with the world that he is both its creator and is created by it, a world he entices to further growth and enrichment; 3) the liturgy is future-directed implying that the worshipper, the worshipping community and the mediating Christ are constantly evolving; 4) the Christ who does the worshipping in the liturgy makes it possible for the community to be the paradigm of the relationship of God and the world; 5) the Church whose spirituality is articulated ritually in liturgy is an event-always-becoming, and 6) the sacraments are those special moments in the Church's life where its relationship to Christ and to the individual members is so expressed that the liturgy becomes a celebration of salvation by appropriating the past, by relating to the present and by responding to the allurement of the future.

Conclusion

How is one to evaluate these models? They are not all equally appropriate to a contemporary liturgical theology. Each model must be judged in terms of its basis in scripture and tradition, the degree that it corresponds to modern religious experience, its ability to give the worshippers a sense of mission and identity, how much it fosters Christian virtues and ecumenical dialog and especially how creative it is for theologizing about worship.

The institutional model rightly emphasizes a structured liturgy although it can lead to a rigid preoccupation with rubrics. The mystery model clearly indicates the importance of the liturgical realism of the ritual action in that worship is the prolongation of Christ's work on earth although this approach runs the risk of viewing the liturgical symbol too Platonically and of viewing the presence of Christ (in distinction from his actions) too statically. The sacramental model highlights very well that it is the community at worship which is the primary symbol of God's salvation, but it can also cause an excessively in-house consideration of the liturgy. The proclamation model sees the liturgy as the primordial place of the event of the Word of God although there is always the danger of a form of fundamentalism. The process model avoids the ever present temptation to separate liturgy from life, but it does not speak as clearly as do some of the other models of the transcendence of God and the eschatological dimension of the Church's worship.

No one model can be the supermodel under which the others are subsumed. The liturgical theologian must work with them all in a complementary fashion. An individual theologian may choose one model as the dominating image if he/she in no way excludes the other models. I do not believe, however, that the institutional model can be taken to be a primary image in a liturgical theology because institutions and structures are subordinate to persons and life. In fact the imperialism of any model in a liturgical theology will be detrimental to that theology because ultimately worship is part of the mystery of Christ and the Church.

HOW TO RECEIVE A SACRAMENT AND MEAN IT

Karl Rahner, S.J.

I propose a new way of thinking about sacraments: instead of seeing in them a spiritual movement outward from the sacramental action to an effect in the world, we should look for a spiritual movement of the world toward the sacrament. This applies to every sacrament which is received with conscious faith—hence only infant baptism is excluded. If we speak primarily of the Eucharist, it is for the sake of brevity; this theory applies proportionately to all the other sacraments.

What does the average Catholic feel at an average reception of the Eucharist? Perhaps something like this: the Christian experiences himself as living in a profane world, bound by divine commandments which are hard to keep, called by God, and put on a path that leads through death into God's eternity. In order to get in touch with God, every now and then he steps out of this profane world into a "fane," a holy place, where a true encounter with God is possible, where God appears not as commanding but as forgiving and strengthening. Having met God and the Lord Jesus, the Christian returns to the profane world, to his daily grind far from God. The sacrament alone puts him in touch with the Lord, and makes his life meaningful and "religious."

In this view the reception of the Eucharist and other sacraments is the real high point of Christian life. This is certainly a legitimate way of looking at it, but it is not the only way.

For one thing it seems to be on the way out. Rightly or wrongly, this way of thinking is suspected of empty ritualism; for Mass and sacraments seem to make no difference in real life. The "pious" person may say they comfort him; the less pious person will think: "That is just what I reject—this escaping into an unreal world. It changes nothing in real life, and anyway the consolation vanishes when you understand the psychic mechanism involved." And if in the Mass we are enjoined to "take Christ's sacrifice out into our daily lives," this only reestablishes an ethical obligation, the futility of which drove man to the sacraments in the first place. For it would not be the sacraments which brought us out into real life, but we who had to take them out with us. Their power would actually consist in our own renewed effort to be good. Furthermore this view puts us in danger of considering the sacraments as "good works" to be accumulated—but mere frequency of reception of the sacraments seems now more than ever of doubtful value.

Contemporary movements to desacralize Christianity may be objectionable in many respects, but they show that a lot of people are uncomfortable with sacral sacramental practices. It can be doubted whether even earnest Christians really experience the Mass as the high point of Christian life, as Vatican II called it.

Our response to the sacraments is inhibited today not only by fashionable ideas of "secularization" but also and more fundamentally by our growing awareness of the difference between authentic existence and the conceptual models we use to reflect on it. For example, a person may sincerely declare, "My God, I want to love you with my whole heart," without actually loving God with his whole heart. In his reflex consciousness he has constructed a conceptual model of such a love and to some extent assented to it. But this replica of whole-hearted love is not itself whole-hearted love. If such love is really present, it is enacted on a more profound level, because freedom is on a more profound level than our reflex representation of it.

What is more, this profound freedom is not able at every moment in an individual's history to accomplish its purpose, namely to make a radical and definitive disposition of the total person. But reception of the sacraments is by its nature an attempt to make a radical disposition of oneself before God in freedom and love. Modern man's experience of freedom tells him that the *kairos* for this basic decision does not come often and cannot be conjured up when he wants it. Hence frequent reception of the sacraments makes him feel dishonest, particularly when it is thought of as decisive for his individual salvation. The problem is not completely solved by what we are proposing, namely that we become aware that the sacramental sign is the manifestation in one's own life of the grace that guides the history of the whole world. But responding to the sacraments will be easier if the recipient is aware that he is already part of the "cosmic" history of grace.

The Eucharist and the other sacraments can be viewed in another way. This view is based on the simple dogmatic fact that sanctifying grace is found *everywhere*, wherever man has not cut himself off from the saving God by a truly culpable "no." Here we will not prove this truth itself but only explore its consequences for a new understanding of the sacraments.

The world is permeated by God's grace. To be sure, the sacraments are grave-events, but not in the sense of discrete discharges of grace into a profane world. The world is permanently graced at its root. It is borne up by God's self-communication even before free creatures decide whether to accept this proffered grace. It is graced, whether or not it seems so to our jaded sensibilities. Without hope and faith in precisely this kind of grace, modern man would never be able to believe in the sacraments as isolated, intermittent acts of grace. He could never overcome the impression that they were phony offers of transcending a brutally profane world.

This radical gracing of reality may seem rather abstract, but there is no way to talk clearly about what enables man to surrender to the unutterable mystery. Still we must stress one thing: this grace is not a particular phenomenon occurring parallel to the rest of human life but simply the ultimate depth of everything the spiritual creature does when he realizes himself—when he laughs and cries, accepts responsibility, loves, lives and dies, stands up for truth, breaks out of preoccupation with self to help the neighbor, hopes against hope, cheerfully refuses to be embittered by the stupidity of daily life, keeps silent not so that evil festers in his heart but so that it dies there—when in a word, man lives as he would like to live, in opposition to his selfishness and to the despair that always assails him. This is where grace occurs, because all this leads man into the infinity and victory that is God.

Something else must be said about this grace which is the depth and mystery of everyday life. It attained its clearest manifestation in Jesus of Nazareth, and precisely in the kind of life in which he became like us in all things, in a life full of ordinariness—birth, hardship, courage, hope, failure, and death. If we had the space we could show how the man who accepts the human life, death, and resurrection of Jesus as God's irrevocable promise of his own personal victory and thus as God's last word, also affirms more or less explicitly the traditional Christology. And thus whoever understands the grace of God as the radicality of his own life accepts the historical manifestation of this grace in Jesus Christ, whether he knows it or not.

Finally, this grace creates solidarity. If we take grace as the deepest meaning, the holiness of all that is profane, then life itself, when accepted sincerely, truly, and lovingly, binds us mysteriously together. In his own fate, each one experiences that of all men; and in the living and dying of others, he discovers himself.

From the above standpoint, the sacraments are the manifestation of the holiness and redeemed status of the profaneness of man and the world. Rather than entering a temple which walls off the Holy from the godless world outside, man sets up in the open expanse of God's world a sign proclaiming that not in Jerusalem alone but everywhere, in Spirit and in truth, God is adored, experienced, and accepted as gracious liberator. It is a perpetual tragic misunderstanding when this little sign, which is to remind us of the limitlessness of God's grace, is made into an enclosure in which alone God and his grace are to be found.

Let us make this concrete by applying it to the Eucharist. The world and its history is the terrifying, sublime, death-and-immolation liturgy which God celebrates unto himself by the agency of mankind. The whole length and breadth of his monstrous history, full of superficiality, stupidity, insufficiency, and hatred on the one side, and silent dedication, faithfulness unto death, joy, and sorrow on the other side, constitutes the liturgy of the world, and the liturgy of the Son on his cross is its culmination. Since man's eye is as blind to this grand liturgy of the world as man's heart is ignorant of itself, it must be clarified and brought into reflex awareness in what we ordinarily call liturgy. This latter, however, can be performed authentically only if we come to it from the existential liturgy of faith, which is identical with the rightly lived history of the world.

The believer knows that his life is implicated in the drama of the world, in the divine tragedy and comedy. And if the secret essence of the world's history, at once stupefying and stimulating, wells up from the depths of his existence and overflows the land of his heart, he is not surprised that thus he experiences the grace of the world. Judgment when refused, blissful future when accepted, this grace permeates history, and in the cross of Jesus it has already reached the point where it can no longer be defeated. In faith he experiences the abiding presence of the cross; he knows that those who sorrow weep the tears of Jesus, the joyful share in Jesus' joy, and so forth. He knows that both mankind and the Son of Man can be understood only in polarity: without Christ mankind's hope is vain, and without mankind Christ degenerates into an abstract ideology. Before he even thinks of it, a person is involved in this drama of the head and members, in which the head is for the sake of the members, because the Spirit of Jesus is from the outset the Spirit of the world as God wills the world to be.

Going to Mass, then, adds nothing to the world but celebrates what is really happening in the world. Jesus' cross is not raised again, but its mysterious presence in the world is put into words. At Mass, the Christian offers the world in bread and wine, knowing that the world is already offering itself in triumph and tears and blood to the incomprehensible, which is God. He gazes into ineffable light, knowing that the real vision is given to eyes blinded with tears or glassy with approaching death. He knows that he proclaims the death of the Lord because this death is ever present in the heart of the world and in everyone who "dies in the Lord." He proclaims the Lord's coming, because He *is* coming in whatever brings the world closer to its goal. He receives the true body of the Lord, knowing it would profit him nothing, were he not in communion with *the* body of God which is the world itself with its fate. He hears and speaks the word of God, aware that it is the verbal expression of the divine word which is the world and of the Word in which God eternally says "yes" to this world.

When a person goes to Mass, he may not be explicitly conscious of his community of destiny with the world, yet his own life relates him to the Absolute. If he loves even when he is not loved in return, if he forgives even when it does not make him feel good to have forgiven, if he is suddenly struck by the majestic inexorability of truth, these everyday events speak to him of God, provided he lets Him set him free.

This Mass-goer need not be alarmed and feel that his faith is in danger if he is tempted to see the sacraments as empty ceremonies and the Mass as a game, like the sacrifice offered by a Vedic priest to approach the gods and keep the world on its hinges. To save these ceremonies, he need not imagine that when they are performed God does something he would not do if they were omitted. Rather he must realize that they spring from, express, and lead to the divine depths of real life. Anyone who is afraid of practicing empty ritualism should recall the experiences of God and of grace which he has had in apparently profane life and say, "This is the experience I am ritualizing in worship." Someone who thinks he has never had such an experience, however, should refrain from the sacraments, for Christian doctrine forbids receiving them without faith. Actually everyone has such experiences, and it is the duty of mystagogical instruction, not to produce them, but to bring them into reflex awareness.

Such a person sees the Mass as only a tiny sign of the Mass of the world, but he does not see it as unimportant.

On the one hand, he can regard it as the "summit and source" of his life only in a very qualified sense. "Summit," yes, but he leaves it up to God which moment, sacred or profane, will be the decisive moment in which he finally succeeds in giving himself to God. "Source," yes, but he knows that it flows from the real source, the transcendent saving God and unique saving death of the Lord, and he needs but to open his heart in faith, hope, and love for the water of eternal life to well up everywhere from the depths of his existence.

This does not mean that he regards the sacrament as superfluous. It bears witness to what is hidden in the darkness of the world and the depths of men's hearts; in the serene recollection of the cultic act we can discern what we lose sight of in the daily struggle. The sacrament is the sign of the *res sacramenti*, the sign of the reality signified, which is identical with the whole history of the world, since, to apply a phrase from Aquinas, the sacrament is a *signum commemorativum, exhibitivum, et prognosticum* for everything that happens in salvation-history from beginning to end.

This in no way denies or obscures the "efficient causality" of the sacraments. It is meaningful, after all, to baptize an adult who is already justified—as Peter baptized Cornelius, not in order to give him the Holy Spirit but *because* he had *already* received the Holy Spirit. And normally the Christian is justified by charity *before* he comes to the sacrament of reconciliation. Thus traditional theology holds that the recipient of a sacrament may already have what the sacrament gives. If we understand what "already having grace" really means—namely, being part of the intimate dynamic which unites all earthly realities and persons in the one history of the world, which is the Coming of God through his self-imparting—then we cannot say that the foregoing attitude toward the sacraments diminishes their significance or necessity.

In this theory, how do the sacraments work? With the best and oldest theological tradition we emphasize the sign-character of the sacraments and insist that efficacy is not something added to the sign-function but belongs to the signs as such. This efficacy involves several stages.

First, when a concrete human being realizes himself in history, the corporeal exterior act is always a sign of something in his basic attitude, his "fundamental option," *and* at the same time it influences this basic attitude. It is always a "real symbol," in which the human being realizes his basic attitude. By expressing, man posits what he expresses.

In the body-spirit unity of man, the "real symbol" is both sign and cause of what it says. It is not a cause which posits something distinct from itself, but it is a cause insofar as the real cause—interior free decision—can realize itself only through such exteriorization.

All this applies to the free act performed in grace. This becomes an event of grace by finding expression, and this expression is (in the sense explained) a cause of the act and of the grace. This is why the Scholastics taught that grace is increased by the fruitful reception of the sacraments, though it is grace itself that makes the reception fruitful.

Finally, this grace is the grace given to the world as such, perpetually offered to it as the inmost finality of its history, appearing in salvation-history, and thus producing what we call sacraments when its appearance coincides with decisive moments in the lives of individuals and takes a form to which the Church as basic sacrament of grace fully commits itself.

This concept of "real symbol" allows us to attribute a true causality to the sacramental signs.

We will understand this better if we reflect on the relation between the Church and the world. According to what is perhaps the most timely as well as the most original statement of Vatican II, the Church is the "sacrament of salvation" for the world. Up to now this has been taken to mean that the Church is a sign of salvation for those who actually belong to her. It is the ark, the sheepfold, while the world outside is the realm of evil, the situation of the unsaved. Now there is certainly some truth to this view. There is a world which is at enmity with God. But today it has become clearer that the historical-social phenomenon called Church is not simply the promise of salvation for those "inside" but also for those who are still "outside" and who perhaps never will belong to the Church in a sociological-empirical sense. For there are those who are sanctified and saved by grace, though they have never belonged empirically to the Church, because God refuses salvation to no one who follows his conscience.

For these anonymous sanctified and redeemed and saved (we don't have to call them "anonymous Christians"), the Church is the social-historical sign of salvation, the fundamental sacrament of the promise which is valid for them, because she is the visible community of those who confess that God offers everyone salvation through the death and resurrection of his Christ. Those who expressly belong to the visible Church are not so much the Elect (as though all others were excluded); rather they are the ones who through their life and churchmanship are to make sacramentally manifest the salvation of the others in the solidarity of the whole human race redeemed by Christ.

The actual members of the Church work out their salvation *by* exercising this sign-function with respect to others. Moreover, in principle all men are called to exercise this function: any man may find himself in the situation where, in order to obtain salvation, he must proclaim it and thus become part of the basic sacrament called Church.

Seen from this standpoint, the world does not stand to the Church as the godless to the holy, the deluge to the ark, but as the undisclosed being, still seeking full historical expression, to that complete historical visibility for which it is destined.

The real finality of the Church is to be found in the world—hidden in its inmost core, but knowable by the Church's faithful. It is not, of course, the "natural" dynamic of history, but God's grace—ultimately, God's imparting of himself to the world. And of course the Church is a very imperfect manifestation of the ultimate victorious entelechy of world history; she is still searching for herself, still has to integrate into herself the particular manifestations of grace which form salvation-history "outside" the Church. We hear of "adapting" the Church to the world: this is not bringing the divine power down to the level of a godless world but recognizing what is anonymously Christian and ecclesial in the world and its history.

Now we see how to conceive of the individual sacraments. They are nothing but acts of the Church, as the basic sacrament of the world's salvation, realizing itself concretely in the life-situation of the individual. The unfailing union of the Church with Christ continues into this concretization of the basic sacrament in the individual sacraments and is there called *opus operatum*. This term does not imply opposition to the *opus operantis*; rather it points to a quality of a particular *opus operantis*—the fact that this *opus operantis Ecclesiae* fully commits the Church and so of itself can never lose the grace of Christ. If, therefore, the sacraments are continuations and actualizations of the sign-function of the Church as fundamental sacrament, then they signify the grace that the Church signifies, the grace that is always at work in the world. We should be aware of this when we receive them. Then they will not seem to be actions extrinsic to the world, affecting an unholy world from without, but actions of the grace of the world, perceived in the world by someone who has experienced how God has always sanctified his life and that of the world.

One can object that this whole view of the sacraments makes excessive demands upon the average churchgoer. But so does every view of the sacraments. It may not seem so to those who think they understand words like "the means of grace" and "causality through signification." But the attitude in receiving the sacraments which I recommend here demands no more than any other theology ever demanded—that is, that one grasp the meaning of God's grace existentially and in such a way that receiving it is believable. I have only tried to present a concept of grace which can be verified by contemporary man, who starts with everyday experience and tries to avoid individualistic narrowness in his way of thinking about grace.

With this attitude in receiving the sacraments, can a person confess and receive Communion as often as traditional piety recommends? Every form of sacramental piety has to answer the same question, for mere frequency of reception without genuine existential participation is meaningless. It would not hurt for traditional piety to modify its almost magical idea that frequent reception is always to be encouraged, as long as one has the proper intention and a little good will, because it increases one's store of grace. A frequency which overburdens the recipient by making excessive demands on his existential awareness is not advisable. But this is an argument against excessive frequency, not against the view of the sacraments proposed here.

The mutually critical relationship between authentic participation and frequent reception of the sacraments must also take account of everyday needs. The high point where one succeeds in taking one's whole life in hand is rare, and yet one must anticipate it and practice for it in daily life. "I love you" really resounds in the great moments of life, but it can and ought to be said on ordinary days, and the same goes for the sacraments. In the liturgy we pray for the poor, the dying, and so forth. These petitions may be perfunctory: should we therefore omit them, or should we rather allow them to warn us against being preoccupied with our own selfish concerns?

Now that our theory has been developed from the starting point of traditional theology, with all the ramifications which that entails, one really ought to go back and, independently of this starting point, explain it quite simply. Then it would be clearer how it can be realized and religiously verified. The man who has no taste for explicit religiosity should then be able to say: "This is what is happening in my life. Much as I am tempted to conceal my religious feelings, I must acknowledge this openly." The "pious" person, in turn, would become aware that his "spiritual life" is no dispensation from the responsibility of his profane life, not even really a high point in relation to his everyday life; but simply taking control of a life that only seems to be profane. And then, without this long theological detour through the traditional conception of the sacraments, a kerygmatic presentation might have some effect on religious life.

INITIATION: BAPTISM AND CONFIRMATION

Aidan Kavanagh, O.S.B.

Phenomenology of Christian Initiation

PART I

Bad liturgy does not create itself. It is the result of social illness and individual pathology or sloth. Good liturgy does not create itself either. It is the result of social health and individual sensitivity, knowledge, and discipline tuned to the true form and content of the liturgical act. Such individuals make up healthy communities of faith. The primary task is, therefore, to prepare individuals who can take part in healthy community life. Individuals are the ones who make liturgy good or bad, relevant or irrelevant, meaningful or meaningless.

This preparation is absolutely critical. It is even more critical than adequate forms of liturgical activity. The Christian community recognized this from the beginning. The early church put far more emphasis on preparation for liturgy than on liturgy itself. Its policy seems to have been that a well-prepared people do not celebrate themselves poorly: if the people are well prepared, the liturgy will perforce take care of itself. Thus, in early Christian writings, one finds much more detail on preparation, or catechesis, than on liturgical details. Yet we know that the power of the act of worship was unsurpassed. Augustine noted that the sight of the people at worship, and the vigor of their "Amens"—which struck him like the sound of an awesome thunder—were major factors in his own conversion to faith in Christ. That sight ravished him, but now we are hard pressed to reconstruct in detail the precise liturgical forms of his day. People then wrote less about them, but they seem to have done them better—because they were prepared to an extent and a degree that we today would find difficult to imagine.

This essay will be about the liturgical aspects of that preparation, that catechesis. It will deal with the process of one's coming into faith—with, that is, conversion—with the "beginnings" of faith not as an exclusively intellectual assent to a list of abstruse doctrines, but with faith as a concrete style of living in a community of faith shared. Unless the Christian liturgy is an act of faith, it is not liturgy but ritual alone—compulsive at best or viciously psychotic at worst.

This essay will deal less with the liturgical details of baptism and confirmation than it will with the whole phenomenon of a person's coming into communal faith. In this generalized context, I hope to point out the forest instead of only one or two trees—that is, I hope to sketch the landscape that alone gives meaning to any one of its details. I ask you, therefore, to think of baptism and confirmation not as two separate acts of ecclesiastical ceremonial but as a single event of Christian consecration whose scope is larger than most of us have thought.

The reality of what a Christian is is laid open to a large degree in the process by which he gets that way. As Tertullian said, "Christians are not born, they are made." The reality of what a Christian is attains primary and radical social expression in the consecration we have come to call Christian initiation—a consecration that is made up specifically of baptism and confirmation. Yet these two sacramental events do not stand at the beginning of the complex process of coming to faith; nor do they, as ceremonial acts, exhaust or complete that process. Baptism and confirmation are in fact one consecratory event of social initiation—initiation of one in whom faith has long been growing, and in whom that same faith must continue to grow in increasingly social and public ways after initiation is over if it is to survive at all. Baptism-confirmation, then, marks the initial point at which individual faith has developed in one sufficiently to be thrown open, so to speak, for social interaction and public participation. One's own private, peculiar, and largely incommunicable faith-experiences must be brought to a point at which that faith is strong enough to bear the rough and tumble of social engagement in the faith of others, and of theirs in it, within a community of faith shared.

It is in this sense, I think, that baptism-confirmation can be called a sacrament, or a liturgical act, of "beginnings." With this crucial reservation: that baptism-confirmation does not initiate the *faith* of an indivual, does not *confect* faith on the spot and out of nothing, to inject it like an unheard of miracle drug or a disembodied heart muscle into the vacant veins or chest cavity of a passive receiver. This surgical-pharmaceutical view of faith, and its correspondingly clinical view of Christian initiation, should be called what it is: it is theological heresy because God calls one to faith as he pleases; it is psychological rubbish; it is pastoral myopia; it is ritual magic. It is a symptom of an administrative mind's passion for neatness having laid waste the rich and raunchy complexness of man's existence— a complexness that is the only soil out of which mystery, fascination, symbol, awe, exhilaration, and a sense of the holy can emerge.

To reduce baptism-confirmation for neatness' sake to a quasi-magical confection of faith on the one hand or a quasi-surgical excision of the great wart known as original sin on the other, and to attempt to make even this somehow compelling in fifteen minute ceremonies done privately in corners with teacups of water and a smear or two of grease is unacceptable. It reaches tragic proportions when this perfunctoriness is made to bear the additional weight of attempting to reflect, actualize, and predict what a Christian truly is in a compelling way. No wonder baptism-confirmation has sunk into a sort of atrophied conventionalism; no wonder we find ourselves groping to rediscover what the full integrity of Christian formation might be; no wonder we find conventionally pious people able without much difficulty to coexist with the vicious paganism within them; and no wonder our ceremonies of ending (such as final anointing of the sick, viaticum and Christian burial) seem so barren even when white is their liturgical color and alleluia their song. Death must be hideous when the life it terminates is as lush as Death Valley. The way we make a Christian by the grace of God—through catechesis, the waters of the font, the perfume of anointing, through pardon and reconciliation, through bread broken and wine poured out, and much else besides—all these transitions and beginnings anew will resolutely determine how we take leave of him. If you really want to see what we think of our Christian selves, then savor the squalor of initiation and death in most of our parishes throughout this land.

We have begun to change: but we have only just begun. And our pain, frustration and confusion is both normal and salutary. We are, perhaps, just beginning to realize that our problem is not primarily liturgical, but social. The problem is with ourselves as a community of faith shared. Liturgical problems are mere symptoms of this more radical malaise. As Pogo said: "We have met the enemy, and he is us."

PART II

This is my standard caution concerning what I detect too often among persons who are most admirably concerned with the state and future of Christian worship. What I detect is perhaps too high an expectation of what ritual can do. Ritual is a great and absolutely necessary behavior pattern that allows a society's most critical values—the values that make it a society—to surface, to be articulated, and to be really shared in by all. A human group that loses its ritual patterns is a group that is already dissolving. And it is not only the ill-meaning that can effect such a loss: the well-meaning may also, inadvertently, cause this to happen. Remember how fundamental the rhythmic regular ways people do things are to their own sense of individual identity and security, and how crucial these factors are to social cohesion. In this game, social cohesion is the absolute condition for social survival. Often, indeed, these patterns of behavior—of which liturgy is one, but only one—need changing if the group is to cohere and survive. I have no argument with this. My only insistence is that such changes must be done with sensitivity, resourcefulness, and a creative patience. People do change, but groups of people change slowly. And before I get the label of being *laissez-faire*, I must point out that these characteristics in the one who would change the liturgy add up more often to a need for vigor than to an excuse for no action at all.

Permit me to illustrate what I mean in terms of what the coming of one into faith as a communal style of life looks like from a liturgically orientated point of view.

Faith has often enough been represented as an ongoing process that terminates according to St. Paul only in the vision of that which has been believed. Faith has also been called a dialogue in tension between the lover and the beloved, the creator and created, God and man. It is carried on in two motions—call and response. God calls, man responds. This is fine, so far as it goes. As far as it goes, it does indeed put the initiative on the caller, and it suggests also that the called is not just passive in the dialogue but is in fact summoned into active converse with God himself. To this extent, man is put on a sort of par with God; he even shares, and is expected to share, in the divine initiative that has called his response forth. God and man thus can be seen as co-operators together, locked into a relationship of true communion that has untold effects on man. This is classic Christian orthodoxy. So far as it goes.

I submit that the evidence of classic Christian orthodoxy, especially as enshrined in the liturgical corpus of the church both east and west, goes beyond this however. This evidence suggests that faith is indeed a process that terminates in vision, but that it involves a trilectic tension between not only God and man the individual, but between God and the social community that preconditions the individual within it both as regards what the divine call is (in terms that are available to the individual) and in terms of what the individual's response to that call must be in order to secure the faith-community's continuing cohesion and survival. This trilogue between God, the individual, and the faith-community is like the keel of a ship. But note that the keel is not the ship. The keel anchors a series of structural ribs that spring off and up and away from it: the ribs carry the material that keeps out the sea so that the ship can function. But all the tensions and stresses meet in the keel, and the keel makes it possible for all these to be met and harnessed so the ship may sail.

As a keel is, the trilogue of ongoing conversion is a dynamic factor even in its stabilizing function. Unlike a ship's keel, however, the trilogue is not to be found in some place: even less is it to be found always in the same place. A society is forever changing its core, howsoever slightly: thus its axis, keel, or criteria-center is always on the move. It is far easier to tell where it has been than where it is or will be. Yet the society can sense about where it is: if it cannot do this—due to trauma or creeping arteriosclerosis in its patterns of communication within itself— it is either on the verge of significant change or already into it, for better or worse.

These are extraordinary changes. But most changes that occur in a society are ordinary, constant and regular. From the normal pressures these changes bring to bear on the society experiencing them, the society—in the depths of its own corporate subconsciousness—obtains constant if obscure readings on where its center is. It is an operational thing above all, just as most individuals sustain a rather submerged operational definition of themselves that they would be hard put to render into words except under unusual conditions (such as analysis, certain forms of drugs, personal traumas, etc.).

Now all this must appear contrived and hopelessly abstruse. I am at fault, if so, because I am straining to bring into motion a whole series of factors that begin to operate when social change occurs. No more regular change occurs in the community of faith shared than the change produced by one's coming into such a community. This begins with radical and often catastrophic releases of psychic energy in the one who has begun to believe. His previous personal focal center has been disrupted and has begun to yaw widely: he is rapidly ceasing to be who he was and is beginning to reach out for support in order to become himself once more by becoming, paradoxically, someone different. The symptoms he exhibits may indicate either a nervous collapse or a religious conversion, or both. Say it is religious conversion: this does not make it any less painful or difficult. Where did he "catch it"? Most probably by some exposure, either direct or indirect, to a community of faith shared. Perhaps he has been stunned by its integrity, its uprightness, its splendor of life. He has been pre-evangelized, and has come down, as it were, with a case of religious conversion praecox.

The community is responsible for this by being what it professes. More critically, it has an obligation to help. It does this by responding to the call of God given the converting one. It enters into its responsibility by doing what modern catechists call evangelization—that is, it draws the conversion crisis to a white-hot point of focussed intensity centered on the gospel of Jesus Christ. It puts at the converting one's disposal its own faith in that gospel as a community, a faith embodied in the here and now, in real people in communion with each other. They must see him through this trauma and not desert him. Conversions at this stage may skid off into a whole swamp of compulsive neuroses. There are many converts who were deserted yet initiated precisely at such a stage, and who have never been whole or Christian since.

Once this critical evangelization stage is past, and only then, does formal catechesis become possible. At this final preparation stage, the convert's previously inchoate stirrings of belief are now brought into some equilibrium *vis-à-vis* the gospel, and can begin to be rendered increasingly social. His faith is ready now to be drawn into a series of interaction situations with his peers in the community that has already begun to receive him. The converts as a group begin to learn how to pray formally and in public by easy stages. They are taught how to reduce their incommunicable experiences of faith into concrete acts of mercy, fasting, almsgiving, of solitude and private prayer—acts that cost them something and that evoke a variety of responses from others. They are slowly eased down into a lifestyle suffused with faith and with the costs that faith demands. Only then are they regarded as capable of consecratory initiation, and all this may have taken years.

The *convert* has responded to God's call by making available to the community of God's faithful ones his own awareness, trust, desire, and ascesis of mind and body. The *community* has responded to God's call in the convert by making available to him its own life of faith and its own professional structures staffed by those who are wise in what faith costs and in how faith must be lived in common. And in their mutual responses to each other, the convert and the community respond to *God* who acts in each. These three merge into one body through the waters of death and life, passing together through the prism of Jesus' passion and death. This is what life costs.

The meshing together of the one converting and the community of ongoing conversion we call the church is a faith-interaction. This interaction begins to occur during catechesis, and it means three things: (1) that the convert begins to stabilize his new identity; (2) that this identity has begun to affect the faith-community into which he is entering; and (3) that neither the convert nor the local faith-community exists as they had before. Both change.

This is the context within which baptism-confirmation begin to become possible. Christian initiation is as of great, if not greater, importance to the community as it is to the convert. He changes it, it changes him, and both meet within the enacted paradigm of that archetypal change at the center of all things—Jesus' passage from death to life.

PART III

The foregoing is a most inadequate sketch of an infinitely complex process. But if my sketch is basically sound, even in its modesty, I can suggest a few fresh angles it seems to reveal concerning baptism-confirmation and much else besides. Allow me merely to list them.

1. It suggests an *operational definition of the church arising from the local level* where alone the faith-conversion context is to be found.

2. It suggests the point from which an existential theology of the church can develop—as distinct from a ponderous, static, and essentialist ecclesiology that is our bequest from the days of a Christendom long past. I might observe that a dynamic, existentialist theology of the church, arising from an operational definition of it, seems to me the only atmosphere in which a really pastoral mode of doing theology—as found in the early church fathers—can be resuscitated. It was the absence of just such an atmosphere, I believe, during our past absorption with Christendom, that has caused pastoral theology to peel off either into legal casuistry or into mere psycho-clinical counselling. Pastoral theology is neither of these two otherwise valid enterprises. It is a way of *doing theology*—not out of books or schools, but out of the living milieu of faith shared, through the pain and cost of conversion, prayer, fasting, repentance, and sacrifice.

3. The sketch might correct the presumption that faith is a static entity locked up in the vaults of the church's administrative offices, offices that never change—a faith that is passed out to converts who receive it passively and only in their brainpans. The "instruction class" to prepare for baptism is symptomatic of this. We must learn all over again that proximate preparation for baptism means catechesis, and that catechesis is not about doctrinal or ecclesiastical data, but about conversion.

4. The sketch suggests that coming into faith is a dynamic process that has the most profound repercussions throughout the faith-community, not just in the convert alone.

5. It suggests that tradition in the church is not a dragging anchor, but a vital force that changes not just converts but the whole of the community of faith and the way in which it sustains its faith as a style of communal living.

6. It suggests that the root meaning of the old saw about *ecclesia semper reformanda* is this: that the community of faith shared has nothing to fear but changelessness itself—so long as all change within it is calibrated by the criteria of the gospel of Jesus Christ and by no others.

7. The sketch sheds some light on the role and meaning of prayer, fasting, works of mercy, and asceticism in general within the communal life of faith. These disciplinary elements are means to further faith-as-shared, and thus to deepen and secure the reality of being "in communion" with God and all his holy ones and holy things in this world. It is this communion alone which makes eucharist possible; this communion alone which the eucharist celebrates; this communion alone which the eucharist reinforces, deepens, and carries further into as yet unexperienced dimensions of stunning intensity. If you have a community of faith shared—a community of prayer, mercy, fasting and of a hard lean asceticism—then you have a community in which the eucharist is not a possibility but an inevitability.

8. Finally, the sketch may provide a grasp on why both baptism and the eucharist, the two premier New Testament rites, are: (a) *community-wide by nature* not by special dispensation from any source; (b) *constitutive of the community*, to the extent that a Christian community with no baptism cannot be a Christian community with eucharist, and vice versa. And a community with neither of these is not Christian. It is Moose, Elks, Odd Fellows, or God knows what; (c) *exhaustive of Christian ritual activity*. There are no other Christian rites that do not flow from these two and that are not reducible to these two. Other rites there indeed are, and this is good. It is even necessary, because these two premier rites of a community of faith shared bring into motion a whole set of cosmic orchestrations, archetypes, primordial stirrings, and humane needs that require a vast chorus of ritual *beaux gestes* even to acknowledge (e.g., the blessing of the baptismal font and its sexual-fertility, even phallic, imagery—a *beau geste*, at least, to some of the loveliest creations of God). Our having forgotten this is as central to the viciously insensitive exploitation of our natural environment as any other factor I know. As we Christians led the pack in de-sacralizing nature, we forgot that the only alternative left was to exploit it. And now we are paying the price. (d) *Rites of change*. Baptism-confirmation is one rite that makes public the community of faith's acceptance of change having been accomplished in

an individual—to the initial degree at least that it can now become the property of all the group, that all may now share in that person's change and profit from it mightily. Its reality is no longer incommunicable, alien, alone. It can now have voice, it can now be spoken of and understood in a language of body and mind that is available to all. This is what Lent is about: to prepare the whole community anew to hear the language of conversion that is spoken by the mind and body of a single human being as he sinks into Jesus' death and rises in him to a new life God has made stunningly ours on Easter.

The eucharist is a rite that intensifies change and causes it to take place continually according to that same pattern of Jesus' own change from death to a life no one had ever lived before. We break the bread of his body, we pour out the cup of his blood in sacrifice. John Paul II and Mrs. Murphy can know this: kings and paupers can know it: professors and freshmen can know it. It isn't hard for lots to know, but it is supremely difficult to live without sham or full-scale retreat. Baptism and eucharist are really one corporate person dying and rising. That is a lot to load onto simple things like water and oil, bread and wine. But they never complain. They have never sinned either. They are faithful and close to God in their original innocence, therefore, to a degree that staggers one's imagination. To become like them is what he came to show us. They are superb as God meant us to be. To get that way is a passion for us who have fallen, as it were, into reason.

The Question of Confirmation

It is within the context of considerations such as the foregoing that the matter of confirmation as a distinct if not separate sacramental event should be viewed. But first some categorical data on what this sacrament has been, and why, seem in order.

First, there is no unambiguous New Testament evidence for what we today recognize as a separate "sacrament of confirmation." What is found in the New Testament is an inchoate and compound pattern of Christian initiation-consecration developing around water immersion—an event that reflects so radical a departure in lifestyle from what went before that this event is regarded as a veritable "new birth." Elements of handlaying are mentioned in this context without much consistency. Also, the vocabulary of "anointing" is used, but it seems this is not to be taken literally so much as figuratively—a manner of speaking to denote one's being consecrated by and set apart for God. Finally, the vocabulary of "spirit" is used, but it is not restricted to a single moment of the initiation-consecration process.

Second, when one turns to the historic evolution of the rites of initiation-consecration, several factors emerge:

A. The sequence of baptism-confirmation-eucharist is with almost no exceptions regarded as intrinsic both to the nature of the initiation process and to the intelligibility of it for catechetical purposes. This sequence is still maintained by all the Eastern Churches, and it was maintained in the West until about the 11th-12th centuries. It is still presumed in Roman canon and conciliar law.[1]

B. The West's understanding of this sacramental sequence shifted for two main reasons: (1) the demise of adult baptism as the norm, together with the atrophying of the adult catechumenate; and (2) continuance of exclusively episcopal ministry of confirmation. Neither of these two reasons arose from breakthrough in understanding the *intrinsic* nature of confirmation or the initiation process. The reasons for a change of practice arose, rather, from *extrinsic* factors.

C. The *intrinsic significance* of the sacramental sequence focused on baptism being consummated by actual entry of the baptized into the Spirit-filled community of faith, the church, most clearly laid bare in the eucharistic action itself. Confirmation, as the solemn conclusion of baptism *as well as* the first public recognition of the newly baptized (often done as they entered the church for the first eucharist of Easter), articulated this pneumatic aspect by the symbolic actions of anointing, hand-laying, and the vocabulary of "giving the Holy Spirit." Thus, the several "explanatory" themes that have developed around confirmation (e.g., maturity, soldier of Christ, engagement in the apostolate, "receiving the Spirit") must be regarded as reflecting complementary aspects of an organic whole whose unity of purpose is initiation into a Spirit-filled community of faith. Isolating these explanatory themes in order to exploit one or another of them speculatively has contributed to diminishing the strict correlation of the sacramental and catechetical stages involved in the process of Christian initiation. This is especially true, for example, of the emphasis on "maturity" and "apostolate" as themes to explain confirmation. It can be argued that no single sacrament is uniquely or separately causative of maturity or apostolicity: rather, evidence indicates these to be characteristics of the whole faith-community attributable more specifically to the eucharist. Thus, even in the case of confirmation and communion of infants what is at issue primarily is their consecratory initiation into a *community whose faith is both mature and apostolic, whose unity is the Spirit present in it, and whose consequent style of corporate life must be eucharistic.* The sacramental sequence is not a "producer" of these traits *ex nihilo.* The sequence formally inserts or splices one, whether infant or adult, into the whole pattern of ecclesial life, a life in communion with which the initiate will grow progressively throughout a lifetime. Maturity and apostolicity are thus not special times or gifts: they are qualities of living in a community of faith which *all* the sacraments support and articulate—and in this way "cause."

This theological principle is important in interpreting sacramental evolution. Sacramental liturgy is indeed always pastoral, but it is not "pastoral" in the sense that what the sacrament *signifies* can undergo substantial change or be manipulated to solve *ad hoc* pastoral or catechetical problems. Its pastoral understanding, modification and development must always be carried on in view of its primal and perennial signification.

D. Historically, confirmation of infants in both East and West would suggest that something more than physical, emotional or even spiritual "maturity" is involved. It is doubtful that confirmation in theory or fact makes even an adult "mature;" it is doubtful that attainment to some degree of maturity (especially physical) even needs a special sacramental expression, and if so, what kind of maturity is to be emphasized? It is simply an assertion, not a demonstrated fact, that social maturity can or should be confirmation's purpose.

Far more urgently, it should be noted that too heavy an emphasis on "maturity" as confirmation's purpose, brings this quite modest rite into serious competition with other sacraments where concerns about maturity are overt—namely, matrimony, holy orders, and the whole parasacramental complex of vows attaching to states of life. Sacraments are not separate spigots that give different flavors of grace; nor are they simply wandering ceremonies that can be manipulated without affecting the whole sacramental economy—a structure embedded in the organic way a community of faith shared lives.

E. Earliest liturgical evidence links confirmation so intimately with baptism that confirmation as a wholly independent sacrament is difficult if not impossible to discern. In this evidence confirmation appears more as the solemn conclusion of the baptismal synaxis, and at the same time as the formal public reception of the initiate into the eucharistic assembly—through the presidential action of the community's chief liturgical minister, the bishop. Confirmation thus appears as a transition—event that hinges baptism (done in relative privacy for adults due to the candidates' nudity) into public eucharist.

In this close relationship with baptism and eucharist, confirmation's words and acts dealing with a giving of the Holy Spirit make sense. To be initiated into a Spirit-filled community is to be "given" that same Spirit, which is the Enabler of the sort of life the community leads both in whole and in part. Separating confirmation unto itself apart from this context raises serious pastoral and theological questions (1) about the nature of baptism, (2) about how a life of faith and sacramental engagement in a community is carried on until the Spirit is finally "given," and (3) about the role of the Spirit in the cohesion of the Church. The new rite of confirmation, strong in its Spirit-emphasis, makes long separation of the sacrament from baptism even more problematic.

Suggestions Concerning Confirmation

1. *The Relation of Confirmation to Baptism and Eucharist.* If infant baptism is proper then there seems no compelling reason why its immediate completion in confirmation should be improper. Physical age has no more significance for confirmation *per se* than for baptism or even the reception of communion in the main line of tradition—until the Middle Ages in the West, and then for extrinsic reasons. Although no person has a right to baptism, the baptized *do* possess rights to confirmation and the eucharist. What is of more radical pastoral consequence is the present practice of what has amounted virtually to *indiscriminate baptism*, done for negative motives (only to remove original sin) or, worse, for purely conventional social reasons without adequate catechesis either before or after the event. The solution to difficulties that confirmation raises on the pastoral level may lie in correcting an inadequate baptismal polity rather than in superficial changes in the ceremonial or canonical regulations concerning confirmation.

2. *The Age of Confirmation*. The age at which confirmation is celebrated depends on the age at which initiation into and consecration for the Christian community is in fact done. At whatever age this is deemed appropriate—in infancy, adolescence or adulthood—the primordial sequence of baptism-confirmation-eucharist should be restored and fostered. At the same time, such a restoration of sequence will remain merely that unless an enlargement of catechetical content and structures is begun. We do not need more Christians so much as we need better ones, and for this not only rites but catechesis keyed to the rites is fundamental.

3. *The Sacrament of Penance*. Penance, seen at its deepest level as reconciling one to God through Christ in his church, *and thus as forgiving of sin*, should not regularly interrupt the sequence of initiation. This sequence in itself, terminating in the eucharist, appears to be more "forgiving of sin" than was often taught in our conventional theology.

. To intrude reconciliation patterns (confession-penance-absolution) into the initiation sequence (baptism-confirmation-eucharist) as regular practice is a questionable redundancy. To make a child who has been baptized and confirmed confess, do penance, and receive absolution as a condition for first communion strikes me as a breakdown in liturgical and sacramental intelligibility. While an awareness of sin and its consequences should be inculcated from an early age, one may doubt whether true childish offenses can be of such grave quality as to rupture the child's union with God in his church. It is even more questionable whether waiting for an older age at which true *sin* becomes possible should be regarded as a regular condition either for initiation into such oneness or for the exercise of rights inherent in that union—e.g., the right to receive the fullness of baptism in confirmation, and the living sacramental presence that is the source and center of Christian existence in holy communion. The sacramental process of confession-penance-absolution is, like baptism-confirmation-eucharist *integratory* at base. The final stage of each sequence is achieved only in the eucharist both as celebrated and as received.

1. Can. 786, 788; also Vatican II: *Const. on Liturgy* 71; *Decree on Missions* 36.

STILL A CASE FOR INFANT BAPTISM?

Eugene Maly (1920-1980)

Our Catholic practice of baptizing infants has provoked objection from the beginning. Tertullian in the third century argued against what had already become "tradition" in his day. And the discussion continues in our own time, because it reflects our continuing struggle to come to grips with the very core of Christian faith.

Through infant Baptism we *initiate* a person into a faith-community long before he or she can choose whether to belong. And through infant Baptism we also *celebrate* a person's salvation long before he or she consciously experiences the need to be saved or can take any responsibility for turning self toward God.

Something about this flies in the face of very basic notions in our culture about individual freedom and the importance of personal choice—in short, our insistence on individualism. We want to believe that we choose God (rather than that God chooses us). We want to believe that we can and should save ourselves (rather than that we are saved).

Therefore, an explanation of the Church's constant affirmation of infant Baptism must be related to a fuller appreciation of the place of *community* in both the Old and New Testaments and how our biblical faith challenges our basic human temptation to individualism. Infant Baptism is just one way we have institutionalized our conviction that community is central to Christian life, to God's plan of salvation.

Community and Salvation
in the Old Testament

Let us consider some of the evidence for the centrality of community
in the Old Testament:

From Community to Disunity (Gn 1-11)

The two stories of origins in the opening chapters of Genesis describe
the original condition of man and woman living in harmonious community. The Priestly author states that the man and woman, made in God's
image, are to be fertile and multiply, to fill the earth and subdue it
(1:27-28). Implied here is the conviction that it was God's will from the
beginning that the human family live in harmony with all creation.

The Yahwist author speaks of this initial community in these terms:
"The man and his wife were both naked, yet they felt no shame" (2:25).
He means these bold words to express a community living in harmony,
with no barriers or walls between them, as is made most clear by the
events that follow. In each of them—the eating of the fruit, Cain and
Abel, Lamech, the flood, the Tower of Babel—there is a disruption of
community on a gradually intensified scale until the peoples were scattered "all over the earth" (11:8). What had begun as community had
ended in disunity.

It seems most likely that the final editor of Genesis intended these 11
chapters as an introduction, not only to the patriarchal narratives that
follow immediately, but also to the whole of "salvation history" as he
knew it at his time. In this case, then, the meaning of that "salvation
history" is clear: *to restore the community shattered so violently by the
escalation of sin in the world.*

The Promise of a Great Nation (Gn 12:1-3)

Abraham's call strongly confirms this understanding of salvation as a
restoration of community. The first words of God's promise to the
patriarch are that he would make of him "a great nation," and the final
words are, "All the communities of the earth shall find blessing in you."
Abraham is being called, not primarily for his own sake, but that a
people—a community—might be formed that would be an exemplar of
blessing to all the communities of the earth.

Covenant Community (Ex 19ff)

At Sinai that first salvation community was called into being through the mediatorship of Moses. God's words to Israel are: "You shall be to me a kingdom of priests, a holy nation" (19:6). There follows the description of the covenant between God and this people, concluding with its solemn ratification by the sprinkling of blood on the altar (representing God) and on the people (24:3-8).

What is significant for our purposes is this: *the covenant is not made with individuals but with the whole people.* They, *as a community,* are the primary object of God's covenant love and saving action.

It is not that individuals were less important; they were very important, but precisely because of their relationship to the community.

In the Priestly writings of the Pentateuch we find frequent reference to individuals who, for various reasons, are to be "cut off from their people" (Lv 7:20, 21, 25, 27). This doubtless included *social* ostracism, but more important to the biblical authors was the exclusion from the liturgy which such a "cutting off" implied. Common liturgy was where the divine favor was poured out upon the community—and its individual members. A psalmist, exiled from his home and people, recalls with nostalgia the times when he "went with the throng and led them in procession to the house of God . . . with the multitude keeping festival" (Ps 42:5).

So strong was the sense of covenant *community* that Israel found it almost unnatural to praise God alone. One of the most poignant lines in the Psalter describes the loneliness of the author who pictures himself as "a desert owl . . . among the ruins" (102:7).

The close-knit community of tribes and of the patriarchal family helped to make this notion of covenant salvation intelligible and meaningful to ancient Israel. But long after Israel had adopted the ways of city life and after the ancient tribes had lost some of their cohesiveness, she remained a "people of God" called by the Lord to covenant community.

Circumcision (Gn 17:9-14)

One of the most striking illustrations of this emphasis on the covenant community was Israel's practice of circumcising male children eight days after they were born. The prescription of this ritual is recorded in Gn 17:9-14.

Circumcision was widespread among the peoples of the ancient Near East. (The Philistines were one exception, referred to contemptuously by the Hebrews as "the uncircumcised"—Jg 15:18.) But it seems that only the Israelites gave a religious significance to it. And the significance was this: admission into the covenant community.

A child who was obviously not able to make a conscious response to God's covenant love was yet considered worthy of membership in the community. It is God's will and the people's acceptance of the child that were the primary determinants of membership.

Covenant Community
in the New Testament

It would be impossible to imagine that Jesus or those first Jewish Christians would not have thought of their new relationship to God in terms of a *new* covenant. This framework was so much a part of their own heritage, so deeply rooted in their own psyches, a clear and conscious rejection of it would be required for us to believe otherwise. No such rejection is recorded in the New Testament, and positive references leave no one in doubt.

Jeremiah, some 600 years before Christ, had pointed to "a new covenant" that God would make with his people in which his law would be written on their hearts (31:31-34). And it's the fulfillment of this promise that Luke (22:2) and Paul (1 Cor 11:25) seem to have in mind when they record Jesus' words at the institution of he Eucharist, "This cup is the new covenant in my blood. . ." There is a reference here not only to Jeremiah's prophecy but also to the words of Moses as he sealed the covenant of old with the blood of animals (Ex 24:3-8). Hence, at one of the most significant moments of his ministry, Jesus speaks of his relationship to his followers in terms of a covenant.

St. Paul, in his famous allegory on freedom, speaks of "the two covenants" (Gal 4:24), meaning, of course, the one made with Israel and that made with the new people of God. And he sees himself as one of the "qualified ministers" of this new covenant (2 Cor 3:6). In the same letter he makes use of an Old Testament passage (Lv 26:12) to describe the nearness of God to his people in the new covenant community (6:16).

Moreover, he sees the remission of sins as one of the major fruits of the new covenant relationship (Rm 11:27).

Practically the whole of the Letter to the Hebrews can be read within the context of a comparison of the two covenants. For this author the risen Lord is the supreme and unique mediator of the new covenant interceding constantly before the Father's throne for his people.

In 1 Peter the author can only describe the new covenant community in the very terms that the Old Testament author had used to describe Israel when she had just been called by God to a covenant relationship: "You, however, are 'a chosen race, a royal priesthood, a holy nation, a people he claims for his own . . .' " (2:9). And, to make it clear that this is a new creation of the Lord's, he adds, "Once you were no people, but now you are God's people . . ." (v. 11).

Another way to understand the continuing importance of community in the New Testament is to examine the concept of Church. The Greek word *ekklēsia* is used in conscious reference to the Hebrew word *qahal*, which described the covenant community at Sinai and, at times, the liturgical assembly of Israel. Both the Hebrew and Greek words imply the notion of a group that has been called together on God's initiative and made one. It is not, therefore, a free association of individuals who happen to profess the same Lord. The group is bound together by an inner bond which is the prior call of God bringing them into a relationship with himself and with one another.

St. Paul develops the theology of Church in a special way. He refers to the community of Christian believers as the body of Christ (cf. 1 Cor 10:17; 12:12-27). By this he means that the risen Christ lives in each Christian so intimately (cf. Gal 2:20: ". . . the life I live now is not my own; Christ is living in me") that all Christians together can be said to constitute his body. This is still further developed in the letter to the Colossians where Christ is said to be the "head of the body, the Church" (1:18).

In this vision, then, the Church cannot be seen simply as a huge umbrella under which stand those individuals who call Jesus "Lord." Rather, *as Church*, Christians enjoy an inner, transcendent bond between them that is so real and so powerful that Paul can even say, "If one member suffers, all the members suffer with it; if one member is honored, all the members share its joy" (1 Cor 12:26).

Some observers of Christianity contend that the Old Testament sense of peoplehood, of community, has, in fact, been displaced by the individual. "Christianity . . . surrenders the concept of a 'holy people' and recognizes only a personal holiness," contends Jewish theologian Martin Buber.

But the surrender of that concept did not take place in the New Testament. And well into the patristic period, the conviction of a covenant people was so strong that the Fathers could not conceive of salvation outside its embracing arms.

Several quotes from a recent study sum up the community consciousness of the early Church: "Like the people of God of the first covenant, the new people owes its existence to God's preferential love. It is his gracious choice and not the intrinsic merits of man that calls this community into being"; ". . . one's first glory as a Christian is to be a member of God's people;" and, "The Church is not simply a free association of individuals; they are members only because of a vocation from God" (J.P. Schanz, *A Theology of Community*).

The Place of Children

In the context of this biblical understanding of a covenant community through which salvation is mediated to individuals, what can we say of the newborn infant? If "one's first glory as a Christian is to be a member of God's people," is the child to be denied that glory?

Is God's elective love to be held in abeyance until the human person determines its scope? Cannot the child be the object of God's preferential love, his gracious choice, even before being able to make a response in faith? (Even adults are unable to make a faith response without God's grace!) "It was not you who chose me, it was I who chose you . . ." (Jn 15:16).

To demand the individual's "I do" before God can enrich his community would be heretical (Pelagian), a good case of the unbiblical individualism charged by Buber. Salvation of the individual is through the community *before* it is consciously accepted by the individual.

It is true there is no evidence of Jesus making disciples of little children. It is interesting to note, however, that some scholars see in

Jesus' blessing of the little children (Mk 10:13-16) an intended anticipation by the biblical author of the practice of infant Baptism.

But the real point is this: There had to be constituted a community by the risen Lord before it could accept its own new members. And the Church, the new covenant community, is only born in the death-resurrection of Jesus and the giving of the Spirit.

Even during that period of Jesus' earthly ministry, however, we notice the sovereignty of Jesus in choosing his own disciples. This is in striking contrast to the custom of young Jewish men going from master to master to determine which they would choose to follow. It is in apparent reference to that custom that the statement of Jesus in John's Gospel, quoted above, has its special meaning. As the Father did with Israel, so does the Son with his own; he chooses whom he will.

Even after the Church had been constituted, there is no explicit reference in the New Testament to the Baptism of infants. Yet we read in the Acts of the Apostles that Paul and Silas baptized the repentant jailer "and his whole household" (16:33). Can we not suppose that the whole family, including children, would have been included? In a preceding verse, where the jailer asks what he need do to be saved, Paul and Silas reply, "Believe in the Lord Jesus and you will be saved, and all your household" (v. 31). The explicit faith act is asked of the jailer who, once brought into the community through Baptism, can then, through that community, mediate salvation to others.

In the post-biblical period allusions to infant Baptism become more common, and in a way that simply supposes it to be an accepted practice. Then, writing in the first part of the third century, Origen openly states it to be an established practice going back to apostolic times.

Combating Individualism

Throughout her history the Church has been plagued with the temptation to individualism. We can see Paul fighting against it in his letters, especially in those to Corinth where the Christians were concerned with going their own individual ways, doing their own thing. His plea for unity in community is based precisely on his conviction of the prior significance of Christ's body, the Church (1 Cor 12).

In our century and in our country, in political and social as well as in religious attitudes, we find a rampant individualism symbolized most vividly perhaps in the Horatio Alger ideal of the one who lifts himself up by his own bootstraps. One of its most popular champions is the novelist Ayn Rand, the self-proclaimed promoter of the "virtue of Selfishness," who concludes her novel *Anthem* with these strong words: "And here, over the portals of my fort, I shall cut in the stone the word which is to be my beacon and my banner. . . . The sacred word: EGO."

To this, biblical Christianity issues an uncompromising "no!" It is the common good, the good of others, the good of the Body that must first be served before there can be any true self-fulfillment. "In my own flesh I fill up what is lacking in the sufferings of Christ for the sake of his body, the Church" (Col 1:24). "To each person the manifestation of the Spirit is given for the common good" (1 Cor 12:7). ". . . Unless the grain of wheat falls to the earth and dies, it remains just a grain of wheat. But if it dies, it produces much fruit" (Jn 12:24).

The Christian vision is clear. Any good of individuals, any power or value they may have, any beauty of their being is determined primarily by their relationship to the community, to the Body of Christ, to which they are called by God's love. It is into the Body that the individual is received through Baptism and attains its first glory. It is this community of God's holy people that takes precedence over the individual and renders the notion of personal salvation viable, not on the terms of the individual, but on those of God's prior choice and the community's acceptance.

If the Church were merely an organization to support and encourage individuals to expend their own personal efforts to attain the saving grace of Jesus Christ, then infant Baptism is indeed a useless rite that has no effect either on infant or on Church. But if the Church is the extension of Jesus Christ into history, as Paul's conviction of the Body implies, then that Church by Christ's power can mediate salvation even to the unconscious spirit and bring it into the Lord's embrace.

* * * * *

Editor's Note: Looking to the day when adult baptism would possibly become more the norm than the exception, what would be the lot of the infant children of Christians? John Gallen suggests a welcoming ritual celebration needs to be developed, inaugurating infants at an early age into a "... catechumenal process of development in faith. This gradual process of formation in faith would be guided by parents and family, then bit by bit by other Church influences and sponsors offered to the growing child. The ritual itself could be a sensitive reworking of the present *Rite of Becoming Catechumens* in which the long formation process would begin, marked by the express commitment of the 'sponsors and the entire assembly,' on behalf of the newly received, 'ready to help them come to know and follow Christ' (n. 77) . . .''

This welcoming ritual for infants would "... achieve the desired socialization so much esteemed by parents who quite correctly wish their newborn to be recognized, welcomed and introduced into the life of the Community. Infants would be marked with the Sign of the Cross, given a Christian name, solemnly welcomed into the Church and started in a long process of formation, supported, nourished, and blessed by the members of the Community. At the same time, introducing infants into the catechumenal process would calm the fears of parents who may be concerned about serious illness or possible threat of death for the infant before baptism. Indeed it is the clear proclamation of the Church's tradition that catechumens already belong to the bosom of the Church and share in its saving life. As the *Rite of Initiation* itself makes clear, 'God showers his grace on them' (n. 14), they are to be 'welcomed by the Church with a mother's love and concern' and 'are joined to the Church and are part of the household of Christ' (n. 18). Finally this welcoming ritual for the infant, followed by the catechumenal process leading to later liturgical celebration of the sacraments of initiation, would place an unmistakable responsibility on parents and sponsors to be agents of the Word, proclaiming the Word of the Lord in every aspect of family life, bringing the children, step by courageous step, to the moment of commitment.''*

*John Gallen, S.J., "The Pastoral Celebration of Initiation," *New Catholic World*, Vol. 222, No. 1330, July/August, 1979, pp. 151-152, © 1979.

THE THEOLOGY OF CONFIRMATION

Thomas Marsh

The ceremony known for centuries now as 'Confirmation' is connected in the Catholic tradition with the gift of the Holy Spirit which Christ promised his Church and fulfilled at Pentecost. Over the centuries there has been little official pronouncement by the Church on this rite. The Council of Trent declared it 'a true and proper sacrament,' one of the seven sacraments of the new law (Denz. 844, 871). The most important official statement on its meaning is that in the *Decree for the Armenians* at the Council of Florence in 1439 (Denz. 697). Confirmation is there described as the giving of the Holy Spirit for strengthening (*ad robur*), as he was given to the apostles on Pentecost, so that the Christian might boldly confess Christ's name. This document draws its doctrine from the sacramental teaching of St. Thomas Aquinas and Aquinas' teaching on Confirmation has thus formed the post-medieval Roman Catholic tradition on this question. This position states:

(a) that in Confirmation there is a giving of the Holy Spirit;
(b) that this gift is the perpetuation of Pentecost in the Church;
(c) that it is directed towards the public profession and witness of the faith;
(d) that it involves a strengthening of the Christian life of the recipients for this mission.

This position leaves a wide area open to theological discussion and interpretation and in recent years Catholic theology has shown considerable interest in this sacrament. The recent discussion has tended to emphasize two points in particular: (a) Confirmation forms part of Christian initiation and represents the liturgical and sacramental completion of Baptism and introduction to the Eucharist; (b) the Spirit given in Confirmation is the prophetic Spirit who, investing with his special force the Christian's living of his faith before the world, enables one to be a witness of Christ in the power of the Spirit. These two points should be seen as complementary.

Though, following ancient tradition, official statements tend to reserve the expression 'gift of the Spirit' for Confirmation, Catholic theology also attributes a gift of the Spirit to Baptism.[1] The Holy Spirit operates in Baptism and is the source and principle of the remission of sin, grace and sanctification there accomplished. Catholic theology thus speaks of two gifts of the Spirit in Christian initiation, a sanctifying gift of the Spirit in Baptism and a supplementary gift of the Spirit, sometimes nowadays described as a gift of the prophetic Spirit, in Confirmation. These two gifts constitute full Christian initiation, make the full Christian and give full membership of the Church.

Not all theologians, however, are convinced that this position satisfactorily solves the question of the relation of Confirmation to Baptism and theological discussion still continues.

Scripture

In its practice and basic interpretation of Confirmation the Catholic Church sees itself as the heir of a long tradition reaching back over the centuries to the Church of the Fathers and the Apostolic Church itself. It claims scriptural warrant for its practice and basic doctrine. There are, inevitably, different ways of seeing and presenting this argument from scripture. The outline presented here is a personal approach.

The question of Confirmation in scripture concerns the sacramental context for the gift of the Spirit. The problem here is the apparent discrepancy between Acts, which seems to attribute this gift to the imposition of hands after Baptism (Ac 8:14-19; 19:1-6) and the Pauline and Johannine literature, which seems to attribute it to Baptism (1 Cor 12:13; Jn 3:5). Exegesis tends to follow confessional lines on this question, Protestant scholars tending to interpret Acts in the light of the Pauline-Johannine position, Catholic scholars doing the opposite, or at least arguing that the silence of Paul and John concerning a post-baptismal rite of the Spirit (generally admitted today) does not amount to a denial of its existence. The assumption common to both approaches is that this discrepancy between Acts and Paul and John is only apparent and that both positions are perfectly reconcilable. This paper will adopt the viewpoint that this assumption is unwarranted.

To interpret the New Testament documents on this question it is necessary to be clear on what 'the gift of the Holy Spirit' means. This is a complex biblical concept. The essential background to the New Testament concept of the gift of the Spirit is found in the Old Testament, Judaism and the life of Jesus.

Old Testament: The Spirit of God is mentioned in the Genesis account of the creation of the world and of man (Gn 1:2; 2:7). It plays a creative role in creation and is the source of man's life. The Spirit of God here is a creative, life-giving Spirit. But since creation is a *semel pro semper* (once for all) action, this role of the Spirit is not repeated in the Old Testament. The Spirit of God is not presented in the Old Testament as a life-giving Spirit in contemporary life and experience.

The Spirit, however, continues to play a very significant role in shaping the history of Israel. Here, it acts not in a life-giving capacity but rather as the power which accomplishes the mighty acts of God and which is communicated, temporarily or permanently, to certain men whom God calls to some role of leadership in the community or to whom he assigns a particular mission. Thus, Moses, Joshua, David, Samson, the judges, the prophets, all receive this gift of the Spirit (1 S 10:5-12; 16:13; 19:20-24; 1 K 22:10-12; Jg 6:34; 14:6; 15:14; Nb 11:25; 27:20; Ne 9:30; Is 34:16; Mc 3:8). Because of its particular association with the prophets, this concept becomes known in Judaism as 'the prophetic Spirit' (Os 9:7).

In the prophetic description of the messianic age, especially under the impact of the exile, a new role is envisaged for the Spirit of God. This new age is described as a new creation, a re-creation of the world and of man, involving a new and interior moral and religious renewal (Jr 31:31-54; Ezk 36:25-27; 35; 37:1-4; Is 11:6-9; 51:3). The agent of this new creation and renewal will be the Spirit of God, here acting once again as a principle of new life (Is 32:15-18; 44:3-5; Ezk 36:25-27; 37:14-15; 39:39).

The eschatological gift of the Spirit in the messianic age is also presented in prophetic terms, as a universal gift of the prophetic Spirit to all God's people (Is 59:21; Jl 2:28-29). This gift of the Spirit will first be evidenced in the Messiah himself and then in all the people (Is 11:1-6; 42:1-4; 61:1-3).

The prophetic literature thus envisages an eschatological gift of the Spirit in the messianic age which is portrayed as both a gift of the life-giving Spirit and a gift of the prophetic Spirit.

Judaism: The concept of the Spirit in the inter-testamental literature and in rabbinical thought is the classic concept of the Old Testament, the concept of the prophetic Spirit. With the cessation of prophecy in Israel after Haggai, Zechariah and Malachi, the Spirit of prophecy is regarded as quenched in Israel, as withdrawn by God because of the people's infidelity. It will return with the Messiah and signal the dawn of the messianic age.

At the time of Christ, then, the general concept of the Spirit is that of the prophetic Spirit temporarily withdrawn from Israel but whose return will signal the arrival of the Messiah and the messianic age. The concept of the life-giving Spirit is not completely forgotten, however, and would seem to live on in circles like the Essene community at Qumran with its notion of 'the spirit of truth and holiness.' But this probably represents a minor current in Judaism as a whole in the first century.

Life of Jesus: The concept of the Holy Spirit in the life of Jesus insofar as this can be recovered from the Gospels, must be sought in: (a) the Baptist's logion concerning 'baptism with the Holy Spirit and fire' (Mt 3:11; Lk 3:16); (b) the illapse of the Spirit upon Jesus after his baptism in the Jordan; (c) references by Jesus to the role of the Spirit in his own life and work (Mt 12:28; Lk 11:20); the promise of the Spirit by Jesus to his followers (Mt 10:20; Mk 13:11; Lk 12:11-12; Jn 14:16-17; 15:26-27; 16:7-11, 13-14; Ac 1:8). The concept of the Spirit in all these passages is that of the prophetic Spirit, the prevailing concept of the Spirit in Judaism at this time. The order of events at the baptism of Jesus is significant, baptism followed by the gift of the Spirit.

New Testament: The early chapters of Acts present us with the authentic attitudes and outlook of the early Christian community. The gift of the promised Spirit takes place at Pentecost. The whole context here emphasizes that this is an event of the prophetic order and the endowment of the community with the promised prophetic Spirit. This is consistently the concept of the Spirit throughout Acts.

When, immediately after Pentecost, the community begins to receive new members, the service of Christian initiation makes its appearance. It consists of two elements, baptism in the name of Jesus Christ for the forgiveness of sins, and the gift of the Holy Spirit (Ac 2:38). The presentation of Baptism and the gift of the Spirit in the rest of the Acts shows that two distinct and successive events are described here. For Acts consistently presents Baptism and the gift of the Spirit as separate and distinct, even if also closely related (cf. 2:38; 8:12, 14-19, 38; 10:44-48; 11:15-17; 19:1-6; esp. 8:16 'they had *only* been baptized in the name of the Lord Jesus' and 19:2). Moreover, the effect of Baptism in Acts is simply the remission of sins whereas the concept of the prophetic Spirit is not essentially connected with this effect. In normal practice the gift of the Spirit is here conveyed by imposition of hands (8:14-19; 19:1-6). Acts, therefore, bears witness to a primitive Christian initiation in the Apostolic Church consisting of Baptism in the name of Jesus Christ for the forgiveness of sins and imposition of hands for the gift of the (prophetic) Spirit. Heb 6:1-5 further supports this conclusion.

One must further ask, however, why the early community adopted *two* rites in their Christian initiation. One must remember here that Christian initiation means new converts becoming members of an already existing community. This community was brought into being by two events. The first of these was the life, death and resurrection of Christ, in short, the event of Christ. He, as leader and savior, is the source of forgiveness of sins for those who adhere to him in repentance and faith (Ac 5:31), i.e., become his disciples. The second event was the gift or event of the Spirit, the event of Pentecost. But already before Pentecost the community existed as the community of the disciples of Christ, of those who had committed themselves to him while he was still on earth. They had already experienced the event of Christ and therefore required no sacramental rite to make them what they already were. Now on Pentecost they experienced the second and distinct event, the gift of the Spirit, and they now exist as the *Spirit-filled* community of the disciples of Christ. When, then, they came to initiate new members into this community, they did so by repeating sacramentally the two foundation events which established it and made it what it was—baptism in the name of Jesus Christ for the forgiveness of sins (the event of Christ) and imposition of hands for the gift of the Spirit (the event of the Spirit). No doubt, they were also influenced here by the exemplar of Jesus' own baptism and the subsequent illapse of the Spirit upon him.

The practice of Christian initiation in the early apostolic community is thus based not on a thought-out theological position—the theology is indeed very primitive—but on the salvation events as the community has experienced them.

When we turn now to the writings of Paul and John, we find that for these writers forgiveness of sins is too negative an expression to fully describe the saving effects of Baptism. Baptism is therefore now presented as a new creation and a new life (Rm 6:3-11; 8:2; 2 Cor 3:2-6; 5:17; Gal 6:15; Jn 3:5). This theological concept of the Christian life immediately brings into the picture the concept of the recreative, life-giving Spirit spoken of by the prophets for the messianic age. The Spirit thus becomes 'the Spirit of life in Christ Jesus' (Rm 8:2). The beginning of this new life in Baptism is therefore the work of the Spirit and the gift of the Spirit is now seen as implied in Baptism (1 Cor 6:11; 12:13; Tt 3:5-7; Jn 3:3-5).

Theological reflection has thus led Paul and John to place the gift of the Spirit in Baptism.[2] It does not follow, however, that they dropped the post-baptismal rite from the liturgy of Christian initiation. Ac 19:1-6; Heb 6:1-5 and the initiation liturgy of the later Church (e.g. Tertullian, Hippolytus, Origen) all provide evidence this was not the case. What they have done is to create the theological problem of Confirmation, though there is no evidence that they ever adverted to this. For the problem now is how to relate the gift of the Spirit implied in Baptism to that which is explicitly expressed in Confirmation.

Later History

In the patristic theology of Christian initiation the Holy Spirit is presented as the source and principle of the effects of Baptism, of the new life and sanctification there accomplished. The explanation of the post-baptismal gift of the Spirit tends to emphasize the prophetic function and aspects of the spirit. When the two rites begin to be separated in the West from the fifth century on, theology begins to speak of two gifts of the Spirit in Christian initiation (a point already anticipated by St. Augustine), making the distinction along these lines. The Spirit is given in Baptism as the principle of new life and in Confirmation as the gift of prophetic force for witness. (It should be remembered that the term 'Confirmation,' introduced in the fifth century in Gaul to describe the separated post-baptismal rite, had a liturgical origin and meant simply 'to complete' the rites of Christian initiation; it did not originally have the theological sense of strengthening.)

In the early medieval period the concept of the post-baptismal gift of the Spirit as a gift of the prophetic Spirit for witness is strongly emphasized. The most complete statement of this concept is to be found in Rabanus Maurus (d. 856). This statement becomes the basic source for the later scholastic theology of Confirmation. St. Thomas Aquinas will later build his theology of Confirmation around this concept and through him it will become the statement on Confirmation in the Decree for the Armenians and thereby determine the post-medieval Roman Catholic doctrine of this sacrament.

Theological Assessment

Christian initiation expresses the basic qualities of the community into which the convert is being received. In its origin initiation expressed the two experientially distinct but intimately connected events which founded the Christian community and maintained it in existence, the event of Christ and the event of the Spirit. In its origin, then, Christian initiation possessed two basic references, christological (Baptism) and pneumatological (the rite of the Spirit). Further theological reflection in the Apostolic Church revealed more and more the intimate connection of these references. The Spirit was the Spirit of Jesus Christ, the Spirit of life in Christ Jesus. The gift of the Spirit, therefore, is already implied in the christological reference, Baptism. Yet, the Church continued to practice the post-baptismal rite specially referring to the gift of the Spirit. The later effort of theology to understand this situation by speaking of two gifts of the Spirit based on the different concepts of the life-giving and prophetic Spirit cannot be considered satisfactory. Though the Bible distinguishes these two concepts this does not lead it to distinguish two gifts of the Spirit. As there is but one Spirit, there is but one gift of the Spirit involving these two aspects. If the gift of the Spirit is therefore given in Baptism, it is totally given in Baptism, insofar as the action of 'giving' is concerned. (The terms 'gift' and 'giving' have theological limitations in this area.) Yet the following considerations should show that the special rite of the Spirit is not thereby reduced to a merely symbolic significance. It is in the light of these considerations, it is suggested, that the Church should now see the meaning and purpose of Confirmation.

(1) This rite recalls and celebrates continually in the Church the second great event which brought it into existence and makes it what it is, viz. the event of the Spirit. It is important that the Church and its members have a continual reminder of this event and its significance. This special moment of remembrance and celebration will clearly have reference to Christian initiation and membership of the Church.

(2) Baptism and Christian initiation are not actions which are over and done with once the rite has been completed; they are but the beginning of a process which must grow and develop and realize itself in the life of the Church. The realization of this process is the work of the Spirit of Christ in the Church. The special rite of the Spirit, intimately linked to Baptism and opening out to the mission of the Church, has a role to play in this process of realization.

(3) All sacramental theology is ecclesiology and the operating concept of the Church determines the character of the sacramental theology. The concept of the Church as institution is a rather static concept and needs to be supplemented by the concept of the Church as event. There is a true sense in which the Church was not merely founded once for all so many years ago but is founded continually every new day. In this sense Christian initiation is something which has to be reactualized in the Church and its members continually. Here again the concept of the Spirit is important and the special rite of the Spirit helps the Church to see and realize herself as continual event.

(4) Christian initiation is concerned with giving membership of the Church. Membership may be regarded in a rather juridical sense, a question of status and rights determining meaning and limits of participation, e.g. participation in the Eucharist. Where this concept operates, Confirmation may be said to be part of Christian initiation but not essentially constitutive of membership in that what Confirmation refers to, the gift of the Spirit, is already contained and given in Baptism. But this also is a rather static concept of membership and needs to be complemented by a more dynamic concept which conceives membership in terms of event, growth, process. Such membership should be seen as

leading the Christian not into a merely passive, docile status within the institution, but into the full freedom of mature human and Christian personality. This is the freedom of the sons of God and it is a freedom of and in the Spirit. Here again the role of the Spirit is fundamental and the special rite of the Spirit becomes significant.

These considerations, which are really but variations on the one theme of the Spirit in the Church, should help us to see that the special rite of the Spirit is not simply a piece of ceremonial within the liturgy of Christian initiation, but a significant action which enables the Church to become aware of herself and realize herself as the Spirit-filled body of Christ. It is an action in which the Church is realizing itself and this is its claim to sacramental status.

The Age for Confirmation

It is in the light of these considerations that the vexed question of the right age for Confirmation should be approached. If Confirmation is seen as conferring its own specific gift of the Spirit distinct from Baptism, the old order of the initiation sacraments, Baptism, Confirmation, Eucharist, must, it would seem, be adhered to. For then Confirmation would constitute the full Christian and clearly it is as such that one should take part in the Eucharist. Confirmation then should be conferred 'about the seventh year,' as Canon 788 required, and precede First Communion.

If, on the other hand, it is one and the same gift of the Spirit which is in question in both Baptism and Confirmation, and if this gift is already implied in Baptism, then the Church is entitled to regard the merely baptized person as an actually full Christian—something which is indeed implied in its legislative practice.

Since Confirmation does not here actually add any new element constitutive of being a Christian, even the merely baptized fully participate in the Eucharist. In this view, therefore, Confirmation is not so necessarily linked with the first Eucharist and the place of Confirmation in the old order of the initiation sacraments need not be regarded as sacrosanct. One is then free to situate Confirmation in the developing life of the young person at the moment which would be most consonant with its meaning. This would be when the young person is capable of personally realizing and appropriating his Christian status in the context of the Church as the Spirit-filled community of Christ. Confirmation would

then appear as the sacramental expression of the unfolding of Christian
initiation into its full ecclesial dimension. It is best conferred then at an
age when this unfolding can be a meaningful reality and this, I would
imagine, would be somewhere in early teenage.

Such a practice with such a meaning carries with it a serious implica-
tion for the Church. The sacrament expresses a concept of the Church and
the Church must seek to live up to and fulfill this concept. The confirmed
person should be able to experience the Church as the Spirit-filled
community of Christ, a terrain where the soil and climate foster the
growth of the Spirit's fruits. It is important that his subsequent experience
of the Church does not contradict the sacrament's meaning and promise,
that he discover the Church to be event, and nor merely institution.

Conclusion

'I believe in the Holy Spirit, in the holy catholic Church . . . :' this
credal profession describes the context which gives its meaning to the
sacrament of Confirmation. The Church is the community animated and
guided by the Spirit of God. The Spirit is here gift, promise and mission:
gift because his presence in us is pure grace; promise because he is God's
pledge to us of our sharing Christ's resurrection; mission because he calls
us and leads us to full Christian life and stature. Confirmation is the
sacramental expression of entry into this community-defined area, this
temple, of the presence and power of the Spirit. The grace of Confirmation should be, in the Christian, in the Church and in the world, the fruit
of the Spirit.

> The fruit of the Spirit is
> love, joy, peace, patience,
> kindness, goodness, faithfulness,
> gentleness, self-control:
> against such there is no law (Gal 5:22-23).

Footnotes

1. The ritual of Baptism carefully avoids any reference to 'the gift of the Spirit' in association with Baptism itself.
2. It is distinctly possible, and I would say even probable, that St. Paul views Christian initiation, consisting liturgically of Baptism and Confirmation, as a unit. This would stem from his close association of Christ and the Spirit. The one reality, participation in Christ and his Spirit, is accomplished in the complex initiation liturgy.

EUCHARIST, MYSTERY OF FAITH AND LOVE

Joseph M. Powers, S.J.

Mystery of Faith

In order to appreciate fully the role of the eucharistic community and its worship in the growth of the Christian in faith, hope and love, it is important to call attention to a significant change in focus for the theology of the sacraments. From the time that Peter Lombard (d. 1160) applied the notion of causality to the sacraments, sacramental theology could be characterized as a "theology of confection." The questions and concerns of sacramental theology centered on the conditions which are required for the sacraments to "produce their effect"—sanctifying grace and the other graces proper to each of the sacramental events. Aside from some marginal considerations of the requirements on the part of the "subject" or "recipient" of the sacrament, the major consideration was devoted to the powers of the minister of the sacrament, his ordination, unity with the Church, and so on. Drawing on a newly developed treatise on the Church which was centered on papal, episcopal and priestly power, sacramental theology emerged as a similar "power theology" largely concerned with who has the power to do what to whom.

This is the spirit in which St. Thomas Aquinas approaches his explanation of the sacraments in his *Commentary on the Sentences*, and it is the emphasis adopted by the Council of Trent in its defense of the theological tradition of the Church in its canon on transubstantiation. Accordingly this is the emphasis which found its way into the theological textbooks of the seventeenth, eighteenth and nineteenth centuries. It is the emphasis which has been found in much of the understanding, preaching and piety of approximately the last seven centuries. As it is applied to the understanding of the Eucharist, this theological style focuses on the power of the priest to "confect" the "real presence" of the Risen Jesus in the Eucharist, with all the consequences this has for the understanding of the Eucharist as sacrament and sacrifice, for the power of the Eucharist to confer the graces and virtues proper to it as sacrament. This is also the emphasis which characterizes Pope Paul VI's encyclical *Mysterium Fidei* in which he stresses the importance of the Eucharist for the fostering of the "sense of being Church" (*sensus ecclesialis*).

But all this emphasis on the effective power of the sacraments has a particular and important context. That context is set by the classical formulation of St. Augustine when he describes the sacraments as "sign of a sacred reality" (*signum rei sacrae) (De Civitate Dei*, X, 5). Peter Lombard certainly develops his understanding of sacraments in this context, because the power and efficacy which he presents is the power and efficacy of a sign (*signum efficax gratiae*). It is in this context that Thomas Aquinas develops his theology of the sacraments in the *Summa Theologica* (q. 60ff.) and the *De Veritate* (q. 26) where he insists that the sacraments "cause" grace by "signifying" grace (*significando causant*). And it is to this context that Vatican II's *Constitution on the Sacred Liturgy* turns. For, rather than repeating Trent's declaration that Christ is "really present" by the "transubstantiation" which takes place by the power of the words of consecration spoken by the priest, Vatican II stresses the fact that it is the presence of Christ *throughout the entire liturgical action* which gives the liturgy its value as an act of worship and sanctification.

For in the constant worship which Christ offers to his Father, he always associates the Church with himself. Thus, he is always present to the Church, especially in its liturgical action. He is present in the minister of the Eucharist, and especially present in the eucharistic elements, in the word proclaimed, and in the singing and praying congregation (n. 7). However, this unfailing presence of Christ to the Church must be matched by the full presence of the faithful to Christ. And that full presence to Christ and through him to the Father, although it should rise to expression in the knowing, active and fruitful participation of the faithful in the Eucharist (n. 10), must also be the pattern of the whole of Christian life, a life of constant conversion and repentance shown in the works of love, piety and apostolate (n. 9). In this statement the Council consciously moves away from the kind of sacramental optimism which would place all the emphasis on the proper performance of the liturgical sacramental act, away from a narrow concern with requisites for validity and liceity of celebration to a strong emphasis on active participation in the Eucharist and, more importantly, to a presentation of the Eucharist as the self-conscious self-articulation of the whole quality of life in the community.

We could characterize this shift of emphasis as a shift from a theology of "confection" in which the principal concern is the proper performance of the ritual, to a theology of "celebration" in which the emphasis is rather on the quality of participation in the Eucharist. This quality of participation includes not only the elements of conscious and active participation in the liturgical action in prayer, song and communion, but extends beyond the liturgical community to encompass the whole life of the worshipping community. And in this, the Council proposes far more than a reformation of liturgy. It calls for far more, for a broad and deep renewal in the faith-life of the Christian community. This is a far more profound pastoral challenge because it calls on us to examine, judge and renew the whole pattern of faith-in-action which is Christian living. For the "celebration" in question is far more than a matter of flowers, balloons and banners. It is the honest assessment, acceptance and confession of who we actually are as believing Christians here and now, an acceptance and confession which looks to a deepening of the bonds of faith, hope and love which make of us a Christian community—an acceptance, too, of the weakness, division and pride which seek to tear those bonds asunder.

St. Paul urges the Christians of Corinth to this kind of "celebration" in 1 Cor 11. What is lacking in that community is precisely the vision which a full life of faith gives to the believer. The divisions, the selfishness and greed, the lack of concern for the brothers and sisters of the community indicate to Paul that the wealthy members of the community do not "discern the body" and thus "eat and drink judgment" (1 Cor 11:29). The judgment is not simply something which awaits these people in the future. It is in their midst in the weakness, neglect and even the death of those who make up the body. It is this judgment which is eaten when one fails to "discern the body." Vatican II calls for this same kind of "celebration," a celebration which includes "examining ourselves, and so eating the bread and drinking the cup" (1 Cor 11:28). For what rises to expression in the Eucharist as Jesus associates us with himself in his worship of the Father is the vision and experience of faith, a vision and experience which is not simply limited to the actual celebration of the Eucharist, but which extends beyond the liturgy to the whole fabric of our lives of faith as Christians. "Mysterium fidei!" ("The mystery of faith!") the deacon cried in the ancient liturgy, and the community responded with praise to God for the life, death and resurrection of Jesus, a mystery lived out daily in the vision and experience of lives of faith. In that experience of the profession of faith in the celebration of the Eucharist, their whole lives of faith rose to humble and jubilant expression and were deepened in their communal confession.

Vision and *experience*: perhaps these two words can best express what we mean by the substance of faith in our lives. Our faith is a perspective on life in the world from which we see ourselves and the world in a certain way, through which we experience ourselves and our world in a certain way, and because of which we find the courage to invest the limited but real power of our own freedom in ourselves and our world the way we do. The central vision of Christian faith springs from the confession that in raising Jesus from the dead and pouring out his Spirit to gather the Christian community together, God has definitively revealed who he is: the God and Father of the Lord Jesus, who raised him from the dead and who will give life to our mortal bodies through the Spirit which dwells in us (Rm 8:11). This mystery of faith is the core of the vision and the experience of the Christian in the world, and it is at the core of the Christian community as it gathers to celebrate the Eucharist. It is this mystery that we celebrate with joy and hope in prayer, song and communion as well as in the confession of our own sinfulness knowing that God is faithful and just (1 Jn 1:9).

This faith-vision and the experience it gives rise to are not something that we can arrive at through our own individual effort. Christian tradition has insisted on this, especially in the context of the Pelagian controversies in which the teaching of the Church laid great emphasis on the fact that faith is always grace, always gift. It is not reason or logic which brings us to Christian faith, but grace and gift. In this context, the importance of the living, worshiping Christian community becomes apparent. There may be those among us who find themselves thrown to the ground like Paul and experience dramatic, miraculous conversion. But for virtually everyone the bearer of the gift and grace of faith is the living worshiping community which says: "That which we have seen and heard we proclaim also to you, so that you may have fellowship with us; and our fellowship is with the Father and his Son Jesus Christ" (1 Jn 1:3). And the "proclamation" in question is far more than a preached word. It is embodied far more powerfully in lives lived in the Spirit of Jesus, the Spirit of him who raised Jesus from the dead.

The power of that Spirit becomes apparent when we look at the description of what fruits that Spirit brings into being in Christian lives. Paul lists them: love, joy, peace, patience, kindness, goodness, faithfulness, gentleness, and self-control (Gal 5:22-23). A community gathered together by the Spirit of the Lord is a community of love, joy and peace. But that love, joy and peace are founded on very concrete human attitudes and commitments (virtues). They are the love, joy and peace which come into being when members of that community commit themselves to one another in patience, kindness, goodness, faithfulness, gentleness and self-control. "Being in the Spirit" is something very real, very concrete with a very clear power to communicate the meaning and power of the resurrection of Jesus in very specific ways in our lives. We can imagine what life in such a community would be like, and to the extent that we do experience this kind of community, we know the power it has for the growth of faith. This kind of community—or, perhaps more realistically, our commitment to bring this kind of community into existence—has real power to share Christian vision and experience Christian faith. For it is in this kind of community that the unfailing love of God becomes incarnate in the sacramental community gathered together by this Spirit.

From this it should be clear how important the Eucharist is for the sustenance and growth of the life of faith. The basic attitudes of our lives cannot remain unexpressed, uncelebrated. What remains unexpressed, uncelebrated soon becomes irrelevant and ceases to function in our lives. Our Christian faith is like this because it is one of our truly basic life-attitudes, the vision which shapes and interprets what it means to believe in God through Christ in the Spirit, which is what we mean when we speak of theologal or theological virtues. It needs articulation, to be brought to communal expression if it is to survive, let alone grow. And this is precisely what the Eucharist is, the celebration of the roots, the shape and the promise of the gift and grace of faith.

Likewise, it should be apparent how necessary the reality of a living faith-community is for a real Eucharist. For this living reality, a community doing the works of faith, is what the Eucharist celebrates, and deepens. Without this, the Eucharist is a hollow and empty sign. As Paul and Aquinas stress, the reality celebrated in the Eucharist and the effect toward which the celebration of the Eucharist looks is the unity of the Church, the unity which the shared vision of faith gives us.

Mysterium fidei, the mystery of faith. Our celebration of the Eucharist brings to expression our oneness in Christ as he unites us with himself in his continuous worship of his Father and ours, binding us into the grace-filled oneness of faith in the life and power of the one Spirit.

Mystery of Love

The life of the Christian is, in the last analysis, the fulfillment of the last testament of Jesus for those who would come to believe in him. That testament is a "new commandment" and that commandment is a commandment of love. "This is my commandment, that you love one another as I have loved you" (Jn 15:12). For the formulation of this for a Greek-speaking and Greek-reading audience, Paul and the evangelists could have used a number of Greek terms for love. They could have used the word *eros*, the wild ecstatic love in which reason is consumed by passionate frenzy. They could have used the more polite and urbane word *philia*, the love of equal for equal, of friend for friend. But they used none of these. Rather, they reached out for the word *agape*, a word of vague meaning. Generally speaking, it means the love in which the one who is loved is raised to the level of the one who loves. It designates a giving, active love, not a possessive love of self-fulfillment.

As interesting as all this philology may be, it does not really spell out in much detail the kind of love to which the follower of Jesus is called. For the commandment of love is very specifically spelled out in the Gospels. Paul stresses the fact that without Christian love, no gift or charism, no devotion or energy spent in the service of the Church is of any value at all (1 Cor 13:1-3). And it is only when the whole life of the Christian has its roots and foundations in love that the Christian can know what the love of Christ really means (Ep 3:17-19). Later theology resumes this conviction in its statement that "charity is the form of the virtues" (e.g., *Summa Theol.* II-IIae, q. 4, a. 3). What this means concretely is that all Christian life must be some form of love, that without love as our foundation, nothing we do is of any value at all.

All through the centuries, there has been a great deal said about love, but the command of Jesus gives love its most startling human shape. The clearest and most unambiguous shape of love is the Jesus who gives his life for those whom he loves. What looks like an execution or a legal murder is actually a supreme act of love, because no one can take Jesus' life from him. Rather, he lays it down out of love (Jn 10:15-18). This is the love of Jesus, and his command is that we love one another as he has loved us, ready to lay down our lives for one another (Jn 15:13).

But this love is more than a human love. It is the love of the Father Incarnate in the life and death of Jesus. For Jesus describes his love for his own as the love of God itself: "As the Father has loved me, so I have loved you" (Jn 15:9). On Mount Horeb, God gave his name to Moses, " 'ehyeh 'aser 'ehyeh," a strange expression which is more of a promise than a name. It means "I shall be there with you; I shall be there as who I am" (J.C. Murray, *The Problem of God*, New Haven, 1963, p. 10). Now, in the death of Jesus, the meaning of that name reaches its full completion. For the faithfulness with which God has promised to be with us takes its final form in the crucified Jesus, dying for love of us. And in this sense, John can say with a staggering wealth of meaning, "God is love" (1 Jn 4:16).

Thus, we can see that the love to which we are called as Christians is not simply another kind of human love. It is to be the very incarnation of the absolutely faithful love of God, a love whose faithfulness takes its final form in Jesus' giving everything for love of us.

This command of Jesus might seem impossible. After all, who of us can love with the very faithfulness of God? Indeed, this would be an impossible command were it imposed upon us in our loneliness as individuals. But this is not the case. For the testament of Jesus comes to us through our communion with those who, in their faith, have seen and touched the Lord. "That . . . which we have seen with our eyes . . . and touched with our own hands concerning the word of life . . . we proclaim also to you so that you may have communion with us. And our communion indeed is with the Father and with his Son, Jesus, the Christ" (1 Jn

1:1-3—my translation). It is in and out of the worshiping community that the command of love is mediated to us and that the power to live out that command is given to us.

In this light, we could read the story of Thomas as a specimen of the power of loving confessions given to those who see and touch the Lord. Jesus does not stand off from the one whose faith is weak. No, Jesus invites the believer, no matter how weak faith is, to see and touch him. And from that seeing and touching, itself a form of loving communion, there arises that startling and saving confession, "My Lord and my God" (Jn 20:28). This is a confession filled with awe—awe not so much at the majesty of the Risen Lord, but awe at the experience of seeing and touching the Lord. For this seeing and touching is an experience in which we discover within our lives a new capacity for faith, hope and love, a new capacity for living which makes of each of us a "new creation" (Gal 6:15). But, as the liturgical character of Thomas' confessions would suggest, the place for this loving and saving encounter is precisely the worshiping community.

Of course, the worshiping community is not a place where a magical transformation takes place in the lives of believers. The power which the eucharistic community has to celebrate and deepen the reality of *agape* (God's love incarnate in ours) does not somehow fall magically out of the heavens. Rather, in its Eucharist, the community celebrates the love which characterizes its life throughout all its days. It is this life of love which gives the power of living truth to celebration of the eucharistic community. For what Paul says about prophecy, tongues, martyrdom and the other gifts and callings of the Spirit is equally true of our Eucharist. We could say with him, "If I celebrated the Eucharist with every possible liturgical splendor and do not have love, it is nothing." Christian love is at the center as the power of all Christian living, and it is at the center, too, of the sacramental life in which that Christian living rises to loving expression and confession.

As a eucharistic community, then, what we celebrate most basically is our response to the command to love one another as Jesus has loved us. This is a humbling consideration because, as unlimited as is the faithfulness of the Lord in his love for us, our faithfulness is, like every other aspect of our lives, limited indeed. It is no wonder that we begin our celebration with a confession of the limited character of our faithfulness and our love. But this is no reason to find the command of love impossible. For, as the *Constitution on the Sacred Liturgy* points out, it is Jesus himself, present in our midst, who renews his claim in the proclamation of the Gospel, and it is also Jesus himself who is present wherever two or three are gathered together in his name, responding to God's love within even the limited love which we have for one another. The love to which we are called is a gift, a gift given to us in the gift of the Spirit, and it is in the power of that Spirit, uniting us with Jesus our priest, that we can profess our love and pray for its deepening.

The works of love, joy and peace which grow out of our commitment to one another in patience, understanding, goodness, meekness and self-control (Gal 5:22-23) are the gift of the Spirit of God, the Spirit of Jesus who gives us the power to love and whose power consecrates our love as it consecrates our offering of bread and wine. The prayer of praise and thanksgiving which our Eucharist raises to God is also a prayer for the deepening of the power of his Spirit in our lives, enlarging our capacity to love and to show the works of love to one another. It is a prayer for a deepening of the love of God which has been poured into our hearts through the holy Spirit which has been given to us (Rm 5:5). It is that Spirit which is at the heart of our power to love and to celebrate our love in the Eucharist. It is our task as Christians to open our lives as fully as possible to that presence and that power.

This, then, is the heart of the meaning of our celebration of the Eucharist: the love of God poured into our hearts through the Holy Spirit which has been given to us. The word proclaimed in the Eucharist is basically the word of love, the love of God made manifest in the life, death and resurrection of Jesus and the love with which we respond to his love by loving one another. The offering we make is the offering of ourselves living out our vocation to be the incarnation of that love for one another with the prayer that this offering, like that of bread and wine, will truly be that of the love of Christ Incarnate in his body. Our memorial, our proclamation of the death of the Lord until he comes, is a recalling of the most startling and unambiguous form of that love—Jesus' laying down his life for love of us. Our proclamation of the mystery of faith is a cry of faith and hope, but it is a cry of love, too. It is a cry in which we shout out our hope to be able to grow into the love of Christ through his Spirit at work in our lives as a community.

This, too, is the meaning of our communion. It is communion in the one body. It is sharing in the life of that body as we break the one bread. It is a celebration and pledge to share in the love which is the very spirit which gives real life to that body. It may be that we no longer share in the *agape* of the early Church in which the sharing of food among the community nourished its spirit of love as well as its bodily life. But we still share in the one Spirit of love in a communion of love. Our bread should taste sweet indeed as we become mindful of what we truly eat. Our Eucharist then is at heart a sacrament of love, the love of God poured into our hearts through the Spirit given to us, a sacrament of the lives of love to which we are called.

The concrete shape of the love to which we are called is not hard to find. It is found in the fruits which the Spirit of the Lord bears in our lives, the fruits of faithful commitment to one another made clear in the patience and understanding which we have for one another in the kindness, goodness and gentleness with which we treat one another. It is out of this pattern of daily Christian living that the peace and joy of the love of God blossom in our lives (Gal 5:22-23).

But there is one aspect of God's love which we should always keep in mind when we reflect on our vocation to Christian love. God's love is not given to those who by some herioic effort have made themselves pleasing in his eyes. God does not direct his love toward those who have somehow made themselves like him, perfect, sinless. No, "God shows his love for us in that *while we were still sinners* Christ died for us" (Rm 5:8). God's love is given to those who are different from him, and he loves them precisely in their difference. This character of God's love is apparent in the love of Jesus. He begins his ministry with a quotation from Isaiah declaring that his mission is to the poor, the oppressed, the blind and the captive (Lk 4:18-19). And in his ministry, his love encompassed even the outcasts of Jewish society, "publicans and sinners" (Mt 9:9-13, 11:9, 21:31). And in the end, God shows who is his "well-beloved Son," Jesus, dying as an outcast on the cross. Perhaps one of the reasons we find the mystery of the cross so difficult to comprehend or accept is the fact that we feel that love is only possible for those who are like us. We cannot understand a love which shows itself in the service of the poor, the oppressed, the outcasts of our own society. Yet the love to which we are called as Christians, the love which we celebrate and pledge ourselves to in the celebration of our Eucharist, is precisely this love, the love of God for all, even the least acceptable.

This may be shocking for us, but as we reflect on the meaning of our eucharistic devotion in this bicentennial era, we would do well to recall a part of the American vision which once was profoundly Christian. It is still inscribed at the base of the Statue of Liberty: "Give me your tired and your poor . . ." Surely one aspect of the renewal is the spirit of love which is at the heart of our celebration, a love which reaches out, healing, lifting up, liberating with all the breadth and depth of God's limitless and unconditional love.

THE UNFOLDING PRESENCE OF CHRIST IN THE CELEBRATION OF THE MASS

Everett A. Diederich, S.J.

An extremely rich doctrinal theme for assimilating, understanding and internalizing our new forms of active participation is that of the gradually unfolding presence of Christ in the celebration of Mass. The importance of the theme is clear from the consistency with which it has appeared in the conciliar and post conciliar documents.[1] The reflections which follow hope to make clear the usefulness of such a theme in reflecting upon the present order of the Mass and in identifying the dynamic of faith which underlies its structure.

The presence of the risen Lord

Our experience of active participation in the new order of the Mass, an experience which may impress us by its diversity, is the object of our reflection. What are we seeking? The answer is that we are seeking the mystery. Perhaps we shall realize better what the mystery is and how we are to search for it if we put the question another way and ask, "Whom are we seeking?" The question so put has a familiar post-resurrection ring. It sounds like the question which the risen Lord put to Mary Magdalene in the garden. It helps us realize that the mystery we are seeking through our reflection is the presence of the Lord, who is alive and present to us because the Father has raised him from the dead. Like God who loves us first, the Lord is present first before we come seeking him. He is present to us, to all mankind, and to all creation as the first born of the dead.

In this post-resurrection time in which we are it is the risen Lord who in countless ways is first asking us, "Whom are you seeking?" It is the Spirit-giving Lord, filling the world with his Holy Spirit, who lays this searching in us. Even as the question is formed by his presence through his Holy Spirit, he is gifting us to believe in him, to confess that he lives, and that it is he whom we seek. He gifts us with faith, but there is a dynamism and a transformation in this gifting. It is a process. It is like growth. It has movement like an unfolding drama. We catch all this when we remember the process in reflection. That is what we are about in our reflection, remembering how the living Lord, present to us first through his resurrection, moves us to believe in his presence through the unfolding of the celebration of Mass.

Of the post-resurrection narratives there is one story, that of the disciples on the way to Emmaus, which catches beautifully the dynamism of the risen Lord's presence, moving us to faith in him. It is a paradigm of the risen Lord gradually unfolding his presence in a way which leads to an inner transformation. The inner transformation ends in faith in him present. The activity through which the Lord gradually reveals this presence strikes us as *liturgical*. It reminds us of the way that Christ is present to us in the celebration of the Eucharist. Christ joins his disciples as they discuss the event of his death and the report that he is alive (Christ's presence in the assembly); he opens the meaning of the Scriptures to them (his presence in the word); he breaks bread with them (his presence in the eucharistic species). Prayerful reflection upon the story is helpful for opening our eyes to the ways in which the Lord reveals his presence gradually in the celebration of Mass.

It is difficult to resist the urge to enter into such a reflection in some detail at this point. Such explicitness of detail, however, runs the risk of spoiling the story for others, much like the retreat director who says too much about the Scriptures which he or she is proposing for a retreatant's prayer. The remarks which follow concerning this story are intended as an invitation to further personal reflection, and the hope is that attention to the Emmaus story will be a fruitful way of entering into a reflection upon the unfolding of Christ's presence in the celebration of Mass.

When the two disciples recount their experience of the risen Lord to the Eleven and the rest of the company, two moments are remembered, "what had happened on the road and how they had come to know him in the breaking of the bread" (cf. Lk 24:35).

Jesus joins them on the road without their recognizing him. He allows them to tell him the events which fill their minds and conversation. What stands out most is the event of his death and the report that he is alive. There is little or nothing in these events that has meaning for them. Jesus passes a saving judgment on them to call them away from their fruitless search for meaning. Then he takes the initiative in attending to the Scriptures, the law and the prophets, whom they had neglected. He searches the Scriptures with them and helps them find the inside of the event of his death which had weighed on them so heavily when they had remembered it simply as an historical fact. Through his presence, through his ministry he transforms their memory of an historical fact of failure and defeat into their faith acceptance of his death as his way of entering into his Father's glory. The interiority of his death was his obedient loving surrender into the Father's hands so that he might have life to the full and that all his brothers and sisters might share in that same fullness. The presence of Jesus on the road, explaining the Scriptures, is a light with which to find meaning and is like a gentle glow warming their hearts and drawing them to him. They have faith and their faith is a kind of obedient surrender to the meaning of his death as the way to glory. It is already the beginning of surrender to the love of the Father as manifested through the death and glorification of Jesus as they now accepted it in faith. They have faith and their hearts burn within them.

There is marvelous continuity in what happens on the road and at the breaking of the bread. The same risen Lord is ministering in both to transform the disciples, but his activity is different in the second. He is breaking bread and it is to this action that they now attend. The breaking of the bread is an action to see rather than an event to be remembered, although it is their faith acceptance of his death as a way to new life which now brings them to recognize him in the breaking of the bread. What happens to them in the presence of Jesus is reported as an opening of their eyes. This is a figurative way of speaking and places the emphasis on the inner quality of their seeing. They see in a new way, they see with recognition. Their seeing is recognizing the Lord through the gift of faith. He is the one whose death they accept as a salvation event rather than a tragedy of history. He is the one who opened the Scriptures to them. He is the one whom they now recognize in the breaking of the bread. In short, Jesus, who suffered and died in fulfillment of the Scriptures, that is, in

loving obedience to the Father, now lives again. These two disciples, like
the Eleven and the rest of the company assembled in Jerusalem, can shout
out the basic kerygma, "The Lord has been raised!" (cf. Lk 24:34). They
can confess their faith in him with the basic credal formula, "Jesus is
Lord."

Of all the appearances of the risen Lord, the one to the disciples on the
way to Emmaus seems most like the unfolding our own faith in the risen
Lord's presence when we celebrate Mass. A prayerful rereading of the
story is a marvelous help in catching the thread of continuity which makes
a unity out of the different modalities of presence of the risen Lord to
which the official Church documents refer. It is to these different ways in
which Christ is present to us in the celebration of Mass that we now turn in
our reflection.

The presence of Christ in the celebration of Mass

There is an ordering in the post conciliar documents of the principal
ways that Christ is present in his Church, and the ordering is based upon
the Order of the Mass, that is on the way that the parts follow each other in
the celebration. Thus, according to the documents, the principal ways
that Christ is present in his Church are *gradually made clear* in the
celebration of Mass.[2] The risen Lord reveals and communicates his
presence through the modalities of signs which follow each other in an
ordered way in the celebration of the Eucharist. In that ordered sequence
there is movement toward greater fullness of presence, which in turn
gives movement to our faith as we appropriate this presence through our
active participation in each part of the celebration.

It is becoming more common to speak of the Church as sacrament, as
the visible sign of mankind's communion with God the Father and of the
unity of all men and women in Christ. It is in the celebration of the
Eucharist that the Church as sacrament is expressed in a privileged way.
It is important, therefore, at the very beginning of the celebration of Mass
to focus upon this local assembly of believers as a manifestation of the
Church and, therefore, to focus upon the mystery of communion and
unity which the assembly expresses and realizes.

The local assembly is this manifestation of the Church by having
come together to unite their hearts and voices in a oneness of prayer to the
Father through Christ in the Holy Spirit. This unity of prayer is pointed to

by Jesus himself as one to which he is present: "Where two or three gather together in my name, I shall be there with them" (Mt 18:20). The presence of Jesus in those praying in his name is his sharing with them the gift of the Holy Spirit, his Spirit, gifting them with oneness in their prayer to the one Father.

The purpose of the introductory rites in the celebration of Mass is to actualize and express in an initial way this unity of prayer in the Spirit. It is ourselves visibly gathered and audibly praying together with real inner spirit which is the sacramentalization, as it were, of Christ's presence in the assembly.

There is a certain complexity of elements involved in the introductory rites. We are actively engaged in them and so have to attend to each of them. We have to have a kind of thread of unity in our faith consciousness as we move through them. The thread is an inner sensitivity or attentiveness to the Spirit gifting us with prayer, a gift we are receiving from Christ and offering to the Father and at the same time sharing it with each other. This inner attentiveness will alert us to the key moments in the opening rites, the moments which maintain the spirit of prayer and move it forward. It will help us also to execute these moments in a manner conducive to maintaining the spirit. It should be obvious that it is of primary importance in appropriating Christ's presence in the assembly that the introductory rites give priority, unambiguously and unapologetically, to prayer. We must have the impression as we participate in them that it is a marvelously good thing, indeed quite enough in itself, to be praying. It will be an almost certainly futile struggle to maintain a spirit of prayer if any of the moments of explicit prayer in the introductory rites are a kind of chatty talk about ourselves with God listening in, or even if it is a highly relevant, theologically contemporaneous discourse about God with us listening in.

One feature of the introductory rites calls for explicit comment in this reflection upon Christ's presence in the assembly. The introductory rites, as well as the whole of the Mass, are now celebrated *toward the people*. In the old rite Mass was celebrated *toward the altar*. Since in the majority of cases the Blessed Sacrament was reserved upon the altar of the celebration, the celebration could also be said to have been *toward the Blessed Sacrament*. The priest and the ministers celebrating toward the altar and toward the Blessed Sacrament drew everyone behind them to a faith awareness in which they were focusing upon the altar, and especially upon the Blessed Sacrament. The mystery of Christ's real presence was there, and the unity of faith and prayer of those assembled was very effectively realized through this physical, visible facing toward the mystery. We have emphasized above that the mystery of Christ's presence as it is unfolded in the introductory rites is within the praying assembly. It is the assembled Church *praying* which is the beginning moment of the mystery of Christ's presence, and as the celebration proceeds, it is within the assembly gathered around the table of the word and the table of the Eucharist that the full revelation of the mystery of Christ's presence unfolds. It is to give a symbolic expression of this that the priest faces *toward the people*. He faces toward the mystery of Christ's presence. The mystery unfolds, not so much out in front, but in the midst of the assembly.

As we move from one part of the celebration of Mass to the next, we come alive with the faith awareness of Christ's presence which has been actualized in the preceding part. So we come to the Liturgy of the Word with the faith we have in the Lord's presence in us as a praying assembly. This will be deepened through his presence in his word.

Our activity in the Liturgy of the Word is primarily proclaiming and listening in faith to the word of God with intervening prayers and chants to support our listening. In this activity there is an underlying dynamic toward progressive internalizing of the word of God. The Scriptures are themselves already a faith record. They come to us already bearing within them that obedience of faith to which we are being moved through the Holy Spirit of the risen Lord. They come with the faith which is normative for our own. It is not historical facts which are being proclaimed in our hearing through the scriptural word, but rather the faithful memory of these once-and-for-all events, shaped with their salvation meaning, and thus an instrument for shaping our own faith. It is the Holy Spirit who is responsible that the events are faithfully remembered with their salvation meaning, and the same Holy Spirit brings the faithful memory alive in us by gifting us with faith.

The word of God is proclaimed by a living person to the listening assembly. The Church's rites for the ordination of deacons and institution of readers imply that the word proclaimed is already a living word in the person proclaiming it.[3] Their proclamation is a kind of extension of their obedience to the word, and their being alive with the faith moves us in our internalizing of the proclamation.

The word is proclaimed, however, as God's word, not as the word of the one proclaiming it, and it is proclaimed so that it may take root in the hearers and produce fruit in them. As Isaiah reminds us, this word goes forth to accomplish the purpose for which it is sent (Is 55:11). With the proclamation of the word and in the hearing of it comes the power of the Spirit of Christ, the risen Lord, to receive it in the heart, opening the heart and mind in obedient faith. This is the word coming alive with the power of the Spirit, carrying the movement of internalizing forward.

The manner in which the readings follow each other, the insertion of the singing of the responsorial psalms, the acclamations, and other ritual signs accompanying the proclamation of the Gospel also help carry the movement of internalizing the word. The risen Lord is present to us through his Holy Spirit, helping us to search the Scriptures to find him in them, as the readings follow each other, just as he did with the disciples on the way to Emmaus. When the first reading is from the Old Testament, we are helped to a deeper faith by seeing the full sweep of God's design, finding the unity of the Old and New Testament. In the "today" of our celebration these Scriptures are fulfilled in our hearing (Lk 4:21). The writings of the apostles speak more directly to us of the "time of the Church," thus helping us to contemporize the saving events in our faith. Between the two readings, or following the first when there is only one reading, comes the responsorial psalm. It too is the inspired word of God, but it is the word prayed, therefore carrying with it all the interior qualities of prayer. It is the Church's prayer and Christ's prayer, prayed like all prayer through his Holy Spirit in our hearts, opening them to the risen Lord revealing himself in a special way in the Gospels. All the ritual surrounding the proclamation of the Gospel is to help us to more reverent faith attentiveness. The Gospels have a unique role in bringing us to faith. They were written that we might believe that Jesus is the Christ, and through this faith have life in his name (Jn 20:31).

The Gospels proclaim the great events of the words and works of Jesus, shaped in the faithful memory of the apostolic Church with their salvation meaning. The Gospels are shaped so that we commit ourselves to this normative salvation meaning. The central event, the one summing up all the rest, is the death and resurrection of Jesus. The inner meaning of this event, which we have already mentioned, is the obedient surrender of Jesus to the Father through death in order to be filled with life for himself and for us. Contained also in that meaning is that this sacrificial obedience of Jesus is for us, not just in the sense that we appropriate its fruit by sharing in the new life, but that we share it through our own obedient dying with Jesus.

This brings us to the final moment in the internalizing of the word, which is the Holy Spirit in us inspiring us to commit ourselves to this full salvation meaning of the death and resurrection of Jesus. The Spirit of the risen Lord is in us as light and truth, calling us to new values, vision, and direction for our lives. He is there as love committing us to Jesus, and through him drawing us to the Father. This is the power and efficaciousness of the word of God, sinking into our lives, transforming them and shaping them to the mind of Christ. All this is the presence of Christ in his word and our committing ourselves to him thus present.

But this transformation and commitment is to be lived out. The word is to become our lives directed toward the Father, lifted up toward him with the heart and mind of his Son. This is the dynamic of the Lord's presence to him in his living word, and this is the dynamic which brings us to the altar table for a unique kind of living out of this word.

We enter into our reflection upon the presence of Christ in the person of the minister by recalling where we are in the celebration of Mass and where we are in the spirit. In the celebration of Mass we have finished the Liturgy of the Word. In the spirit we are alive with an obedient and loving faith to surrender and empty ourselves so that we too may receive from the risen Lord's fullness of Life from the Father. The word presence of Jesus the Lord has gifted us with the transofrmed inner meaning, direction, and willing dedication for this surrender.

It remains to live out this inner gift, coming from the Lord's presence in his word. The dynamic of receiving the word is *to do* it, *to keep* it. We have a word from the Lord to keep, his command, "Do this, in memory of me." The Lord who lives again as the first born of the dead commands us to do the memorial of his own obedient sacrifice to the Father, his emptying of himself in loving surrender for Father to fill his humanity with life and the Holy Spirit. He wants us to do the memorial of his obedient sacrificial love so that his sacrifice of loving obedience and worship may be ours. Handing over his worship to us is his culminating gift of presence. This gifting takes place at the Lord's table where he is both host and food. His worship not only becomes our worship but our sacramental food and drink.

With gracious consideration for us flesh and blood people who are his Church, the risen Lord has prepared us for his culminating gift of presence in the sacrificial meal by gradually unfolding his presence in the assembly and in his word. As a final preparation he gifts us with his presence in the flesh and blood person of the priest who presides at the Lord's table. The priest is gifted through Christ's presence in his person to lead us in the obedient doing of the Lord's memorial by being gifted to represent Christ. In his visible, audible, tangible person he brings the presence of the risen Lord so that the Lord's own sacrifice may be accomplished for us to appropriate as our worship and our spiritual food and drink.

Our awareness in faith of the presence of Christ in the person of the priest, who now moves to preside at the altar table, is an enriching as well as a kind of focusing of that atmosphere of presence surrounding and penetrating our celebration, a focusing now upon the altar table where we shall come to recognize the Lord in the breaking of the bread.

Jungmann pointed out in his commentary on the text of the *Constitution on the Liturgy* that, when the draft of the document was debated, there was some opposition, to speaking of the fourfold presence of Christ. This, he says, came from the anxiety that "the faith in the Eucharistic Presence could be belittled."[4] Hopefully our reflection up to this point shows that faith in the eucharistic presence of Christ is not belittled but heightened by our faith awareness of Christ's real presence in the assembly, his word, and in the person of his minister. It is true that it was possible in the celebration of Mass before the changes, when the celebration was toward the Blessed Sacrament reserved upon the altar, to keep our faith attention more sharply focused upon the eucharistic presence than it is today. Such strict focusing upon the eucharistic presence, however, could miss the richness of the mystery. By attending to Christ's presence in the introductory rites and Liturgy of the Word we come resonating and permeated, as it were, with the mystery of Christ's presence, precisely because it has been mediated through signs and symbols which are suited to us flesh and blood persons. We are spiritually sensitized to signs and symbols as ways in which the risen Lord fills us more and more with the mystery of his presence, and now in the Liturgy of the Eucharist we come to the unique sign. In the Liturgy of the Word it was through his word alive *within* us that his sacrificial obedient death as a way to fullness of life from the Father for himself and for us became transparent for our obedient faith acceptance. In the Liturgy of the Eucharist it is through his presence in the material elements of bread and wine *outside* of us that this obedient death becomes transparent first to offer as our worship to the Father and then to take*within* us as our spiritual food and drink.

It seems obvious yet it is important to state clearly from the outset that the Liturgy of the Eucharist is centered upon the material elements of bread and wine. The memorial action begins and ends in the handling of these material elements. It is in that which transpires in and through this symbolic handling of these elements that the mystery of the memorial action consists. They are brought to the altar as our gifts of bread and wine, and they are taken and received from the altar as the risen Lord's gift of his Body and Blood. The mystery of the memorial action, therefore, is how the risen Lord's presence transpires in the symbolic handling of these material elements, how his sacrificial obedient death becomes transparent for our faith acceptance.

The changes introduced in the Liturgy of the Eucharist are to make clearer to us that the several parts of the celebration of this part of Mass have been arranged by the Church to correspond to the words and actions of Christ at the Last Supper. The clarity comes to us through our active participation in the structured ordering of the celebration, which ordering we acknowledge in faith as originating in the Lord's command to do what he did on the night before he suffered. In obedient faith we acknowledge *all* the doing involved in the several parts of the Liturgy of the Eucharist as corresponding to the several moments in the Lord's doing in the Last Supper. A faithful memory of *his* doing permeates all three parts of the eucharistic liturgy.

The preparation of the gifts is truly an ordered and shared doing, and as a first handling of the material elements of bread and wine it is richly symbolic. What is richest in that symbolism is the action of the assembly bringing the material elements of bread and wine to be placed on the altar where Christ's representative receives them. The gifts come from the assembly already twice gifted and thereby doubly transformed by the presence of the risen Lord. His presence abides in the spiritual reality of their renewed readiness to surrender their lives in sacrificial obedience to the Father and faithful service of each other with and through his Son. The material elements for the memorial sacrifice bear symbolically within them the spiritual element for the sacrifice, the sacrificial readiness of the assembly. Christ's fullness of presence transforming the material elements into his Body and Blood will at the same time bring the sacrificial mindedness of his Church to greater fullness. Christ is present in the priest receiving symbolically what is already his own, namely, his gift to us of his own mind and heart toward his Father and toward our brothers and sisters.

Such is the rich sacramentality of the preparation of the gifts. It is an action originating out of the assembly, already gifted with the risen Lord's presence, coming forward to the priest already gifted in his person with Christ's presence. This brings the whole Church united together at the Lord's table, his people, and his ministers, ready for the next step in the doing.

The Eucharistic Prayer is the next step in the doing. It is the "climax and the very heart of the entire celebration." The changes introduced are to help us realize this by the way we enter actively in the praying of the great Prayer.

Distinction of role is expressed in the praying of the Prayer, and yet a marvelous unity of prayer is heard, especially when it is the voice of the priest which we hear. Throughout the Eucharistic Prayer he designates the praying subject as "we." It is not a condescending editorial "we." It is the "we" of the Church united to the risen Christ in his Holy Spirit, praying to the Father. It is spoken by the one in whose flesh and blood person the risen Lord is present to his Church. It is obvious from the very introductory dialogue that it is the priest's intention to draw us into the Prayer. Christ is present in the person of his minister not to pray alone to the Father with us listening in, but rather he is inviting us to be united with him in the prayer as well as with one another.

Having reflected upon the mystery of the unity of ourselves with the risen Lord and with each other which is expressed in the "we" of the Prayer, we can now attend to how the Prayer moves and how the unique presence of Christ in the eucharistic species unfolds in the movement.

The Prayer is described in the *General Instruction* as "a prayer of thanksgiving and sanctification.'' The Prayer begins with very explicit thanksgiving and ends in a climaxing praise of the Father in the doxology. What moves this praise and thanksgiving to the climax is expressed in the gesture of lifting the consecrated Gifts from the altar as we pray the climax of praise in the doxology. We begin the Eucharistic Prayer with *uplifted hearts*, and we end it with *uplifted Gifts*. The climax comes through the sanctification of the material gifts of bread and wine over which our Prayer is spoken and through the presence of Christ in the person of the priest leading us.

The central moment of explicit sanctification of the gifts is unfolded in the cluster of those constituent parts of the Prayer which are called the *epiclesis*, the *institution narrative and consecration*, and the *anamnesis*. The *epiclesis*, the invocation of the Holy Spirit upon the gifts for them to become the Body and Blood of Christ, introduces the central movement. This explicit invocation of the Holy Spirit occurs only in the three new eucharistic prayers and calls for some attention. The Holy Spirit is the Father's gift to us through the glorification of his Son. As we saw earlier, through his presence in his word the risen Lord gifts us with his Holy Spirit so that we can accept in faith his obedient death as a way to life for himself and for us. Before his death the Holy Spirit filled the human mind and will of the Son with obedient love unto death. From his glorified, spirit-filled humanity he fills us with the same sacrificial mindedness. It is this same Holy Spirit that we now call down upon the gifts which are to be transformed into the sacramental sign of the glorified Son's once-and-for-all sacrifice. We are asking that this same Holy Spirit fill these material gifts with sacramental fullness. The epiclesis leads us prayerfully into a dense moment of sacramental mystery, drawing ourselves and our gifts into the transforming presence of the already lived out surrender of the Son to the Father. The fullness of presence of the Spirit brings the fullness of that transforming presence of the risen Lord.

The epiclesis is a gracious entrance into the dense moment of sacramental sanctification because it takes us all into the moment. In the unity of Christ and his Church praying to the Father, expressed by the ''we'' of our Prayer, the emphasis shifts so unobtrusively from Christ to his Church that we notice the shift only in our faith reflection. So humbly does our great High Priest minister to us his sisters and brothers. In the *epiclesis* the emphasis is more on the Spirit-filled Church, in the *institu-*

tion narrative there is a bridge shifting the emphasis to the Spirit-filled Christ in the *consecration*. But the union of Christ and his Church remain as the bonding mystery, and this is expressed in the "we" of the Prayer.

The climax in the central moment of explicit sanctification is the *institution narrative and consecration*. They are our most conscious effort to do what the Lord did on the night before he suffered. They contain the *verba domini*, the words of the Lord. The priest in whose person the Lord is present, speaks them with the risen Lord's attention to and intention for these material elements of bread and wine. The risen Lord's presence fills the words of the persons who represent him, and the words of the Lord accomplish what the Lord wants to accomplish through them. He wills that these material elements of bread and wine are to be totally changed into his Body and Blood as the sacramentalization of his sacrificial, life-giving death and glorious resurrection. He wills that it be a sign of his sacrificial worship as well as the life-giving fruitfulness of that worship. He also wills that his Body and Blood be handed over to us for us to eat and drink as a sign that he wants us to be united with him in his worship and also as a sign that this communion with his worship is going to be our ongoing communion of life with him and through him with the Father and with each other. The risen Lord has gifted his priest with his presence to accomplish what he wills, and so the *verba domini*, spoken in conscious faith obedience to the Lord, accomplish what the Lord wills. The material elements of bread and wine become the Body and Blood of Christ. Thus we come to the culminating mode of presence in the celebration of Mass, Christ present under the eucharistic species.

The final constituent part of the central moment of explicit sanctification of the gifts is the *anamnesis*, the memorial prayer. In the unity of the risen Lord and the Church praying the emphasis shifts again to the Church. It is in this anamnesis and in the oblation, which is inseparably linked to it, that the abiding spiritual reality with which Christ gifted us through his presence in his word enters, as it were, into Christ's presence in the Eucharist. The anamnesis is a part of the explicit sanctification of the gifts because it brings the faithful *memory* of the Lord's saving death and resurrection to explicit expression. In doing so, it explicitates the Church's faith in the holy reality which the consecrated gifts signify, the central saving mystery of the Lord's death and resurrection. In a true sense the anamnesis guarantees that our sacramental doing is faithful, that is, faith-filled. It was Christ's presence in his word which made possible our faith acceptance of the death of the Lord as a saving event for him and us, and even in the anamnesis this word presence is still operative to recognize the same saving event now present in the consecrated gifts.

Again it is a kind of prolongation of Christ's word presence that at this point in the celebration we also recognize the Body and Blood of Christ upon the altar as a sign which we can appropriate to ourselves for actualizing our sacrificial mindedness by offering these holy Gifts to the Father in the *oblation* prayer. The consecrated Gifts are a sign of Christ's timelessly abiding sacrifice. We express their sacrificial directedness by offering them to the Father in the oblation prayer before we take them to ourselves in the eucharistic meal. There is also our own sacrificial mindedness to be lived out here and now in our lives. That too we hold up to the Father in the oblation prayer. Next we move on to the explicit expression of our needs in living out what we offer. The emphasis in the intercessions is clearly on the Church.

Finally, we come to a marvelous concluding expression of the unity of Christ and his Church in the Eucharistic Prayer, of oneness in the sacrifice of praise. The priest in whose person Christ is visibly and audibly present lifts the sacramental sign of the risen Lord's once-and-for-all sacrifice toward the Father and offers all the praise of the Church on earth and in heaven to him through, with, and in the Son in the unity of the Holy Spirit. This gesture and these words show how deeply the Church is resonating to the presence of the glorified High Priest and Victim in these Gifts. But the Gifts are also to be our food and drink for ongoing lived out union with Christ and through him with the Father and with each other, and so we come to the last part of the doing of the Lord's command, eating and drinking his Body and Blood in the company of our brothers and sisters.

We ended the Eucharistic Prayer appropriating Christ's eucharistic presence by offering all our worship to the Father through him. In the communion rite we complete, as it were, our appropriation of this presence. The modality of his presence under the eucharistic species calls for this completion. Christ is present totally and permanently under the sign of food, and we are faithful to his command to take and eat and drink.

The culmination of Christ's unfolding presence thus ends in a culmination of union, of union with him and through him of union with the

Father and with our brothers and sisters. This communion of Body and Blood of Christ completes the gift of unity in the opening introductory rites upon which we reflected. The unfolding of Christ's presence brings the Church to its fullness, expresses that fullness and effects it as well.

It also brings the mystery of the Lord's resurrection to its fullest expression. This is the banquet of life because life which is already fully possessed by the Lord in his glorified humanity is shared with us. Because the risen Lord is present at the banquet, the eucharistic meal is eschatological doing, it is end-time living. It is already living out the fruitfulness of our surrender to the Father in obedient worship. Just as the Lord entered into fullness of life in his glorified humanity through his sacrificial obedience, which was his worship of the Father, so in the celebration of the Liturgy of the Eucharist we have entered into this sacramental sharing in the fullness of life by first entering into a sacramental offering of our worship to the Father through Christ.

The changes introduced in the celebration of the communion rite are intended to help us enter as fully and as consciously as possible into this mystery of holy fellowship with the risen Lord and with each other through him. The changes have brought greater clarity in the ordering of the meal as well. The rite of peace and the breaking of the bread are given greater prominence. It is expected that there will be song to make the sharing of the Body and Blood of Christ more festive. All this is to help us maintain an atmosphere of mystery, a mystery to be received with faith and reverence, which are surely not opposed to a spirit of fellowship and joy. The mystery is something wherein the risen Lord gifts us with his peace and unity, as the prayer before the sign of peace reminds us, rather than something we ourselves create.

We are pilgrims journeying toward the complete fullness of life which the risen Lord already possesses in his glorified humanity. The Lord stays with us on the journey to be our daily bread. His culminating gift of presence is permanent, as the sign of food signifies. His presence is prolonged in the reserved Blessed Sacrament, and it there bears with all the mystery upon which we have just reflected. It is prolonged for our reverent, adoring, thankful, praise-filled, and prayerful contemplation. This prolonged eucharistic presence is an extension of the culminating gift of the risen Lord's presence. Our response in devoted worship of this Holy Sacrament outside of the time of celebration is the prayerful space we need in our lives to reflect upon this great mystery and remain faithful to its celebration in Mass. The mystery is great, and the time of celebration is all too short. We need a time of added contemplation in the presence of the Blessed Sacrament to absorb it.

It is of primary importance to recognize in our contemplation that the eucharistic presence of Christ comes from the celebration of Mass. It bears all the aspects of the mystery of that celebration with it. We should therefore make it our aim in our contemplation to resonate with all the faith response which the unfolding presence of Christ in the celebration evoked in us. We should renew our prayer for all we need to live out that sacrificial mindedness with which we were gifted in the celebration. We should also remember our needs for living out the mystery of holy fellowship in the service of our sisters and brothers. Above all we should resonate with praise and thanksgiving. "To him whose power now at work in us can do immeasurably more than we ask or imagine" (Ep 3:20).

Footnotes

1. Cf. *Constitution on the Sacred Liturgy*, n. 7: AAS 56 (1964), pp. 100-101; Paul VI, "Mysterium Fidei," September 3, 1965: AAS 57 (1965), pp. 762-764; Congregation of Rites, *Instruction on Eucharistic Worship*, "Eucharisticum Mysterium," May 25, 1967, n. 9 and 55: AAS 59 (1967), pp. 547, 568-569; *General Instruction on the Roman Missal*, ch. 2, n. 7; *Holy Communion and Worship of the Eucharist Outside of Mass*, June 21, 1973, n. 6. The last document quotes from the *Instruction*, "Eucharisticum Mysterium."
2. Cf. Congregation of Rites, *Instruction on Eucharistic Worship*, "Eucharisticum Mysterium," n. 55: AAS 59 (1967), pp. 568-569; *Holy Communion and Worship of the Eucharist Outside of Mass*, n. 6.
3. Cf. *Ordination Rite for Deacons*, n. 24: "Believe what you read, teach what you believe, and practice what you teach." *See* also *Institution of Reader*, nn. 4 and 6.
4. *Commentary on the Documents of Vatican II*, Vol. I (New York: Herder and Herder, 1967), p. 13.

THE EUCHARIST:
SYMBOL OF COHERENCE

Paul Quenon, O.C.S.O.

Symbols express meaning. Symbols also contain meaning, and some symbols are so fundamental that without the symbol the meaning behind it is lost altogether. Such would be a symbol of coherence. By it, a whole society, a culture, or a civilization grasps the meaning of its own existence. Remove the symbol and the unity of that society begins to disintegrate.

The Eucharist can be appreciated more fully as a symbolic reality when it too is considered as a *symbol of coherence*. Not only does it serve this function for the Church, but through the Church it is brought to bear upon the historical process as a whole. Considered merely as a symbol, the Eucharist is "the means whereby the world of isolated things and actions is brought together into a framework of meaning."[1] Considered as a symbol of coherence, it binds together a certain cultural development and is inseparable from that culture in its particularity and universality. A culture consists of the totality of human products.[2] What makes it a whole instead of a scattered fragmentation of human products is a central symbol of coherence. By this symbol a society understands itself as a unity and tries to explain why it is what it is. It does this by spelling out in mythological form the story of its own origin, which in certain instances coincides with the origin of the world. In explaining the world, a culture explains itself and its own view of reality.

The story of the American Revolution has this kind of symbolic function: in recounting our origins we explain why such notions as freedom and independence are so important to us as a people. Our observance of the recent Bicentennial was a way of retelling the story of the United States in a ritual fashion, situating that story in the context of contemporary experience, and reflecting upon our future as a nation.

The Eucharist and the story of the Last Supper have the function of symbolizing why the Church exists and what it is all about. They take us back to the central events of the crucifixion, death, and resurrection of Christ, in the ritual re-enactment of that moment when Jesus could look upon his destiny and say: "It is for you." By this rite we are brought into the unity of Christ which binds us together. What unites those who engage in this particular cultural activity and identifies them as a group is their common participation in Jesus Christ. He as a person, bodily, is the principle binding these people together and giving them coherence. He is the reason why they are what they are and as such, the primary symbol of social coherence. Were we to ask why there is such a people here rather than no people at all, the reason would be Jesus.

The Eucharist, in the words of Anscar Vonier, "is a particular instance of the more universal problem of the mode of our union with Christ."[3] In some sense the Eucharist is the particular instance of our union as a social reality because it deals thematically with this unification and does so as a symbol of coherence.[4] What are the intrinsic factors that make the Eucharist a principle and sign of unity between Christ and ourselves? What are the structural properties that make the Eucharist a unitive symbol? This is the main interest of the following study, for we see that in the Eucharist the broad and universal reality of our social and personal union with Christ takes on particular lines and features that define it as a uniquely powerful symbol.

Memorial

The most obvious fact in our eucharistic celebration is the disunity caused by the obvious absence of Jesus. If there is any unity with him, it is by a bridge across the gap caused by Jesus' death and his separation from us in time. By no means is he present in the eucharistic celebration as we are present. Yet the death that separates us is, in a deeper sense, the very thing that unites us. It is in his death that we find the union we celebrate. The Eucharist is not a spiritual substitute for a union of which death has deprived us; it does not bypass the reality of death but hinges upon it. In the Spirit and in the power of the Resurrection, the thing that separates us is the very thing that unites us. To speak of the presence of the risen Lord means nothing except in conjunction with his death. His risen state is not some other mode of presence than his death but rises out of his death. The Resurrection is the unitive power of that death, making of it more than just a moving tragedy of a great historical figure, but a life-giving power.

One of the basic structural properties of the Eucharist, then, is its form as a memorial of an historically determined event. When Jesus had offered the bread and wine he said: "Do this in remembrance of me." The Jewish concept of a ritual memorial was not so much a matter of reaching back into the past, as of making the past reach into the present. It was a re-enactment or a re-presentation of the past in the present, so that the divine power that was manifested takes effect in the present.

> It is a celebration commanded by God like the celebration-memorials of the Old Testament, the *zikkaron*. What is peculiar about these memorials is that God is present in them, renewing the covenant with His people as He establishes it in the great events of Israel's history.[5]

Because of its nature as a memorial in this sense, the Eucharist contains a narrative recitation of the events of the Last Supper. The air of memorial is strongly evoked in the eucharistic prayer: "On the night of his Last Supper, taking bread. . . ." This glance toward the past is a return to the source. It explains why we are all together now by telling how it all started. And in remembering its own origins, the celebrating community recreates itself. Yet the memorial also has a forward thrust. The Eucharist employs a psychological technique which is as old as ritual reality itself and which is found in the ceremonial re-enactment of creation stories all around the world. The Eucharist enlists deeply human powers to achieve union between Christ and ourselves.[6]

This remembrance is not remembrance *about* Jesus, but it involves Jesus himself in our remembrance. The whole Liturgy of the Word functions as remembrance, expanding the institution narrative in the eucharistic prayer so as to include everything Jesus said and did. It tells us more of who did these things and what he meant. The whole of his life is brought to bear upon the meaning of the Eucharist, and the Eucharist makes that meaning present. To understand the Eucharist means to understand Jesus. He is the informative principle of the sacrament, and we should interpret it in the light of what we know of him.

Covenant Renewal

As a memorial, the Eucharist is unitive in the same sense as the covenant renewal of the Old Testament. Just as the union of God with his people expressed in terms of the covenant was renewed in the paschal celebration, so too the Eucharist is a renewal of the union effected in Christ. In the earlier accounts of the Last Supper found in Paul and Luke, the covenant is closely associated with the rite by the words "This cup is the new covenant in my blood" (1 Cor 11:25), as if, read literally, to partake of the cup is to drink in the new covenant. Covenant is mentioned in all the accounts, but in Mark and Matthew it is more closely linked with the event of the crucifixion: "This is my blood of the covenant which shall be poured out for many" (Mk 14:24).

To remember the covenant does more than bring the past up to date. It drives one forward into a further realization of the covenant for the future. Thus when God heard the groanings of the people of Israel under bondage in Egypt, "God remembered his covenant with Abraham, with Isaac, and with Jacob" (Ex 2:24); and that was the beginning of an intervention on their behalf. So too, for us to remember is to be motivated to a greater fidelity to the covenant for the future. It is to live out that union, so that life is ever more an actualization of covenant. Thus the Eucharist lays the spiritual basis for change in the sense of conversion for the Kingdom. To return to the source means to seek out the future; remembrance of the past becomes eschatological hope for the future.

Berakah

On the most material level the Eucharist is a unitive symbol because it is a meal. The common participation in food and drink is, regardless of historical implications, an event which brings people together. For the Jew a meal was a sacred event, because the sustenance was received as a gift from God. The family meal was preceded by a blessing, *berakah*, said over the bread symbolizing the whole meal, and addressed to God who was acknowledged as the source of all goods: "Blessed art Thou, O Lord, our God, King of the Universe, who feedest the whole world with goodness with grace and with mercy."[7] Notice how naturally the thought flows out from the immediate good to the whole of creation, and how it shifts from food to spiritual goods. By prayer the whole context is enlarged, so that what serves the individuals at table is seen as connected with life everywhere.

The blessing Jesus spoke over the bread was doubtlessly in words such as these, and for that reason this level of meaning composes an integral part of the meaning of the Eucharist. By this meaning we are placed in the context of a common participation in a life that comes from God. The Eucharist is the unifying occasion where all creatures are symbolically present, and God is present with his creation. The most elementary human meanings are taken up into the Eucharist and personalized. I once heard a rabbi tell what his Jewish grandmother would say while feeding the babies: "Now take a bite for Grandpa . . . Now take a bite for Grandma. . . ." Thus the act of eating itself is made replete with personal meaning.[8]

Sign-Action

The actions of the Eucharist, as described, are also unitive in significance. What did it mean for Jesus to take bread into his hands? Was it only a utilitarian action? Was it not mentioned explicitly in all four accounts because the same action was repeated continually by the Church as a symbolic action? To take is to touch, to close the separation between the human and the material; and breaking bread is to raise up the material as a gesture of the most human of things, death. To give away something, one has to hold it in possession; and in taking bread, it was as if Jesus were taking into his hands the fragile life that was his to give away.

In recounting and repeating this gesture, the Church re-enacts Christ's self-gift. In the action of the priest, the self-giving of Christ is extended to the community present.

Again, in the words "take this," there is complementary giving and receiving: the gift is not thrust upon the other, it is freely taken by the other. One has the option of not taking. But by freely taking, one responds to the gift freely given. How much more expressive of the dignity of this loving action is communion in the hand, which allows for a more ample and human mode of expressing this gift-taking.[9]

The most striking of sign-actions having a unitive force is the communion itself, the eating of the bread and drinking of the cup. By it we are taking the offered life of Jesus as the nourishment of our life. He enters into union with us through symbols on the most elementary level, symbols which permeate our flesh and fill our bloodstream. He allows us to become the outward form of his presence through our becoming inwardly conformed to him. The community—we ourselves—becomes the expression of Christ's presence on the empirical level. This statement does not mean that his presence is empirical, verifiable by the senses, but that Eucharistic union draws into itself all the concrete and human realities of our life.

The significance of communion, as we have just described it, is not only a union but also unification. It is a sign-action, representing a process, a unification by assimilation into Christ. So what establishes the identity of the worshiping community is its participation in a growing process which brings about unification: the making *one*. What the Eucharistic symbol of coherence does is to span time and the process of change within it, in order to give it meaning and direction. Thus the Eucharist is eschatological in the sense that it contains, to some extent, what it anticipates. The future is already present.

Sign of Transformation

As an eschatological symbol, the Eucharist does not define a limit so much as point out a direction. In this regard it is different from ideologies or national and social ideals. It transcends cultural forms, although it can enter into and assume various cultural forms, as is evident from the variety of Christian liturgies in the East and West. The Eucharist does function in a limiting way in the sense that the historical source and inspiration of the Eucharist is determined once and for all in Jesus. But it functions directionally because it is transcendent, having no particular specifications as to how unification is to be brought about. The way will vary from one situation to another. The Eucharist bestows the predispositions and the power for such a unification and, as such, it falls under the category of *praxis*.

How is this category to be understood? The difference between ethics and praxis is the difference between knowing "I should do" and determining "I will do." A symbol contains meaning which gives rise to a cognitive truth and a moral truth. In showing us life it also shows us the proper ordering of life. An action-symbol also involves us personally in the ethical meaning it embodies and serves as a praxis, or determination, of change. By receiving the eucharist, for example, we commit ourselves to the charity that it signifies, and so we are brought to action by the praxis of the sacrament. Unless the sign-action is performed in hypocrisy or in a purely passive manner, it engages the person in a commitment to its meaning and its fulfillment. The purpose of the rite is to give the power for that fulfillment. One becomes "enthused," *entheazo*, in the sense of being filled by the "god," or by the power to do something, as, for example, in fertility rites where power for producing offspring is conferred. In the Christian context, what is given is the Spirit and the gift of charity to live a Christian life. What is given really amounts to more than an openness to, or a decision for a Christian life. It *is* that life in potentiality as it comes from God. The rite bridges the gap between the intentional level and the level of actual practice. It belongs more to praxis than does, say, ability, skill, or a proper method, for one can have these and never employ them.

The Eucharist is delimited by the historical point in time from which it originates; but also it is open ended, always reaching forward to a future realization of its own immanent meaning. Its drive is always towards what is not yet and it opens up the possibility for that which is not yet. As praxis, it is something broader than method: it is not directed towards a task to be achieved, but towards a mystery to be lived. Like method, it brings about a result; but its results can never be planned and objectified ahead of time, since it proceeds by our free personal involvement. The results are not predictable, as if, once God showed forth his image in Christ, the sacraments afterwards go on like a machine drably making exact copies off the same metal casting. The transcendence of the sacrament consists precisely in provoking the creative and the personal. That is why it is a unitive sign. It gives birth to new life in its diversity, and that diversity finds its source in the Eucharist. The unity it offers cannot be destroyed by diversity, for it is the transcendent source of all diversity.

Of course, in actual practice unity can be confused with uniformity, and the liturgy can be stiffened into a formal and unchanging mold, but that is because the society itself has become formalistic.

The reality of the Eucharist as praxis is implied in the Scholastic statement that the sacraments are instrumental causes of grace. What is conveyed is a grace which brings about conversion and carries it forward.

The power takes effect in a change of life, Christ being the formal cause, the sacrament the instrumental cause, grace the efficient cause. The final cause of the sacrament can be defined in treating more fully the conversion it brings about.

Conversion

In the Eucharist, Christ is present to us as one who serves others. When it is said, "This is my body which shall be given for you" (Lk 22:19), these words are being pointed directly to us, inviting a response. The meaning of the Eucharist, viewed in the context of the life of Christ, is that of a sacrificial love, a giving-over of what begins as "my" body and becomes "for you." Here there is a transformation in Christ of what was "of one" into what is now "for the many:" "mine" becomes "yours" and is shared by the many as "ours." The servant, by his performance of service, becomes an integrating principle for the many. The action of giving-for-others is the dynamic gift that we receive in the body of Christ. The gift and the giving are inseparable; what we receive is not a corpse but an act of love.

The direct offer of this love is simultaneously an impulse to give love in return, for love gives rise to love. While the words "for you" tell us something about Jesus as the Servant of Yahweh (Is 53:5), they very directly contain the service of which they speak and they apply it to us. They employ the unitive dynamics in ritual action and say in words what the action of eating consecrated bread means.

It has often been noted that, although John's Gospel has no account of the institution of the Eucharist, his Last Supper account contains the same essential meaning in the episode of the washing of the feet.

Service is the meaning of the Eucharist. What we derive from the Eucharist is not simply the message "Jesus is the man for others"—a theological statement; we derive, rather, the message "This is my body which is given for you"—a religious statement. A similar difference exists between "God is pure being" and "I am," as John's Gospel uses the phrase. As soon as one hears the latter, one is already involved in it personally.

Eschatological Action

By understanding the present repercussions of the Eucharist as praxis, we are brought to an understanding of its repercussions for the future. Texts which deal more explicitly with the eschatological reference of the sacrament merit consideration. All four accounts of the institution contain some statement about the future, and it is impossible here to discuss adequately the variations among them. But we can note how this future reference is present and what its structural role is in the sacrament as a unitive reality.

Except for Paul, the accounts in the Synoptics tell us about Jesus' own personal disposition towards the future at the moment of the Eucharist. For example, in Mk 14:26 we find: "Truly, I say to you, I shall not drink again of the vine until that day when I drink it new in the kingdom of God." Two features are common to these accounts. First, there is an intervening "time until"—a period when Jesus abstains from eating of the same portion or drinking of the same cup as those to whom it is given. Secondly, there will be a time when he does partake, though when that time will be—at the crucifixion, after the resurrection, on the Last Day, at the Last Supper itself—remains unclear.[10]

In any case, Jesus clearly attended the Last Supper expecting it to be his last meal until the coming of God's kingdom. Whether he himself abstained, as Joachim Jeremias claims,[11] or simply partook as one who would not do so again until that future time, we can see that for Jesus this event marked a final moment, which was also the beginning of a new age. His words convey assurance and an anticipation of victory. The obvious signs of humiliation and failure gathering all around him do not dim the conviction that "I will follow this meal with the banquet held in the Father's kingdom."

The Eucharist, then, is a sign of what is to come. As there is an eating and drinking now, there will be an eating and drinking again in the tomorrow of God. No matter how often we celebrate the Eucharist, it is always the day before the tomorrow of God which is not the day that follows on the calendar but one which comes when Christ comes. This day is so "other" that it makes all our days seem the same. We are continually celebrating within the same day, despite two thousand years of eucharistic celebration. Each day of ours is no further away from God's tomorrow than any other. This tomorrow is not merely an ever-present eternity, for there is a continual changing of our today into God's tomorrow, as one day leads into another. A dynamic transition occurs between what is and what is to come. God has made himself the "absolute future" of humanity, to use the language of the theologian, Michael Schmaus. The Eucharist defines this dynamic for us and brings us into its current.

Hope and Eucharist

Whenever we celebrate the Eucharist, we again hear of Jesus' expectation to eat with us once more in God's kingdom. We enter into the ambit of God's promise where it is offered to us again. Thus, we are brought to live by the promise. The whole dynamics of hope, so well described by Moltmann, is here expressed sacramentally.[12]

What is experienced is not a vicarious glimpse of a future existence. Rather, it is a turning toward present reality lived in the promise of God which far exceeds anything we could conceive by ourselves. The experience is an entering into the potentialities of the present which we would miss completely if it were not for God's promise.

Because in hope God is our absolute future, nothing else is absolute to us. No finite being can be our ultimate end. So our love becomes universal. The possibility for change, conversion, is opened up, for no present state of well-being is final.

What specifically does the Eucharist add to this dynamic of hope? It shows us that this hope is a *collective* possibility. Since it is in community that we affirm this hope, we thereby hold it in common with others. Here again is the great cohesive value of this sacrament. In putting forward a common meaning, the Eucharist gives a sense of direction that transcends social divisions. Divisions will remain, of course, but in the midst of them is the realization that in God's kingdom there lies a unity that is deeper than our separations. The Eucharist is meant to reorient us towards the unity beyond. Of itself it cannot completely remove disunity but where necessary it disposes us for unity.

From this basis, we can reconsider the value of intercommunion among the churches. If the union the Eucharist symbolizes is truly eschatological and transcendent, it would not be a misuse to share it across church lines. This would not contradict the meaning of the Eucharist, since the unity it symbolizes is never identical to a unity we have here and now. Sufficient for intercommunion should be the participants' intention to enter into the potentialities for a unity that lies in God's future.

Another eschatological aspect of the Eucharist is its universalism. The sacrament is ordered toward that final banquet when Christ will again sit with his own in the kingdom of God. The unity for which it hopes can never be limited to the unity achieved in the present celebration, as if to be outside the sacramental unity is, of itself, to be in disunity. Rather, the sacrament seeks for a unity wider than its own—a unity that can be achieved only finally in the Kingdom. Without this eschatological orientation, the Eucharist would lapse into the defect of every symbol of coherence, namely, to become a sign of division and limitation over against another unified group. In the Christian context, unity is defined in terms of service and a universal mission of unification.

Summary

As an expectation of the future Kingdom, the Eucharist is a sacrament of hope. As a remembrance of, and a response to, God's fidelity in the past, it is a sacrament of faith. As service offered in the present, it is a sacrament of charity. In a word, it is the sacrament of Christian life. It unifies past, present, and future into a symbol of coherence that is at once temporal and spatial. Those who went before us and those who will come after us are related to the present in the Eucharist. It is the symbolic presence of the communion of saints.

I have tried to show how the Eucharist is a symbol of coherence and a sign of unification, having an historical limitation and an unlimited openness towards the future. This transcendence is intrinsically structured into the Eucharist as an efficacious process and as a praxis of transformation of history in Christ. History means primarily people and groups of people, but it also means the process of becoming which a people goes through. The Eucharist cannot be understood in its efficacy apart from this broad context. It is a consecration of time, just as much as it is a consecration of individuals and communities. By it Christ is brought from the past, through the present, into the future, effecting a unification and transformation of history.

Footnotes

1. Zachary Hayes, "Man and the Paschal Mystery" *Worship* (1971): 153.
2. Peter Berger, *The Sacred Canopy* (New York: Doubleday & Co., 1967), p. 6.
3. *A Key to the Doctrine of the Eucharist* (Westminster, Md.: Newman Press, 1956), p. 1.
4. Vonier deals primarily with the individual's mode of union.
5. Joseph M. Powers, *Eucharistic Theology* (New York: Seabury Press, 1967), p. 119.
6. This assertion disagrees with J. Jeremias, *The Eucharistic Words of Jesus* (London: SCM Press, 1966), pp. 237-55, where the subject who remembers is God. In reply to his argument: "Was Jesus afraid that his disciples would forget him?" we might answer that Jesus was calling for a response that involved more than a mental act, but a total self-engagement on the part of his disciples.
7. Louis Finklestein, "The Birkat Ha-mazon," *Jewish Quarterly Review* 19 (1928): 215.
8. "In the Eucharist, Christ gives His bodily personal reality to be received under the form of food and drink, a form which suggests the most complete entrance of one personality into another and of the most unique oneness. In the Eucharist, Christ is given as one to many in the context of one meal. Of course, the mere act of eating or drinking does not bring about this intense personal communion. In common with the other sacraments, this bodily presence of Christ is an invitation, not an accomplished fact. Full communion demands full mutuality, and a man can refuse Christ, even in the Eucharist" (Powers, p. 124).
9. Possibly the action of taking bread was a sign of presiding at the table as well.
10. Cf. crucifixion and resurrection scenes: Lk 24:28-31, Mk 15:36-37, Mt 27:48-50, Jn 19:28-30; 21:9-14.
11. J. Jeremias, *op.cit.*, pp. 165-72.
12. *See* J. Moltmann, *Theology of Hope* (New York: Harper & Row, 1967); also E. Schillebeeckx, "The Interpretation of Eschatology," in E. Schillebeeckx and B. Willems, eds., *The Problem of Eschatology*, Concilium 41 (New York: Paulist Press, 1969), pp. 42-56.

WHAT IS A PRIEST?

Walter J. Burghardt, S.J.

My task in this article is to address the question: What is the *Church's* experience of priesthood, as the Church has lived its priestly existence through the ages? It is a formidable task, because it must weld together Scripture and history and theology—yes, and the secular sciences.

I shall develop my theme in three stages. The first stage focuses on Scripture; here is the earliest evidence of the Church's experience of a specialized ministry. The second stage is a search into history; here is the Church's (postapostolic) tradition of a specialized ministry. The third stage revolves around contemporary theology; here is the Church's experience today and her reflection thereon.

I

My first stage, then, focuses on Scripture, the earliest evidence of the Church's experience of a specialized ministry. Here my springboard is the working paper on the ministerial priesthood that was prepared for the 1971 Synod of Bishops (fortunately, the final draft did not contain these "working" ideas). This schema ascribed the current crisis of priestly identity primarily to the effects of secularization. Secularization the schema defined as "the process which gradually comes to take seriously the values of this world, its structures, its goals, and its norms." On a radical level, secularization leaves no room for transcendent realities; "a closed world is established, without any dependence upon a source or a goal, a world which . . . acknowledges no goods except those which it creates.'' In line with this destructive secularization you have the seductive influence of the social sciences, which tend to cast doubt on the Church's mission and the priest's ministry.

The solution? Give history, psychology, sociology a pat on the head for their slight contributions and get back to God's revelation. And precisely here lies a defective methodology. The working paper assumed that there is a determinate essence of ministerial priesthood, a core idea of the Church's specialized ministry, that can be easily uncovered in Scripture and in the authoritative documents of Church tradition, without recourse to human disciplines such as history.

The assumption is as astonishing as it is unexamined. Revelation does not give us a clearly articulated notion of ministerial priesthood; the Bible does not offer a clearly defined view of the essence and forms of the Christian priesthood, does not furnish a detailed and fixed concept of the ministry. Take, for example, the report, commissioned by the American bishops, on the biblical theology of the priesthood. This summary, based on the best available scriptural scholarship, should be sobering:

> From what has been said it should be evident that we can expect to find in the Scriptures an evolution in the concept of ministry that is eminently in keeping with the nature of a pilgrim people of God. . . It will mean, first of all, that we cannot use the Old Testament as a primary referent for our conception of Christian ministry. . . . Acceptance of the concept of evolution will mean, secondly, that even in the New Testament we should not expect to find a clearly formulated definition of Christian ministry from the beginning, or at any single point in the development of New Testament revelation. Christian ministry was never "frozen" in any one mold but continued to develop and to be adapted in the succeeding moments of history. This does not mean that there is no normative character to the New Testament canon. But the normative character will not be seen in a definitive "canonizing" of one exercise of ministry without regard for another, or of one historical manifestation at one time or place in isolation from other such manifestations. Development itself is canonical and therefore normative.[1]

But if we do not get from the New Testament, from the deposit of revealed truth, some unchangeable specific essence of priesthood, where does this leave us? Is there anything we can uncover from Christ's own tenting among men, from the early Christian experience of ministry? Yes, indeed. The New Testament furnishes four facets of Christian ministry which the Church sees as basic in her priests. Not all were present from the very beginning in one and the same person; but the Church has gradually brought them together to help fashion her notion of what a priest is.[2]

First, the priest is a *disciple*—always a disciple. To be a disciple means to be "called," as the first companions of Jesus were called, as Peter and James and John were called—to have a vocation that stems from Jesus: "Follow me." For the priest, as for the original disciples, there can be only one master: Jesus. And the response to Him must be total: "Follow me, and let the dead bury their own dead" (Mt 8:21-22). Not just for today: "No one who has put his hand to the plow and looks back is fit for the kingdom of God" (Lk 9:62). Not part time: discipleship is his whole life; there is nothing else, there is no one else. You have that harsh sentence of Jesus: "If anyone comes to me and does not hate his own father and mother and wife and children and brothers and sisters, yes, and even his own life, he cannot be my disciple" (Lk 14:26). Exaggeration, yes; deliberate exaggeration—to make an unmistakable point: you are not a disciple of Jesus if Jesus is not your whole life.

And to be a disciple is to be called to hardships too cruel for most men: to leave everything and embrace a cross, to have nothing as your own save Jesus. To be a disciple is to pattern yourself after the one master— and this master is a bloodstained, crucified master who came not to be served but to serve, who warned His disciples against honors and first places, who turned savagely on Peter when he rebelled against the passion of his Lord.

Second, the priest is an *apostle*—always an apostle. If to be a disciple means to be "called," called to follow Jesus, to be an apostle means to be "sent," as the original apostles were sent, to serve others. The keynote is service. Remember St. Paul: "I will most gladly spend and be spent for you" (2 Cor 12:15). And what the priest carries to others is always Jesus—not only His message but His presence. "We preach," St. Paul declared, "not ourselves but Jesus Christ as Lord, with ourselves as your servants for Jesus' sake" (2 Cor 4:5).

It is always Jesus who is preached. By word and work, by sacraments and sacrifice. But in a special way, by prayer and suffering. A priest who has forgotten how to pray is a priest who cannot preach Jesus—whatever else he may preach. And a priest, like St. Paul, will present Jesus to others effectively only if he bears the death pangs of Jesus in his own body. Only if he is constantly restless because, like Paul, he is "afflicted at every turn, from struggles without and anxieties within" (2 Cor 7:5). Anxieties within: I mean a loneliness that is in itself no reason for forsaking the priestly life; a lack of appreciation, especially today when priesthood has no special status; an anguish that tears his heart because he is so weak and the forces of evil are so strong, because his words are wasted on the wind, because so few seem to care.

Third, a priest is what the New Testament calls a *presbyter*. The New Testament presbyters were a group responsible for the pastoral care of the churches. And the qualities the New Testament prescribes for the presbyter are sober indeed, even stuffy. He must be above reproach, temperate, sensible, dignified, hospitable, an apt teacher, gentle, not quarrelsome. His task is to organize, to stabilize, to prevent dangerous innovation. "He must hold firm to the sure word he was taught, so that he may be able to give instruction in sound doctrine and confute those who contradict it" (Tt 1:9). His task calls for authority that does not dominate, that is softened by being wonderfully warm and human.

The point is, the priest does represent an institution. No matter how charismatic, how prophetic, even if called to protest the sins and corruption of institutions, of the Church itself, the priest must represent more than his personal insights. Like it or not, I am a churchman. I cannot, as a priest, stand outside my institution; I am an official part of it. Not that the institution is always right, is beyond criticism or censure. Rather that this institution is the setting where faith is born and grows; this institution is the locus and focus of worship; this institution is the community of love. This is what the priest represents.

Fourth, a priest *presides at the Eucharist*. It is not his total task, but it is a central preoccupation of priesthood. For here the priest does what St. Paul insisted must be done: "proclaim the Lord's death until He comes" (1 Cor 11:26). He has a sacramental ministry that revolves around the bread of life and the cup of the new covenant. Around this liturgy the Church has built man's access to the life that is Christ, from the water of baptism through the ashes of penance to the oil of the last anointing. And in this process of life the priest plays a unique role—a role that comes to focus each time he proclaims "This is my body, which will be given up for you. . . . This is the cup of my blood."

Here, in a very real sense, is the heart of a man's priesthood. Even if he works at much else besides—in school or slum, in collective bargaining or the halls of Congress—at some point the priest gathers his people around an altar, around a table, to share with them a thanksgiving where the work of redemption is accomplished and in unparalleled fashion man is made one with his God.

II

My second stage focuses on history: here is the Church's tradition of a specialized ministry. As with Scripture, so with tradition, many an approach operates out of a defective methodology. It assumes that, to uncover what a priest is, to distinguish his priesthood from the priesthood of all Christians, all you have to do is read Roman documents; the index to Denzinger will tell you all. Out of the Church's history will come a core concept of priest that focuses his function and isolates it from all that is not priest.

The joker here is history itself. If you are thinking of priesthood in terms of unique powers and unique functions, the Church's experience of ministry is chockfull (perhaps even shock-full) of change, of diversity, of adaptation. Take, for openers, the ordination ritual that spelled out my specific priestness in 1941, and set it side by side with the ritual for the ordination of presbyters in third-century Rome. If anything specified my Christian ministry in 1941, it was a twin power: the power to offer sacrifice for the living and the dead, and the power to forgive sin in the name of Christ. In third-century Rome these powers were specifically episcopal. The crucial sentence on the power of a presbyter runs like this: "O God and Father of our Lord Jesus Christ . . . look upon this thy servant and impart to him the spirit of grace and the gift of presbyterate, that he may be able to direct thy people with a pure heart."[3] In this connection the remarks of Gregory Dix are highly pertinent:

The primitive Christian presbytery, like the Jewish presbytery from which it derived, was a corporate judicial and administrative body, and the bishop as *ruler* of his church was simply its president, a presbyter among his fellow-presbyters. The primitive Christian presbyter, like his Jewish prototype, *had as such no liturgical functions.* . . . But the *episkopē*, the bishop's own office as bishop, was from the first *primarily liturgical.* . . . The history of the episcopate is in one sense the history of the steady breaking down of its primitive liturgical monopoly. It was inevitable that as the Church grew this should be so by the mere necessity of numbers. By the fourth century only the power of ordaining remains a strictly episcopal preserve, and attempts were even being made . . . to extend that to presbyters. In the end the presbyters did break down the episcopal monopoly so far as minor orders were concerned. But all this is something *new*, not contemplated by ancient documents like the *Apostolic Tradition* or the *Didascalia*. So far as I can see there is nothing in the *Apostolic Tradition* which directly suggests that there is any liturgical function a presbyter can perform which a deacon cannot, except for the one privilege of joining in the imposition of hands in the ordination of a presybter, a natural right of the presbyter since by derivation the *ruling* presbyterate was a corporate body. But in return for this parcelling out of his liturgical functions among the presbyters the bishop had by the fourth century practically monopolized the whole governmental power of the old corporate presbytery. The two offices had by then become in appearance assimilated to a large extent, though not in fact because the bishop has gained very largely in practical power by the exchange. . . .[4]

The point I am making is this: in different periods of the Church's history different theologies of ministry, different models of priesthood, have come into prominence.[5] Of such theologies, of such models, at least five merit mention here.

1) *The Jurisdictional Model.* For several centuries after the Council of Trent, in the context of a predominantly juridical view of the Church and a hierarchical doctrine of social order, the priest was seen as the one who holds the plenitude of authority in a "perfect society." (This vision

is still strong in certain segments of the Catholic population.) The pope and bishops, and after them the pastors, are the chief priests who habitually possess that fullness of authority known as jurisdiction. The preaching and teaching offices of the clergy are assimilated to their jurisdictional role: to teach is to impose authoritative doctrine as a matter of obedience. Even admission to and denial of sacraments comes to be seen through quasi-juridical glasses.

2) *The Cultic Model.* In much patristic and medieval theology the Church was seen primarily as a worshiping or sacramental community. In terms of this model the priest came to be regarded as the hierophant, the performer of sacred mysteries. He offered to God, in the name of the community, the totally pleasing sacrifice of Christ. On some theories, the priest was seen as cultic leader; on others, as the mediator or substitute who offered sacrifice in place of the community.

3) *The Pastoral Model.* According to certain New Testament insights, recovered in large measure by Vatican II, the Church is seen as an interpersonal communion, an intercommunion of persons, effected through divine love poured out by Christ and the Spirit. In this type of theology the priest comes to be viewed primarily as pastor or community leader. He brings people together and seeks to activate in them the graces and charisms which the Holy Spirit bestows upon each for the benefit of all. In this vision the attributes of the pastor are analyzed in terms of the doctrine of Jn 10, Ac 20, and 1 P.

4) *The Prophetic Model.* In modern Protestant theology, especially the kind typified by Barth, the ordained minister is seen predominantly as proclaimer of the word of God. To believers and unbelievers he issues a resounding call to repentance and conversion. While some proponents of this theology would shun the term "priest," as excessively freighted with cultic overtones, they still accept a high doctrine of ordained ministry, based on the conceptions of prophet and apostle found in the Old and New Testaments.

5) *The Monastic Model.* In some Christian traditions the priest is viewed primarily as the holy man, the guru, the spiritual director. In this perspective the religious priest is often considered to be the normal case; monastic spirituality is in great part transferred to diocesan seminaries and diocesan priests. Thus practices such as meditation, recitation of breviary, community life, and celibacy are extended to all priests without

exception. The priest is expected to be withdrawn from the world and its vanities and to live in a manner that anticipates the blessings of the life to come.

Now these models are not necessarily in conflict; but the choice of one model will overshadow aspects of priesthood that seem central in another model. More importantly for us here, this quick foray into history should suggest how difficult, how impossible, it is to isolate some function, something a priest and only a priest can do, and proclaim that this is priesthood, here is the ordained ministry, utterly changeless, unaffected by history, unconditioned by culture. You know, you might end up with a function that takes a half hour of your time, once a week, exclusive of vacation!

But precisely here lies the priestly peril; for precisely here lies the unexamined assumption: there *is* this eternal role, this immutable essence, discoverable in God's revelation, and it is in harmony with this role and essence that a priest's life is organized for him—where he lives and what he wears, how he works and with whom he relaxes, the obligations he has taken on and the rights he has given up, the whole gamut of relationships from pope through pastor to people. It is because of these unexamined assumptions that the Synod schema of 1971 could assert so confidently: "Priestly ministry is a mystery . . . which the people of God clearly grasped from the beginning. . . ." Or: "From this gospel picture of priestly ministry, it is clear that a priest's involvement in political problems, even though they are serious, cannot be ordered to his goal." Or: "Because of celibacy, priests can dedicate themselves more freely and more easily to the work of proclaiming the word of God, since they have firm control of themselves." To the credit of the bishops in synod, these affirmations are toned down in the ultimate document.

III

This brings me to my third stage, contemporary theology: here is the Church's experience today and her reflection thereon. Not that today's experience dispenses with yesterday's; it does not. Ideally, it gathers up the best of the past and enriches that with the insights of the present, with a view to an even more Christian tomorrow. What, then, does today's theology (not all, but some) say about ministerial priesthoood?

First, a priest has a fresh relationship to Christ. This is suggested by the New Testament itself. And in the vision of Vatican II, Christ is the heart and soul of the priesthood. It is His service I enter; it is His ministry I share; it is in His name I act, in His person.[6] For one purpose: to build up the Body of Christ, until the full measure of His manhood is achieved.

And so, secondly, a priest has a special relationship to the Church. Precisely here, in our understanding of the Church, we learn (or do not learn) what it means for a human being to be ordained a priest. For this Church has a mission, this Church *is* mission, and only in view of this mission can you define her ministry—the ministry of *all* Christians and the ministry of *some* Christians.

I have no room here for a rounded ecclesiology. But this much must be said. The Church, in Vatican II's favorite image, is not so much a pyramid as a people, primarily a people, the people of God. This people is a community, a community of persons who accept and confess God's revelation in Jesus as Lord, a community united to the Father and to one another through Christ in the Spirit. This community is more than a casual encounter of freewheeling, like-minded individuals: it is a visible society, and so it has a structure of authority, a juridical order, and a common mission. That mission is a service to all humanity; for this interpersonal community has for function to reach out, through the love that is its inner form, so as to draw all men into the communion of love, so that all men will respond in faith and love to the love whereby the Father loves His own people. This people, therefore, is essentially a missionary people, with a catholic mission of love. Here I find stimulating the summary given in the Report of the Subcommittee on the Systematic Theology of the Priesthood:

> The Church, as a people, witnesses to the Word by proclaiming faith in the Lordship of Jesus (*kerygma*), manifests itself to the world as a community of unity and charity (*koinonia*), positively relates to the world in terms of service (*diakonia*), and worships God by offering the sacrifice of praise and thanks (*eucharistia*).[7]

Only in terms of this mission can you define the Church's ministry; for ministry relates to mission as means to end. But first note this: the

Church's ministry is one common enterprise, where all Christians continue the work of Christ, each with his or her calling, his or her charism, his or her competence. Christian ministry is a shared responsibility. There is no Christian who is not a minister of the gospel.

But within this general ministry there is a specialized ministry, the ordained ministry. Within the universal priesthood of all Christians there is an ordained priesthood. But what does it mean to be ordained a priest? As I grew up, the emphasis was on functions, on roles. We defined an ordained priest in terms of what he could *do* which an unordained person could *not* do. And here the crisis of identity has torn the guts of uncounted priests. They search for priesthood in terms of something specific to themselves, powers proper to priests, functions which distinguish them from laymen. These powers and functions become narrower and narrower, so that they wonder if there *is* anything like this. And if they do find what they alone can do ("This is my body," "I absolve you"), it seems so narrow in scope that it takes little time, little of their life. The rest of their existence (preaching, teaching, building, organizing, counseling. . .) is lived in the suspicion that some man or woman in the pews could do it better. "Of all social roles," B.R. Wilson noted acutely, "the priest's calls for the widest use of his untrained capacities, and calls into play, more than any profession, his personality dispositions."[8]

At this point contemporary theologians break in. For a viable theology of priesthood, they insist, you must get behind the functions. Don't disregard them; get behind them! Get behind Church function to Church office. Not office in the sense of bureaucratic structure; not a mere division of jurisdictional authority. No, Church office here is a relationship of responsibility. The essence of presbyteral priesthood is a new relationship to the mission of the Church. "The ordination of a priest is that solemn sacramental celebration by which a person is received into the order of presbyters, assumes public office in the Church, and is enabled to act in the name of Christ and of the Christian community with the promised assistance of the Holy Spirit."[9]

The point is, priesthood is a social reality, an institutional reality, an ecclesiastical reality. Its heart is a stable relationship, a ratified relationship, between the Church and the individual. By the act of ordination the Christian community at large commits itself to the ordinand and he commits himself to it. Through its responsible officers, in some approved fashion, the community declares that, having observed in him the basic competences and spiritual gifts desirable for the Church's mission at a given moment in history, it trusts him as its representative leader in its official actions. And he engages himself publicly to a life of dedicated service in an official capacity, professes his willingness to shape his life to the needs of the gospel as the Church sees them. He is now a *public* servant, in a sense in which the layman can never be.

Understand me: when I say "officeholder," when I say "representative," I am not saying "one who parrots the party line." The priest may have to stand *over against* the community, over against bishop or pope. Not *outside* the community, not outside bishop or pope, but conceivably over against them, even as public servant, precisely as public servant.

But what is it that office demands of the priest? What public service does it qualify him for? One service, one responsibility, before all else. Since the mission of the Church is to reconcile all men with God and with one another through the one mediator Christ, the priest's primary office is to be a personal, living, effective sign, witness, agent of the reconciling Christ who works through him. Once again the Report of the Subcommittee on the Systematic Theology of the Priesthood offers a splendid vision:

> Unity in Christ is not only a personal, but above all, a communal achievement. The People of God is made up of many interlocking and interdependent communities. If one were to visualize the scope of the priest's responsibility for reconciliation in Christ, the image of concentric, ever-widening circles might serve the purpose. At the center is Christ. The first circle is that of the particular community which the priest serves; he is to be the point of rest for the union of the congregation with one another in Christ. The next circle broadens out to the larger Christian grouping which is the diocese. By his union with the bishop as head of the presbyterate, the priest witnesses to the communion of his congregation with a cluster of similar congregations, thus overcoming the danger of sectarianism or exclusivism. The third circle widens to that of the universal Church, for the presbyteral order as a whole is called to assist the episcopal order in the latter's collegial care for the universal Church. The priest represents the bishop in his collegial responsibility for the whole Church as well as in his pastoral guidance of the

particular Church. Finally, the last circle expands to include all mankind, and here the priest, by his concern for peace and justice in the world, points to the hope that some day all men will be brothers and sisters in the same Kingdom. In a word, the priest is a public, sacramentally designated witness to the unifying presence of Christ in all these communities. This is his office: to be a sign and agent of the reconciling work of Christ.

Because this is not simply his Christian calling but his public office, the priest can be called to account, in a way the lay person rarely can, for the clarity, the authenticity, the wholeness of his witness. The community can demand of him a certain level of performance, a ceaseless reaching for heights of holiness, a way of life that reflects Him who was so utterly human and yet more than human. Because much is given to him, by Christ and the community, much can be expected of him.

All well and good: the priest is the Church's officeholder, and his primary office is to represent, to re-present, the reconciling Christ. But this office is not static; it must express itself in, flow into, functions. Even if we dare not identify priesthood with some single function or several, in isolation from history and historical evolution, still the Church has come to a point in development where certain functions are regarded as special responsibilities of the ordained priest. I shall mention four in generic terms, to distinguish them from a much more arguable area: the specific means different priests may take to implement these roles.

First, a priest is ordained to proclaim the word of God. Not simply—in a pluralistic society, perhaps not primarily—by formal preaching. The model of proclamation may be dialogue; it may be priestly presence; it may be prophetic speech and action in the tradition of Isaiah and Jesus.

Second, a priest is ordained to build up the Christian community. Here lies his responsibility for leadership. But a leader in our time is not one who commands; a leader is one who can move the hearts and minds of men. It is his to co-ordinate the charisms of the community as found in the individual members. He is accountable because his is the office which looks not merely to the care of individuals but primarily, as Vatican II put it, to "the formation of a genuine Christian community."[10]

Third, a priest is ordained to serve mankind. Here Vatican II opened up new vistas: "Because the human race today is joining more and more into a civic, economic, and social unity, it is that much more necessary that priests . . . wipe out every kind of division, so that the whole human race may be brought into the unity of the family of God.''[11] This vision harmonizes splendidly with the fourth aim of the Council: ''The Church will build a bridge to the contemporary world.'' It ties in with Paul VI's address opening the second session in 1963; ''let the world know this: the Church looks at the world with profound understanding, with sincere admiration, and with the sincere intention not of conquering it, but of serving it; not of despising it, but of appreciating it; not of condemning it, but of strengthening and saving it.'' A priest's parish is indeed the world; for the Church's mission is simply . . . man.

Fourth, a priest is ordained to preside at worship, especially the Eucharist. Here is the cultic role of the priest at its most proper. Here he effects the Church's most powerful expression of unity—the unity of the worshiping congregation within itself, with the diocese, with the universal Church, and with all mankind. Here is foreshadowed and promised the Christian hope: that the earth and all who bleed and joy thereon will be transformed into the kingdom of God and His Christ.

To proclaim God's word, to build up the Christian community, to serve mankind, to preside at community worship—these four generic functions of a priest are based on ceaseless, universal needs of God's people; they flow from the gospel dynamic. Not to be involved somehow in these functions is to be a less than responsible representative of Christ and the community. The gut issue, however is not generic but specific: How do you implement these roles concretely, and in such fashion that the implementation is ''priestly''?

Here I leave you with no more than principles and cautions. (1) It is impossible to devise an objective definition or draw up a descriptive list of specifically priestly works. (2) In the perspectives of my presentation, within the theology of priesthood I have outlined, there is no such person as a ''hyphenated priest;'' he is a priest in a specialized ministry, serving God and man in an age of specialization. (3) A ''part-time priest'' calls for clarification. Either the secular job is integrated with his ministry or it is not. If it is—e.g., because it provides financial support unobtainable from the Christian community—then I see nothing but a vehicle for his ministry. If it is not, if he is living two lives in two airtight compartments, there could be a problem—not so much theological as psychological. (4)

How each priest is to specify his generic functions can only come from awareness of a community's needs, dialogue with priests and laity, guidance from superiors, prayerful reflection, and God's grace.

Footnotes

1. Eugene Maly, ed., *The Priest and Sacred Scripture* (Washington, D.C.: National Conference of Catholic Bishops, 1971) pp. 4-6.
2. Cf. Raymond E. Brown, S.S., *Priest and Bishop: Biblical Reflections* (New York: Paulist Press, 1970) pp. 21-43.
3. Cf. Joseph Crehan, S.J., "Ministerial Priesthood," *Theological Studies* 32 (1971) 491.
4. *The Treatise on the Apostolic Tradition of St. Hippolytus of Rome* (New York: Macmillan, 1937) pp. lxxix-lxxx.
5. For the following observations on models of priesthood and ministry, I am indebted to an unpublished paper (1971) of Avery Dulles, S.J., entitled "What Is a Priest?"
6. Cf. Decree on the Ministry and Life of Priests, nos. 1 and 2.
7. This Report, dated Sept. 15, 1971, was commissioned by the American episcopate but was never published.
8. "The Paul Report Examined," *Theology* 68 (1965) 89-103.
9. Report (n. 7 above).
10. Decree on Priests, no. 6.
11. Constitution on the Church, no. 8.

THE PRIEST: A SIMPLE REMINDER

George McCauley, S.J.*

Who is a priest? What function does he serve in the secular city? As the answer to the first question will help us answer the second, it is necessary to inquire into the central intention of Christ in giving his Church a priesthood. No doubt, Christ's desire to continue his own priesthood figures highly in determining this central intention. Priests are living instruments of his priesthood. But if we assume also that Christ takes concrete activities which *already* signify something truly human, and subsumes, incorporates, and fulfills this secular signification in his sacramental gestures, what human value is affirmed in the institution of the priesthood? Is it merely an organizational value, a hardnosed acceptance of the fact that some few men must lead, or speak for, or tidy up after others if the job is to be done really well? Or is Christ respecting personality traits which inevitably show up only in certain individuals, by giving such individuals scope for the exercise of their highly personal endowments in the priesthood? Or does the existence of the priesthood insure the unfolding of the whole community's personality on levels far deeper than the organizational?

Even before the Christian priesthood, it was not clear to everyone that men needed priests. One Roman sage said that he could not see how two priests could pass each other on the street without bursting out laughing.

---

*The reader's attention is also called to Fr. McCauley's recent reflections on priesthood appearing in *The God of the Group*, pp. 83-94 (Argus Communications: Illinois, 1975) and the *Kingdom Come* series (Argus, 1979).

We have come a long way from poking about entrails and such, but priests still seem to many people to form a vast system whose psychological supports are fear and superstition, and whose questionable premise seems to be that some men can be a crutch or substitute for other men's failings. What we need is a realistic understanding of Christian priesthood.

One underlying assumption of the priest makes him extremely vulnerable. To understand and to formulate correctly this central assumption will go a long way to help us understand what a priest is and what Christ meant him to be; for it is at the point of his greatest vulnerability that his real identity becomes apparent. What, then, is the priest's central conviction which sustains him and at the same time imperils him? We would define it as the belief that *love is possible in all directions and that he, the priest, indicates that love in a unique, public way.* That is why we have chosen to characterize the priesthood as a "simple reminder."

This means, therefore, that the priest is not a kind of supersacristan whom we have described adequately once we have said that "he performs cultic acts." This characterization is accurate enough in an external way, but no priesthood is sufficiently explained simply by noting what it does externally. We must, therefore, as a second point, explore the priest's inner motivation. Here we will normally find a conscious identification with the priesthood of Christ, a relationship that is not always evident. Seeing a priest in a parish involved at every level of human problems and activities (family, business, sport, study, social services, education, politics) tends to obscure the relationship to Christ which is central to his thinking on the priesthood. Yet a moment's reflection will show that other members of the geographical parish might be equally or more involved than the priest in the problems and activities enumerated. Hence such activities do not uniquely characterize him, nor do they offer us the key to his motivation. Neither can we admit that the expenditure of time, energy, and talent on the Church is the unique contribution of the priest.

This point logically brings us to a consideration of how the priest looks on the priesthood of Christ. Here his thinking is guided in part by the Scriptures. The classical scriptural locus on Christ's priesthood is the Letter to the Hebrews. Unfortunately this letter presents his priesthood in the imagery of a cosmic liturgy, with confusing references to late-Jewish temple practices. We find it difficult to cut through the scenario to the central affirmations. And yet, this letter and the other scriptural data define Christ's priesthood precisely by seeing it as a break with the normal way in which men understood priesthood up to that time. A key aspect of Christ's priesthood in the New Testament is the common bond between Christ and other men which his priesthood presupposes. Common ties of flesh, blood, suffering, trial, and temptation are absolutely basic to the reality of his priesthood (Heb 2:14; 4:15). For these ties are what make Christ merciful, faithful, and compassionate to men (2:17-18). They also allow us to describe Christ's love as one which moves in all directions, to all men and in all aspects of human life. He is almost greedy in the interests of men (Heb 1:2; 2:8). He pre-tastes death for them to show them how ultimately harmless death is (Heb 2:9; 2:15). He is the prayer-man. He lives to take their part before God (Heb 7:25). All these qualities offer a more accurate description of Christ's priesthood than does his physical dying; they supply the essential motivation for his sacrificial death. Where they are missing, as in some elements of the Jewish priesthood of his day, priesthood becomes meaningless. And indeed the laws and commandments of the Jewish priesthood are rejected by Christ to the extent that that priesthood no longer witnesses to God's compassionate concern for men (Heb 7:12; 7:18; 8:13; Mt 12:5; Lk 10:31; Jn 17:23).

Today's priest, then, tries to capture in his own life some of the motivation that Christ the priest had. He tries to share Christ's kind of love for men—love in all directions. But is this not true of all Christians? We have not yet determined what specifically sets the priest apart. To do so, we must consider one further aspect of Christ's priesthood: its communal and public nature.

The logic of Christ's kind of love led him, as he knew it would, to a central act of death and resurrection. It was not that his love was limited to his dying and rising. At every point we must remember that Christ lived, worked, and spoke in the towns and cities he knew and loved. In the central act of dying and rising, however, the full dimensions of his love for men appear. He defines, in an *absolute* and *human* fashion, the possibilities and the validity of human love, as well as the validity of all that he had done *in the city*. What we wish to emphasize here is that his total priesthood was carried through with the specific needs and concerns of his small community of followers in mind. He led them gradually towards his passion and resurrection. In innumerable concrete situations he taught them, served them, formed and forged them: he allowed for their doubts, their gross ignorances, their selfish expectations. He adapted himself to what he can reasonably expect from them by way of belief, outlook, and adherence. The unfolding of *his priesthood*, then, was determined by the needs of the small community he was forming and with whom he was dealing. More than that, Christ wished to communicate to all men, through this small community, the nature and extent of his Father's love for men. He wanted the world to know!

Now when Christ had "gone," when he was no longer visibly present to the community, or when the original members of the community had come and gone, where was there to be a public unifying version, in or out of the community, of his kind of love? Again, where would there be room, in or out of the community, for a gradually developing realization and acceptance of God's love for men? (The very fact that God's love provided for such a gradual realization is one of the greatest indications that his love is man-centered, that it leaves room for what is historical, evolving, becoming, creative, both in the individual and in society itself.)

We are tempted to answer these questions by saying that public witness of Christ's progressive love is found in the lives of individual Christians themselves, that their lives provide the only valid public gesture which insures the continuity of the Word and the action of Christ in history. Or we might be inclined to say that the Word preserved in the scriptural writings is a sufficient guarantee of the kind of continuing public witness that we need. But is this enough? Will the full dimensions and stature of his kind of commitment to men be guarded in a sufficiently tangible fashion without the reminding gesture of priesthood? The history and the sociology of communities indicate rather the need for a more specific kind of gesture, one which is more expressive than the written word, one that is more pointed or focussed than the day-by-day lives of the community members.

It is from this viewpoint that we are led to conclude that the priest becomes the community's public reminder of the word and action of Christ. By instituting this sacrament Christ attached to the community's needs and desires his efficacious promise to be present in the Word and action which they have received and *wish to perpetuate* through the priest. The human values, then, which are affirmed in the Christian priesthood are complex: there is, on the part of the community, a need and willingness to tell the story over again to itself and to re-enact its central action; there is, on the part of Christ, the effective willingness to respect this human need of the community; there is, on the part of the priest, a basic willingness to serve the developing community as its self-reminder; further, a fascination and respect for the community's founder is at the heart both of his willingness to serve and of the community's invitation to him to serve; finally, the priest is bound by common ties of need and aspiration to the members of the community whose gesture of reminding he is.

In the Christian community, these human values are strained to the extreme. The community is potentially the world. The common lot which the priest shares with others is one of sin, of futile good wishes, of meek failure, or of pure selfishness, but also a common bond of hope and belief and love of love in all directions. The priest who responds to the community's invitation to recall for it *its* ideal finds himself at the service of what is almost an impossible (to believe and execute) love: Christ's love. To deliver Christ's lines without sounding too hypocritical, to keep up Christ's memory when, because of *our* own myopic mistrust, that memory often seems to condemn *us* more than it consoles us to be called upon to recount a story by a community that often loses interest after a few chapters—this is a terrible, or a wonderful thing. The priestly gesture can so easily turn into a posture, a sign that has been jarred awry or gone rusty, a pointer that shakes in the hand, even a betrayal. But if Paul says that *we* are saved in hope, then we must be priests in hope, too. We must be convinced that the gesture is worth making.

We must remember that the need and desire for such a "reminder" is found in the community as a whole. It is not Christ's need: nor is it only the priest's personal need. Hence priests are made, as it were, by public demand. (This is perhaps why people get just about the kind of priests they deserve.) By this we mean that the community, presumably in full agreement with the necessity of the sort of gesture of self-reminding, invites some of its members to perform the task. Priests, therefore, are not substitutes for the community, but reminders; not so much mediators for the community, but reminders, in the sacrifice, of the one mediator

Christ; not even particularly great lovers of the community, but voices that repeat for the community the good news and the absolution pronounced by Christ. Let no one give the priest roles that do not, in the revelation of Christ, really belong to him.

In his function of reminding the community, at its request, of the kind of love that Christ the priest first showed, the priest must spell out all over again what Christ's priesthood was all about. He must reconstruct the main actions of Christ's priesthood. This rewording and reproduction of Christ's priesthood is done, of course, primarily in the sacrifice, in the preaching of the Word, and in the sacraments. These activities are not accidental to the priest's ministry; they identify him in the deepest sense. It is in them above all that the priest answers the invitation of the community (ultimately the invitation of Christ) to tell the story of Christ's love over again and to re-enact it in the sacrifice and the absolution.

In calling the priest a "reminder" we presuppose that the Word and the sacrifice and absolution are efficacious apart from the moral and psychological integrity of individual priests (though not apart from the priest's willingness to represent the community's belief). But this is simply to say that Christ has made himself available to men in still another magnificent gesture; or that Christ's devotedness is greater than our powers of betrayal, distraction, and failure; or that he makes his presence felt where perhaps it is not always welcome; or that his is ultimately the only expression of human love in all directions that is held by no barriers. Our point, then, is not to defend the efficacy of the sacraments or the inspiration of the Word, but to describe that human action to which Christ attaches his promise of grace, and to capture that aspect of a priest's calling which will give him a basic understanding of himself in the Church.

By thus characterizing the priest, have we so restricted his service to the Christian community that we have thereby cut him off from the secular world to which many modern priests feel such a strong sense of responsibility? We are familiar with the trials of the priest-workers (worker-priests, if this will solve anything) in other countries. Seminarians express the desire to acquire a specialization, often in a secular field, if their priesthood is to be effective. Others, in the tradition of Paul, want to maintain a spiritual independence by earning their own livelihood. No one wants to be "kept" in any sense of the word. On the other hand, priests who are engaged in secular tasks often feel disjointed in these undertakings, as though they were not "priestly" enough. What can we conclude about the priest's role in the secular city?

Part of the problem is to weigh the importance of the priest's role within the community against the fact that the community, the Church, has a mission to the secular city. Because the priest preaches the Word and administers the sacraments for the Church, it seems that people in the Church have acquired a prior right to his energies and that the priest's primary role is within the community. The community, however, does not hear the Word or live its life in a void. It is at every point rooted in the city. Hence the expression "primary role" tends to become meaningless when we look at the Church as a movement into the world.

These are not simply academic and airy distinctions. Is the priest to get involved in the secular city only when the community fails to do so? Or is the city his natural habitat from which he has somehow become a stranger? Certainly, people resent his presence in some of the great secular movements of our times. Up to the present, the priest has been visibly and largely attached to his function of exercising the community's cult. He usually lives in a rectory near the liturgical and sacramental center of the community. His wardrobe designates him as a representative of that community rather than as the one who has a job to do in the secular city. His training equips him with the in-language of his community. But the pattern is changing. The priest wants to live in an apartment; he wants to dress normally; he wants no part of a curious curial lingo. Is this changing pattern a sign that the priest today wants to neglect or betray his "primary" commitment to the community?

Perhaps rather we are dealing with a mild, if sometimes painful, realignment of a long-standing and constantly changing relationship between priest, community, and secular city. When the world's problems were problems of sanitation, education, law, public order, recreation, or politics, the clergy, by reason of their education (perhaps by reason of their *Christian* charity?), frequently undertook leadership in these secular tasks. Such involvement was almost always contested by other Christians, so history tells us, in the name of some pietistic understanding of the Church's relationship to the world. But the clergy went ahead, to the undeniable profit of civilization. But the temptation for the clergy was to become entrenched in their secular tasks, to give them up grudgingly, to invent reasons for maintaining the status quo long after the original reasons for their involvement ceased to exist. The latter phenomenon of entrenchment has always been a problem. But it does not negate the tradition of some sort of clerical involvement in the secular city. On the contrary, involvement has been so continuous and so deep-seated in the Church that it must give the lie to those who, in the name of the faith, would keep the priest in the sacristy and limit his involvement in the secular city. Therefore, in attempting to assess the modern situation it would be historically naïve and religiously questionable (in the light of the traditional pattern of secular involvement practiced by priests) to reject new forms of priestly involvement in the secular or to show an angry unwillingness to give up tasks long ago assumed. Where is the priest to be involved in the secular city today? In civil rights movements? At the peace conferences? In education? In communications media? In the arts? In publishing? In medical research? In developing the Third World? Such questions can best be answered on the basis of local need, or individual talent or inclination or similar considerations. We must also include the general value of mutual communication and understanding that can be developed between priests and laymen, between priests and non-Catholics, when priests work side by side with these groups. This value alone is so precious that it would be worthwhile for priests to continue doing certain tasks for which, as a matter of fact, the layman is equally or better suited. The real enemy here is to deny the priest a role in the secular city because he never had *that* particular role in the past.

Where does celibacy fit into the description of priesthood given above? In what sense is the priest's celibacy complicating his simple gesture? This is a difficult question, in which it is often impossible to distinguish the inarticulate groans of the Spirit (Rm 8:27) from the equally inarticulate groans of, shall we say, another spirit.

It is generally admitted that there is no necessary connection between fidelity to what God has revealed concerning the priesthood and the current practice of mandatory celibacy in the Roman rite of the Catholic Church. Hence discussions about celibacy in its relationship to priesthood are really discussions about the *convenientia* of the present legislation. While this legislation is being defended and attacked, it would be profitable to remember that, behind this debate and affecting it, even weightier issues are involved, such as the nature and formation of ecclesiastical legislation, the permanency of ordination itself, the whole Church's appreciation of marriage and sexuality, and others. In much of the debate, moreover, the pity of the liberal for the celibate priest is as illogical as is the fear of the conservative. What is called for beyond pity and fear is cool and clear thinking about how celibacy is linked to the service of public reminder that the priest performs in the community.

Now it seems difficult to deny that, generally speaking, the priest has more time, mobility, and independence for his function of community reminder and focus if he is not married. Arguments against celibacy, therefore, usually concern rather the confidence the celibate priest can instill, and his effectiveness as a reminder of Christ's love. It is often said that lay people today find it difficult to have confidence in the judgment and advice of the priest because their own problems center about living the Christian life in the married state, of which the priest has no personal experience. Such statements are difficult to evaluate. On the one hand, it is true that there is no substitute for experience. On the other hand, one wonders whether the same mentality is at work in the above complaint that would also, for example, claim that the priest cannot speak objectively about fair housing for Blacks because he has no property or family to "defend." It is the experience of many priests that the problems married people have frequently are not problems that require them to learn from anyone what to *do*. They know what to do already, and the priest who offers "answers" risks misinterpreting his whole relationship with them. Most often, it is priests with an exaggerated notion of the priest as an authority figure who suffer most when they "cannot" give people the answers people seem to want. People need rather to talk to someone whom they can trust and who can sympathize with them. In general, do they trust each other the way they trust a priest? Again we have a question of fact. It is at least arguable that the basis of people's trust in the priest seems in large part from his celibacy, which is a *sign* of his commitment to them. The sympathy which people seek is not so specific as to demand a similar pattern of life in their listeners, but demands rather someone who accepts them as persons, as valued in themselves—and someone who can communicate this acceptance to them. The priest does not win the trust of the people only on the basis of his personality, virtue, or talent, but also by the fact that he has been willing publicly to report and register the love of Christ and has made his celibacy a gesture of this willingness.

On the other hand, it can be argued that the priest has no real opportunity to learn what human love is because he does not participate in the tangible, body-and-soul kind of love that is found only in marriage. Yet many married people remain utterly impervious to the implications of their own union. Moreover, Christ himself did not marry, and only those whose thinking is cryptically docetist or apolinarist would find this point irrelevant. The priest must preach the good news, which means that he must demythologize it in that basic and traditional sense of showing how it speaks from start to finish of the love of God for men. He must also mediate the forgiveness of Christ in the sacrament of reconciliation, and in this encounter he must learn well the dimensions and nuances of love. For some individuals it is probably true that marriage would improve the efficiency of their ministry, but here we are speaking in terms not of time, energy, or mobility, but of the inner qualifications that, practically speaking, a man needs if he is to stand for the kind of love which Christians esteem and celebrate in their Word and sacraments.

Human love between a man and a woman remains, therefore, for the priest an all important analogy for understanding God's love for men. Its concrete and immediate quality could be a way for the priest to understand better "the holy city, a new Jerusalem, come down out of heaven from God, like a bride dressed and ready to meet her husband" (Rv 21:22).

We have tried to pare away to a stark, simple structure the figure of the priest. It is our hope that the understanding of priesthood which we offer here succeeds in doing two things. First, in protecting the priest against certain alien roles in which people today try to cast him but which he accepts at his own great risk: the holy man, the man who is alienated from the secular, the ecclesiastical bureaucrat, the substitute offering, someone with special, almost magical insight. Second, to encourage priests to cut through to the central issue of their priesthood: whether or not they think it worthwhile to make the gesture of reminder that the priesthood is. The priest is a reminder *of* the saving, secular words and actions of Christ. When he makes his gesture of reminding or, more properly, when he becomes that gesture, his faith tells him that this gesture is graced with the promise of Christ to be there, speaking again to the hearts of men and acting in their lives. He is most a priest, just as

Christ is most present, when he recalls the supper that Christ gave not for his servants, but for his friends. The priest is also a reminder *for* a community of believers who are thrown together in Christ, sometimes in incredible confusion, inequality, time-serving, routine and indifference, but at other times with astonishing vitality, good humor, dedication, and peace. The priest is one with that community, in its weaknesses and in its strengths, in its reflective moments and in its mission to the world. He could do a lot worse.

MARRIAGE:AN HISTORICAL AND THEOLOGICAL OVERVIEW

Jared Wicks, S.J.

The Old Testament and marriage

The Bible reflects a notable evolution in the Jewish and Christian understanding of marriage. We can trace marriage from a time when early Israel hardly differed from her pagan neighbors down to the momentous connection made in the letter to the Ephesians between marital love and Christ's self-sacrificing love for those he has redeemed.

Jesus himself commented how the ancient laws were adapted to Israel's "hardness of heart" (Mt 19:8). Polygamy was tolerated (e.g., 1 S 1, 2); certain marriages between in-laws were even required in order to perpetuate physical descent (Dt 5:5-10); and the husband could repudiate his wife for a number of defects (Dt 24:1-4). The earliest meaning of the commandment, "Thou shalt not commit adultery," was that a man should not violate the proprietary rights a husband held over his wife. The husband did not sin by intercourse outside marriage, unless he laid with the wife of another man and so violated the other husband's rights—the notion of a double standard has a long history.

Later portions of the Old Testament reflect a growing purification of Israel's ideals concerning marriage. The second account of creation (Gn 2) indicates that marriage is not just an arrangement for procreation, but that man and woman are made to support each other in intimate companionship. Each completes the other as they live together and become one flesh. Marriage is a partnership intended by God in spite of the elements of pain introduced by the couple's sin.

In spite of the Law's provisions for divorce by repudiation, the writer of Proverbs urged men to live in loving fidelity to the wife of their youth (5:15-20). The prophet Malachi inveighed against divorce as a practice the Lord hates (2:15), and took the significant step of calling marriage a covenant witnessed by the Lord (2:14). If marriage is a covenant, then suddenly a wealth of religious meaning—mutual trust, sacred commitment, God's own fidelity—clusters around the relation between husband and wife. The covenant theme was the powerful purifying force that brought forth the full Christian ideal of marriage in the Lord. Almost on the eve of the Christian era, the Book of Tobit presented a highly spiritual picture of a couple living before God in prayer and fidelity, dedicated to the ideal of a lifelong and godly marriage (especially Tb 8:5-8).

Jesus and the New Testament

Jesus stood in the reforming tradition mirrored in Malachi and Tobit when he laid down the unqualified principle, "What God has joined together, let no man put asunder" (Mt 19:6). Jesus made obligatory for his followers the ideal of the Lord's covenant with Israel, in which the Lord remains faithful even when Israel wanders off in sin. In the gospel of Mark, Jesus stated the revolutionary principle that the wife too has rights in marriage that are violated by her husband's infidelity: "Whoever divorces his wife and marries another commits adultery against her" (Mk 10:11). According to Matthew, Jesus harkened back to God's original intention in making man and woman to live not as two but as one in a union consecrated by God himself.

Along with these insistent words of Jesus we must take account of the quality of loving dedication he manifested as he went to death on behalf of sinful mankind. Jesus' love for those he redeems is the true foundation of Christian married love. The New Testament, in fact, came to refer to the redeemed as the body Christ loves as his own bride (2 Cor 11:2; Rv 19:7; 21:9).

In an early letter, St. Paul gave Jesus' teaching on lifelong obligation of both husband and wife within marriage—a dramatic, though unappreciated blow for feminine equality: "the wife does not rule over her own body, but the husband does; likewise the husband does not rule over his own body, but the wife does" (1 Cor 7:4).

Then in the later letter to the Ephesians (ch. 5) we come to the climactic biblical passage on marriage. The context is the extended exhortation that Christians, as those chosen and reborn by God's grace, walk worthy of the vocation to which they are called (4:1). We should "walk in love, as Christ loved us and gave himself up for us, a fragrant offering and sacrifice of God" (5:2). Within marriage, this Christ-like love is to transform the relation between husband and wife (5:21-23). But there is more here than ethical injunction. The two-in-one relation intended by God from the beginning is a great mystery that expresses Christ's relation to the redeemed (5:32). Marriage itself can image forth Christ's own loving fidelity and thus be a sign or sacrament of Christ the redeemer who gave himself up for sinful mankind.

We have clearly travelled a long distance from the mentality reflected in the ancient laws of Israel. The meaning of marriage has grown in richness, depth, and beauty. When one looks around himself in the Western world of the 1980's, the thought arises that many of us Christians need to retrace this path. We need urgently to recapture the vision of marriage as a sacred covenant, witnessed by God, that links husband and wife for the life-long companionship in a love mirroring Christ's self-sacrificing love for those he redeemed.

Early Christian tradition

Writers of the first generations after the apostles made only fleeting references to marriage, but even in these we sense that Christian marriages are different. Christ's redemptive love is the norm; marriage is a concern of the bishop; the civil laws allowing divorce are merely human laws that do not apply to Christians.

Some spiritualist movements of early Christianity—more inspired by Plato and Stoicism than by Scripture—came to look down on the bodily aspect of human existence. The notion that the body is the hostile prison of the soul led to suspicions that marriage was gross and carnal. In spite of the exalted blessings with which the church "sealed" Christian marriages, Christian thinking was infected with a preference for the purer asceticism of virginity. A teacher like St. Augustine knew and cited the verses of Ephesians on the Christlike love and fidelity of the married, but at the same time he believed that original sin had so deeply wounded human sexuality that marital intercourse was always infected with some evil. Only the procreative purpose could override this evil and make marital intercourse morally tolerable.

In late antiquity an important development took place in the areas of the Eastern Roman Empire ruled from Constantinople. As the church came more and more under the influence of imperial authority a spirit of accomodation led to modifications in the rigorous stance previously taken by the church against divorce and remarriage. Churchmen of the East came to cite the words of Jesus in Matthew (5:32; 19:9) that appear to introduce an exception to the rule against divorce, i.e., "except on the ground of unchastity." Civil law allowed remarriage after adultery, and the Eastern Christian tradition came to tolerate the remarriage of the "innocent party" after a first marriage collapsed on the rocks of infidelity. Thus, in contemporary Orthodox Christianity there is a special liturgy for a second marriage, however, a liturgy punctuated with penitential prayers for pardon and cleansing.

The development in the Middle Ages

The most important development in the West in the middle ages was not the inclusion of marriage in the definitive list of the seven sacraments. Rather, it was the entry of a legal and contractual mentality into Christian thinking about marriage. By the late middle ages, references to marriage as a sacred covenant of fidelity had become rare, and marriage was more often seen as a contract formed by mutual consent exchanging exclusive rights over each other's body for procreative acts. The language of contract made it possible to speak of marriage with amazing clarity, but at the cost of reducing it to an almost commercial exchange of goods and services. Echoing Augustine, the medieval tradition also reiterated the primacy of the procreative purpose in marital love.

As canon law grew in extent and refinement, the Western medieval church developed wide-ranging stipulations about the legal requirements of a proper marriage contract, especially concerning the "impediments" hindering certain kinds of marriages.

The Reformation

The Protestant reformers of the sixteenth century launched a fierce attack on the competence of papal and episcopal authority to lay down binding stipulations concerning marriage. The Reformation view of a sacrament as a word and sign promising the forgiveness of sins made it impossible for most Protestants to see marriage as a sacrament of Christ and the church. The Protestant tradition holds rather that marriage is an ordinance of creation, a unique human relationship instituted by God but not included integrally in the dispensation of redemption through Christ. Marriage remains basically a secular reality. The church can clarify God's mandate and exhort couples to live in fidelity, but Christian marriage itself is not an articulation of the mystery of Christ's redemptive love.

In responding to the Reformation, the Council of Trent reaffirmed that marriage between Christians is a sacrament of Christ, a teaching said to be indicated in the letter to the Ephesians. The Council rejected the notion that the church had exceeded her competence both in developing a marriage law and in insisting on the lifelong character of Christian marriage. Trent was careful not to condemn outright the Eastern church's tolerance toward divorce with remarriage, but it showed no readiness to admit this into the Catholic tradition.

In recent times, this Catholic tradition was remarkable for its impressive rigor and consistency concerning marriage. Every marriage between two baptized persons is viewed as a sacramental union enduring until death. No compromise was admitted on divorce, except where it turned out that a first marriage was in fact no marriage in the sacramental sense. Within marriage the prime purpose was the procreation of children, a purpose that had to be respected in every expression of love through marital intercourse. In the very recent past this Catholic tradition has been subjected to questioning from a number of sides. Consequently, Catholics are today traversing the biblical road of pilgrimage in quest of new depth and clarity concerning marriage in the Lord.

In what sense is marriage indissoluble?

We single out this question for treatment prior to stating the fundamental meaning of sacramental marriage. A reflective approach to the lifelong character of *some* marriages is the best way to mark out the precise area where one can speak of the meaning of marriage in the perspective of a Christian vision of our life on earth.

Many today wish to interpret Jesus' prohibition of divorce as the statement of a high ideal toward which Christians must strive, but which in fact cannot be attained. Matthew placed this prohibition in the Sermon on the Mount, beside the ethical commands to love our enemies and to turn the other cheek. These are goals to seek, but hardly norms we can make legally binding. Does not considerable "hardness of heart" still continue in the Christian era? Therefore, there would seem to be warrant in Scripture for coming to terms with an ordered practice of divorce and remarriage in our imperfect world.

In considering this argument for tolerating the solubility of marriages, a number of important points have to be made. Centrally, we question whether it is enough to simply treat divorce as an ethical question. The New Testament has more to say about marriage than is recorded in the Gospels. The idealism taught by Jesus is more than a simple imperative imposed as law on his followers. We have a wider and richer vision of marriage given us by Scriptures and church teaching. If the marriage of two baptized believers is in fact a covenant witnessed and guarded by God, and if such a marriage images forth Christ's love for the redeemed, then a truly Christian marriage is a reality that simply does not waste away and become negligible, whatever the subsequent change in the persons involved.

Instances of Moderation

But while we ponder the lifelong character of a covenant marriage, we must take careful note of the many instances of moderation in the church's treatment of divorced persons. A patristic writer like Origen (died 254) relates, albeit unapprovingly, that some bishops permit women to remarry during the lifetime of their husbands. We saw that the Eastern Church chose to accomodate itself to the Roman law of divorce. In the troubled days of the early medieval West, the penitential books allowed remarriage in certain cases after the collapse or destruction of a couple's life together. Although the late medieval church refused to dissolve sacramental marriages, the many canonical impediments provided ways of subsequently determining that a broken marriage was no marriage at all. Canon law often worked to free people for a new marriage. In recent centuries, popes have exercised competence to declare dissolved many marriages in which one or both of the parties was not baptized. Paralleled with this latter practice is the "Pauline privilege" granting freedom to remarry to a convert to Christianity, if the non-baptized spouse does not wish to continue the marriage (1 Cor 7:15).

Tolerant Concern

We find in these practices a long tradition of tolerant concern for persons involved in broken marriages. There are two elements in this concern (1) the full Christian view of marriage as a lifelong covenant is not verified in every kind of marriage. Some marriages, as among the unbaptized, are in fact *not* marriages in the Lord. These marriages are thus not indissoluble in the strict sense—however much we must lament the deep wounds in the lives of couples and children caught in divorces and broken homes. (2) Even when a first marriage appears to have been a sacramental dedication of believing Christians, there are signs that at times the church has tolerated a second marriage to avoid worse evils. Frequently, the church has been quite rigorous in refusing the blessings of full communion to persons in such a union. Many have seen such second marriages as little more than organized adultery. But this rigor is not the whole story. The church has never completely forgotten her mission of healing to her members still weakened by sin.

Because there are such elements in our tradition, and because the tragedies of broken Christian marriages surround us, there is an increased urgency to the question about the church's ministry to her members in intolerable marriage situations. The signs are clear all around us that the rigor toward those in second marriages is abating and that the channels for forgiveness are opening. This is not to call for the solemn celebration of second marriages as covenantal unions in Christ, but it is a development in the direction of restoring to a fuller sacramental life those Christians living in stable second marriages.

The fundamental meaning of Christian marriage

A couple enter a Christian marriage by their pledge of lifelong love and fidelity. They do not merely exchange rights and duties, but rather confer themselves in a total way. Each takes on a new identity for the other. Under the influence of Scripture, we are constrained to see this pledge of love as the sealing of a covenant before God. As the Lord selected Israel from the other nations to live in a covenant relationship, so also the spouses select each other, forsaking and excluding all others for the rest of their lives. As a covenant, such a marriage has God as its author and witness. Because the new husband and wife are members of the priestly people, God is the guarantor and guard of their union.

The biblical strictures against divorce bring out a central aspect of marriage in the Lord. However, they only have complete meaning if such marriages are in fact godly covenants. If these marriages are contracts, then they can be broken by mutual agreement, lack of compliance, or civil intervention. But covenants are not broken by anyone. Rather, they are violated by a breach of the fidelity promised. Scripture insists on God's fidelity when Israel turned to alien gods. Such fidelity belongs to the covenant pledge of couples entering Christian marriages.

Clearly not everyone is capable of such loving dedication to life together. No little maturity is required for a person to enter such a life partnership. Beyond a certain psychological development and stability, this maturity must include a real vision of faith if a couple are to call upon God to witness and seal their pledge to each other. The mere fact of baptism does not insure this. Today, not a few apparently Christian marriages are in fact the union of baptized "unbelievers" and should not be treated as covenants in the Lord.

Covenant Love

Such a pledge—and the life together that ensues—is a sacrament of Christ because of what the husband and wife articulate to each other. This is so because their pledge of covenant love can only arise out of the deepest levels of their freedom. Such a dedication can only be an engagement made in the power of a transformed identity under the Holy Spirit. Marital love is sacramental when it is vowed by persons assimilated to Christ and consecrated by him in his priestly people. Each partner expresses to the other the self-forgetting and redemptive love that Christ manifested in going to death on our behalf. Because their love is such an engagement of their persons, it is sanctifying and enriching for a lifetime—as the partners prove responsive to each other's sacred commitment.

The full expression of self-giving in Christian marriage does not occur in the ceremonial words of the wedding. Such words give a marriage a public visibility that enriches both the church and the wider society. But the covenant love of a married couple is pre-eminently articulated in the intensely personal interchange of sexual union. Here their mutual gift of self and their new identity for the other find a language of deeper engagement and fuller personal dedication. Again, the assimilation of the couple's love to Christ's dedication issues in a requirement, that of openness to the creation of new life. As Christ's love bears fruit in the conferral of life and more abundant life (Jn 10:10), so the conjugal love of those pledged to each other must be oriented to the gift of and growth of life. In their children, the partners of a Christian marriage find that their mutual pledge to each other has issued in new persons expressive of and responsive to their parents' dedicated giving.

The grace of married love is thus enrichening for the couple whose love is sealed, deepened, and strengthened by the Spirit. Within the priestly people married couples offer a forceful articulation of the loving fidelity to which all are called. But the ultimate service they render is not only to the church, but to the whole of humanity as they image forth in their love the one foundation of a fulfilling life in this world. For life—whether in marriage or outside it—only unfolds its riches when we overcome egotism and self-regard to become persons for others.

THE SACRAMENT OF MARRIAGE
Leonardo Boff, O.F.M.

There is a well-defined theological doctrine on the sacramental nature of marriage. Marriage, this doctrine states, is properly and truly a sacrament of the evangelical rule (DS 1801). Like all sacraments, it is a sign that contains in itself and brings about that which it signifies. The sign is the realization of marriage itself on the level of a union of two wills and two bodies. This sign produces what it signifies: the indissoluble union of the two partners. This union is in turn a sign of a deeper union between Christ and the Church. Marriage is thus an image of the marriage between God and humanity, or between Christ and the Church; this forms the *res et sacramentum* of matrimony. Finally, both the exterior sign (*sacramentum*) and the interior sign (*res et sacramentum*) produce the grace specific to the sacrament (*res sacramenti*): the grace proper to the married state, which enables the partners to live their sacramental union in such a way that it mirrors the mystical union between Christ and his Church. This grace furthermore assists them in the tasks, temptations and vicissitudes of married life. Such is the set of assertions that forms the kernel of classical theology of the sacrament of matrimony. Despite its undeniable virtues, it is difficult today to see how this doctrine applies the concept of sacrament to the fact of marriage. The task of theology is not to elaborate or defend doctrines with ever-increasing refinements of argument, but essentially to reflect radically on the religious reality from which all doctrines must spring. Marriage is such a profound human reality that it cannot be grasped adequately through the doctrinal coordinates of one system of thought. It is a "great mystery" (Ep 5:32), and theology, if it is to grasp its mysterious nature, must always be questing beyond the realms of doctrine. It is on the level of mystery that marriage takes on its sacramental character, and also in this dimension that it can be seen as a matter of grace and salvation.

From this, a number of questions immediately follow. Does the mysterious character of marriage, for example, only apply when it is celebrated as a sacrament, in the marriage of two baptized persons? Is, in other words, only the marriage of two baptized persons a sacrament? Or is the sacramental character inherent in marriage by virtue of its human reality alone? Can the sacramental reality be held to be always one and the same thing, or can it exist on different levels of perfection and in different degrees of wholeness? What is specific to Christian sacramentality in its fullest form?

These questions do not arise merely from an ecumenical interest, as subjects for discussion among the Churches, but stem from the very reality of marriage as an important anthropological fact, as we shall see later.

What is a Sacrament?

Perhaps a deeper look at what a sacrament is will bring us closer to the sacramental reality of all marriages. We have become used to the classical definition of a sacrament: "an outward sign of inward grace," or St. Augustine's *"Sacramentum est sacrae rei signum"* (Epist. 138. I), or Trent's "A sacrament is the visible sign of invisible grace, to which is given the power of making holy" (DS 1639). Behind all these rigid formulations stands a whole thought system, a whole manner of approaching reality. It is a primitive and savage way of thinking, as Claude Lévi-Strauss[1] has pointed out; primitive not only because it belongs chronologically to the early stages of man's development, but also because it is closest to the origins of our modes of thought and speech. Technological man, thinking in scientific formulae and planning with computers, is still *sauvage et primitif.* This way of thinking involves signs, symbols and sacraments; it has been called simply sacramental thinking. In it, things are not thought of as things in themselves, nor the world simply as the world, but everything has to be a sign, symbol, or image of a higher reality. Reality is not only transcendent and immanent, but also transparent: one has to look through it to something beyond.

Now, this way of thinking is specific to mythical and theological thought, in which everything is seen from the starting-point of God. Then everything becomes transparent and changes into a sacrament of God. In the words of St. Irenaeus: "in God there is no emptiness, but everything is a sign" (*Adv. Haer.* 4:21). This habit of thought extends into the personal domain: the basic realities of life, such as spirit, freedom, love, friendship, encounter, etc., can only be expressed adequately through signs and images. These make the realities they signify present, but also refer back beyond them. Everything that touches man deeply becomes surrounded with rites and ceremonies that reveal both its mystery and its links with a deeper reality.

There are, for example, certain nodal points in human life that are truly sacraments, and these are endowed with rites that enhance their importance and emphasize their transcendence: birth, marriage, sickness, death, eating and drinking. . . . In these situations, which belong in the physical, not the spiritual sphere, man feels his insertion into the mystery of life. He feels that there is a power that transcends him and on which he always depends; he realizes that he does not create his own being, but receives it continually from the world—from food and drink, from other people who make up his life and without whom he would lose the basis of his existence. These situations are charged with a sacramental content: eating is not just eating; it is also a sign that makes present and communicates a power that is greater than the action of eating and cannot be manipulated by it. So eating becomes a sacrament of the divine and eternal God who sustains all and penetrates and confers meaning on existence. The basic life situations—birth, marriage, death, eating, etc.—form the basic sacraments of creation. These essential life situations are sublimated, "a sublimation because in the sacrament, these vital situations are seen from the standpoint of their ultimate basis, the point where they meet with the divine."[2] In these basic sacraments, situated at the points where man realizes the potential of his biological nature, he experiences his links with God. This is why he surrounds them with marks of respect, sacralizes them.

The sacraments, then, express a symbolic understanding of the world. This is not to deny the consistency of material things in themselves, but to discover in them a dimension that transcends analysis of their physical-chemical components and that makes present in the world the reality of the transcendent and the eternal. Man is called to grasp the divine message that calls to him from all reality. He is not only a worker in and fashioner of the world; he is also the one being who can see through the transparency of the world to its ultimate ground: God.

Marriage: A Natural Sacrament

Marriage is undoubtedly one of the nodal points referred to. As for the well-known phenomenologist of religion G. van der Leeuw wrote: "The old primitive world knew marriage as a sacrament in the literal sense of the word. This implies that in some ways the end of marriage is not mutual comfort or procreation, but the salvation to be found through it."[3] In fact, marriage seen on its own is already a sacramental sign of the love of two lives. Through it, the meeting and flowering in love of an I and a Thou are expressed on the personal and social levels. Human love, therefore, seen in its totality, possesses a transcendent need and dimension. In love, man experiences fullness, the generosity of living for another, and the encounter that makes two one. Nevertheless, he also knows that love can be threatened by infidelity, by separation and by death; he can also find that the other is not the full and exhaustive answer to the longings of his heart. Man sighs for a deep and lasting love. What he loves is not in fact just another person, but the mystery of personality, revealed and made flesh in the loved one, but also veiled and withdrawn. In marriage, both husband and wife feel called to transcend themselves and to unite in the deeper reality that lies above them, the answer to their latent quest and the principle of union between them. Religions have seen God as the supreme and ineffable mystery that penetrates everything and encompasses everything, in which everything is revealed and kept. So the real Thou to whom man is radically open is not a human Thou but a divine Thou, and, ultimately, man is married by and to God. The other person is the sacrament of God: the personal vehicle for the communication of the divine love in history. One person becomes the sacrament for another when God is seen to be near because he is felt in the excellence of their love, and also felt to be distant, because he is veiled under the sacrament.

Human love, we can see, is always supported and surrounded by divine love; it is never a merely human love, since its link with the transcendent gives it a saving aspect. In other words, whenever a marriage contains genuine love, there will also *de facto* be the grace of God within the human love, making it possible, keeping it open in its transcendence and ensuring that, through the love of one person for another, God's saving action is brought about.

This reality is brought about even when God is not explicitly or systematically involved in the human love. The structure of marriage itself, when it is lived with sincerity, naturally embodies permanent reference to and inclusion of God.

This transcendent dimension of marriage is already contained in the priestly account of creation, in which God gives the man and the woman the commandment to grow, multiply and fill the earth, in the image and likeness of God (Gn 1:27-8). The human reality of marriage is sacramental by its nature; it refers back to the mystery of God. In the prophets the idea of the alliance between God and his people is expressed in terms of marriage. Yahweh is the faithful husband establishing a community of love and faithfulness with Israel. The latter is unfaithful and breaks the bond (Ho 2-3; Jr 3; Ezk 16-23; Is 54). Yahweh still professes his faithfulness in tender terms that overcome human faithlessness: "I have loved you with an everlasting love; therefore I have continued my faithfulness to you. Again I will build you, and you shall be built, O virgin Israel" (Jr 31:22). The eschatological dimension of the wife's eternal faithfulness is also expressed in terms of prophetic desire: "For the Lord has created a new thing on the earth: a woman protects a man" (Jr 31:22).

In conclusion, we can state: marriage as a human order possesses a sacramental character; it does not merely express the loving union of a man and a woman, but also the loving and gracious union of God with mankind, as the prophets clearly saw. It is theologically accurate to say that it is the love of God for men that makes possible true love between man and woman. For this reason, marriage, in the final analysis, is part of God's alliance with his people and so becomes, of itself, a permanent sacrament, which makes present and communicates the love, grace and salvation that come to us from God.

Marriage as a Christian Sacrament

If every marriage is a sacrament *per se*, what is specifically sacramental in marriage between Christians?

The Council of Trent taught that marriage was instituted by God and not invented by men (DS 1801). But it did not indicate what such a statement might mean. The New Testament gives no indication of any words of Jesus that might be taken as instituting this sacrament, any more than it does about other sacraments of the Church. Modern sacramental theology holds that formal institution is not necessary for a sacrament to be considered as having been instituted by Christ. Christ left the Church as the primordial sacrament of his saving, victorious presence in the world. All its actions possess a sacramental character, particularly the seven principal rites through which it actualizes the saving power of Christ in the basic situations of human existence. Christ and the Church took up the natural human sacraments that already implied a reference to God and placed them in a context of special relationship to the Christian mystery. The institution of a sacrament by Jesus Christ should be understood in this way.

Such an understanding fits better with Jesus' attitude to Jewish marriage. He breaks with the casuistry ruling at the time, which distorted the human order, and appealed to the divine origin of matrimony. He did not institute anything new, but restored the ancient form in its original theocentricity, recalling the words of Gn 2:24: "A man shall leave father and mother and be joined to his wife, and the two shall be one flesh; so they are no longer two, but one flesh. What therefore God has joined together, let no man put asunder" (Mt 19:5; Mk 10:1-11; Lk 16:18).

This *parti pris* of Christ's against the legislation of his time should not be seen as an attempt to impose new legislation in his turn; it is of a prophetic, not a legalistic nature. Indissolubility as a sign and a precept is an ethical requirement—man *should* not put asunder—rather than a statement of fact—man *cannot* put asunder. Voluntary separation is said to be a sin, re-marriage no longer permitted, but this is not an immutable law. Man does not have the right to separate what God has united, but this does not exclude the possibility of what God has united being separated, whether by unfaithfulness, death, or the causes contained in 1 Cor 7:11. The absolute character of Christ's precept is as an ethical demand to which man must always pay attention, and not a juridical law of absolute validity.

So in what specifically does the Christian sacrament reside? We have seen that Christ did not institute a sacramental sign proper to matrimony, but built on marriage as it existed, restoring its original human dimension. Christ did not come to build a new cultural pattern and new forms of interrelationship between men. He left the world as he found it, displaying a notable indifference to the social, political and economic structures of his time. And yet he introduced a new spirit and a new ethic with which to confront all things. So Paul can write that the Christian slave is the freed man of the Lord, and the free Christian is the slave of Christ (cf. 1 Cor 7:22). What Christ introduced was a new capacity for transforming human relationships from the master-slave pattern to the brotherly pattern.

Likewise with marriage: Christian marriage is like other marriages in its structure and pattern of organization. But it is lived in a new spirit: marrying, Paul says, is marrying in the Lord (1 Cor 7:39), and if one can understand this, one will understand what is special to Christian marriage.

In the Epistle to the Ephesians (5:21-33) Paul explains the underlying meaning of marriage: "He who loves his wife loves himself. For no man hates his own flesh, but nourishes it and cherishes it, as Christ does the Church, because we are members of his body. For this reason a man shall leave his father and mother and be joined to his wife, and the two shall become one. This is a great mystery and I take it to mean Christ and the Church" (28-32). *Mystery* here is based on the Hebrew word *sôdh*, and means the latent divine plan that gradually manifests itself in history. Marriage, as the intimate joining together of two loves, shows its true meaning in the light of Christ and his Church, Paul says; it does not only signify the union of God with mankind, as the priestly account of creation states in Gn 1:27, nor is it just a figure of the alliance between God and Israel, but it has a deeper meaning, revealed with the Christ event: it prefigures the unity between Christ and his Church in one mystical body (flesh). The words of Gn 2:24—"they shall be one flesh"—take on a more radical meaning referring to the unity of one body with Christ. "In this vision," as Schillebeeckx has observed, "Creation, the covenant and redemption are intermingled. Christ is the bridegroom whose bride is the Church. Christ, the one who loves, redeems and cares for the Church, is presented as a model for the husband in his married relationship with his wife."[4]

Marriage as a human reality gains its final dimension in the light of Christ. It was ordained to Jesus Christ. Grace exists in nature, and nature in grace. Nature was created by and for Christ (Col 1:16). He is the firstborn of creation and the mediator of all creation (Col 1:15; Jn 1:3). Wherever Christians marry, they should see it from this christological viewpoint, as orientated and penetrated by the reality of Christ and his Church.

The sacrament is not, therefore, something added to marriage; it is marriage itself seen from the standpoint of Christian faith. The more it is seen from this point of view, the more it emerges as a sacrament; faith detects and reveals a dimension that was already present in human marriage (Gn 2:24; Ep 5:31-2); now, with Christ, it declares itself and becomes clear. In other words, marriage does not become a saving action only where it is seen and identified as a sacrament by Christian faith; it is a sacrament whenever it is lived in the true human order of two in one flesh. In this case its sacramentality may not be obvious (though it tends of its nature towards this aspect that the Christian faith defines), but this does not make it any the less the means and the place for God's saving communication of his love for men and union with them. Certainly it was only in Christianity that this sacrament reached its full revelation, but wherever it is lived in a right order it achieves what the full and complete sacrament in the bosom of the Church achieves: the grace and communication of God.

What belongs specifically to Christian marriage is the full revelation, in Christ and the Church, of the ultimate meaning of love in the created order between husband and wife: the love of Christ and his saving covenant with mankind, particularly with the believing section of mankind, the Church. The sacrament reaches its fullness when it is brought about in the bosom of the Church-Sacrament of the Lord. The sacrament of marriage is a moment and a particular means of realizing the primordial sacrament that is the Church. Then the sacramental sign, through its participation in the Church, confers *ex opere operato* the grace of God that is always and indefectibly present in the Church.

Sexuality, Eros and Agape as Components of the Sacrament of Marriage

If the sacrament of marriage is marriage itself in its human state, then the human components of married love are also taken up into the sacrament. *Eros*, as the Song of Songs vigorously proclaims, is a natural force by which man is drawn to woman and vice versa. They are called to form one flesh not only in the bodily sense, but also in the fusion of two wills, two minds, two lives. *Eros*, reveals man's transcendence over himself and his openness to another. This openness is a sacrament of even greater transcendence when man aspires to the absolute and the divine. *Eros* reveals the riches and the poverty of human life: the riches of being able to give oneself in the happy joy of a meeting of two hearts and two loves; the poverty of longing to be completed and to accept joyously the gift of the other. Living the erotic dimension, in the giving and receiving of love, allows man to glimpse the meaning of God's grace. It is a gift to be able to give and receive; it is not in our power to win love or ensure a meeting; we live in the gratuitousness of the gift.

Sexuality, which is always more than genital sexuality, expresses the fundamental fact that human beings live as male or as female, relating to each other not as two incomplete beings that only become complete when they unite, but complementing each other. Each exemplifies *humanitas* in a particular way, and reveals different facets of the mystery of human- ity, to their mutual enrichment. Genital exercise of sex, in God's plan, is always within the context of marriage, crowning the deep closeness and union of the two partners at all levels of their lives, and now in their corporeality too.

Agape should not be seen as a reality extrinsic to marriage in con- tradistinction to *eros*. *Agape*, as a being "in the Lord" (1 Cor 7:39), means being able to live the conjugal union in its final essence, as an expression of Christ's love for men: "Husbands, love your wives, as Christ loved the Church and gave himself up for her" (Ep 5:25). Christ makes his presence felt in the married state and in marital relations. These can be practiced according to the pattern laid down by prevailing social norms, but through *agape*, being "in the Lord," they are transformed in their inner nature: this again is a form of grace in the world. "As the covenant without creation would be empty, so *agape* without *eros* is inhuman."[5]

Marriage as a sacramental earthly reality shares in the ambiguity common to every condition of fallen humanity. It is love, but also domination; it is self-sacrifice, but also a power structure; it is giving, but egoism at the same time. Married love, in fact, is lived with the psychological burden inherited from earliest childhood, with the frustra- tions and personal failings that hinder or obstruct our purity of vision and experience of this great mystery. Because of this, marriage, more than the other sacraments, is lived under the aegis of the cross of Christ. So the *agape* expressed in married life takes on the nature of a medicine for the wounds humanity inflicts on the sacrament, and of a revitalizing force for the underlying meaning of marriage as a sacrament of union between Christ and humanity. By virtue of this, love between man and woman should always and continually be in a process of purification from egoism and every hint of the will to power. The sacrament of matrimony is truly a sacrament that lasts throughout the life of the partners, and not a moment that marks the start of married life.

Conclusion: Marriage as a "Domestic Church"

One thing should be clear from these reflections: when two baptized persons validly contract matrimony, they receive the sacrament *ipso facto*. The love that unites them is not just a symbol of the love of Christ for the Church. They make this love visible and actual; then, as baptized Christians, take part in the building up of the Church. In one way they form what *Lumen Gentium*, n. 11, calls a "domestic Church;" in another, they are manifestations of the Church, which accommodates them in its bosom. The Church is present in the sacrament of marriage, not through its sacred ministry, but through the contracting partners themselves. The sacred ministry completes the sacrament in the sense that it provides the liturgical rite through which the implicit sign of marriage is made explicit on the level of profession of faith, and the juridical-canonical form in which the partners express their consent. The juridical-canonical form belongs to the *full* sacrament, in the sense that marriage is never merely a private affair or one of love between an I and a Thou, but always includes a social dimension and is naturally subject to the order and rules of society.

Just as the universal sacrament of the Church knows various degrees of actualization and explicitness, from the atheists in good faith *(Lumen Gentium*, n. 16) to Catholic Christians in a state of sanctifying grace, so marriage likewise expresses its sacramental character in various ways, from the imperfect but real forms of the world's various civilizations and other religions, to its perfect and complete form within the Church.

This perspective forces us to look with the eyes of faith not only at Christian marriage, but at all validly contracted marriages. All marriage is a sign of the transcendent and an incomplete realization of the mystery of Christ and the Church, moving towards an ever greater explicitation of its religious entelechy and inner Christianity.

Footnotes

1. Cf. *The Savage Mind*, (London, 1966).
2. G. van der Leeuw, *Phänomenologie der Religion*, (Tübingen, 1956), ch. 52.
3. G. van der Leeuw, *Sakramentales Denken*, (Kassel, 1959), p. 152.
4. Schillebeeckx, *Marriage*, London, 1965, p. 170.
5. J. Ratzinger, "Zur Theologie der Ehe," in *Theologie der Ehe*, 1969, p. 102.

COMMENTS ON THE NEW FORM
OF CONFESSION

Tad W. Guzie

The ritual of confession has been a mixed experience for most Catholics. Sometimes confession has been a real release from the burden of sin. At other times it has been simply a burden.

Any ritual is like that, to some extent. Sometimes participants get caught up in the spirit of a good celebration; at other times they remain unmoved, even bored. The particular difficulty with confession is that it has seldom been liturgy. Too many Catholics have had mostly negative experiences with this sacrament; no doubt many good and otherwise practicing Catholics have entirely given up going to confession. Some see the hand of God in this ritual, others do not. Some see it as an occasion of grace. Others cannot see how a ritual which they have found so consistently distasteful could possibly be a true occasion of grace.

The church now has a new rite of penance. Much has already been written about it. By this time most Catholics know about the external features of the new rite. A confessional room instead of the dark box. The option of face-to-face confession without a screen. Scripture readings and new prayers.

But there is more to implementing a rite than moving furniture or rewriting prayers. The recent past years have taught everyone, sometimes through painful and divisive experiences, that the revision of liturgy is much more than the revision of books and rites. A truly renewed liturgy calls for renewed attitudes, even entirely new attitudes, on the part of all the faithful and their ministers. Experience over the past decade comes to a head in the new rite of confession. Unlike the liturgy of the Mass, where there can always be safety in numbers there is no way to avoid the challenge of full participation which a one-to-one encounter raises.

The new rite of penance does not change the doctrine of the forgiveness of sin. But the experience of forgiveness through sacramental confession is now meant to be a new kind of experience, for penitent and confessor alike.

Back in the days of the Reformation, in 1551, the Council of Trent wrote a decree on penance which defended the practice of confession against the attacks of various reformers. Yes, said Trent, confession is a true sacrament, and the church has the authority of Christ to proclaim the forgiveness of sin in this form. Trent dealt with the doctrinal question, but its decree did not lead to the kind of liturgical revision which is occurring now. Trent did not address the question of the quality and shape of the ritual itself. Vatican II took up the task that the Council of Trent left undone, and the *Constitution on the Sacred Liturgy* called for a revision of the rite of penance which would take account of questions like these: How can confession be pastorally effective? How should the rite be structured in a way that will best meet the needs of the faithful? How can the sacrament become a genuine celebration of the mercy and forgiveness of God?

Negative experiences of confession have been very substantially a result of what Trent left undone. One thing in particular has plagued the practice of confession: legalism. Church law is good and useful; it is the community's summary of its wisdom and experience regarding the rights and responsibilities of membership in the community of faith. But laws are always the servant of the church, never its master. So trouble arises whenever people see their relationship with God primarily in terms of observing laws. Much of Jesus's preaching was directed against this attitude toward law.

Long before Trent, legalism came along to distort the Christian idea of "satisfaction for sin." In the course of the centuries, confession came to be understood as a kind of sacramental courtroom. Especially during the Dark Ages (roughly 600 to 1000 A.D.) the church's ministry of forgiveness became tied up and confused with society's way of dealing with wrongdoing. During these centuries, when civil society was in chaos, church law made up for the absence of civil law and became intermingled with it. The sacramental penances for theft or murder, for instance, came to be little different from the sentences which the civil courts of that rough age would hand out (fasting on bread and water, imprisonment, even physical punishment). The result was that confession came to be understood according to the procedures of human justice. In civil society, criminals are pardoned after they have served their sentence or paid their debt to society for the wrong they have done. This is the same model that has been implicit in the practice of confession: A sinner is pardoned by reason of making due satisfaction for the offense.

There is no doubt that people are obliged to make up for any wrong they have done. They have to make restitution, have to reconcile themselves with those whom they have harmed. But in no sense is the Lord's forgiveness earned. When legalism comes into play, and when confession is thought of in terms of the procedures of human justice, it runs counter to the gospel idea of God's justice, which does not work on the basis of tit-for-tat. God's forgiveness is freely offered, and it is the Lord who takes the initiative in love, not penitents. "Doing penance" can mean many good things. Above all it is a sign that sacramental absolution never dispenses people from the effort of seeking real-life reconciliation with those they have hurt. But never does penance "earn" or "obtain" the Lord's forgiveness, which is his free gift.

The heritage of legalism has also distorted the idea of what the forgiveness of sin is. Many Catholics have used confession as a forum for straightening out violations of law even when there has been no sin. Take the example of a man who confesses missing Sunday Mass several times; he then adds that this happened because he was in the hospital for an operation. The confessor might ask, "Do you think this was sinful?" And the penitent answers, "Oh no, Father, I know it wasn't a sin. I just thought I'd better mention it."

I suspect most Catholics have confessed things "just to make sure." This practice, and the example given, illustrates the serious confusion that has often existed between the forgiveness of sin and a kind of legal pardon which might relieve a certain feeling of guilt, but which has nothing to do with sin. Catalogues of sin—the famous "grocery lists" found in many old catechisms and prayer books—fostered this confusion, insofar as they approached the experience of sin in a heavily legalistic way.

Trent's decree on penance insisted that sins should be confessed by number and kind. The council was calling for sincerity, and it was reacting against the practice of seeking absolution for no confession at all (e.g., "I have failed in my duties to God and neighbor," period). Unfortunately the fathers of Trent wrote with the model of the law court in mind; they even spoke of the penitent as a "defendant." Their rule about naming and numbering one's sins was well intentioned, but it had the effect of fostering the grocery-list approach to confession.

Most Catholics grew up paying far more attention to sins than to sinfulness. Many confessors have had the experience of hearing a list of sins recited by a penitent, and suspecting from the whole tone of the confession that the list has little to do with what is really bothering the person. The list of sins, in other words, seems to have little resemblance to the penitent's real experience of sinfulness. If the confessor asks, "Which of the things you mentioned really matter to you, really affect your life?" he will sometimes get an answer like, "Well, Father, what really bothers me is this. . . ." And the penitent will go on to talk of a deeply felt experience of failure or inadequacy which simply doesn't fit into neat categories of number and kind.

As the practice of confession focused more on sins than on sinfulness, acts rather than attitudes, it dealt with symptoms rather than the real disease. Individual acts are usually symptoms. Not to say that symptoms aren't real; sometimes they are very harmful indeed. But the real disease of sin most often stems from the half-conscious attitudes and complex situations in which a person's freedom—or lack ot it—becomes involved.

I have been drawing a grim picture of the past. There have fortunately been confessors and spiritual directors who have led many people beyond the pitfalls arising from legalism. Still, it is against this background that the following question must be answered: "Will the new rite change anything?"

I believe the new rite can bring about great change. But this will depend on how much serious prayer and reflection is given over the next few years to the new rite, which presents a whole new understanding of the church's ministry of reconciliation, a vision which will not be absorbed overnight.

In the new rite, individual confession is one among several forms of the sacrament of penance. The other forms involve communal celebration, and on certain occasions general absolution. These forms open a new chapter in the history of the sacrament, and only the future will tell what that history will be. I shall confine my remarks here to the rite for individual confession. I have grouped my remarks, somewhat arbitrarily, under five key topics.

(1) *Confession is a celebration of God's mercy, not a court of judgement.* From the moment the confessor welcomes the penitent to the concluding prayer of thanksgiving, it is inescapable that a new atmosphere exists, an atmosphere of healing and prayer. The rite, in fact, insists that the priest (as well as the penitent) should prepare himself with prayer to celebrate the sacrament.

The story of the prodigal son (Luke 15) is helpful for understanding the atmosphere of the new rite. The repentant son had a speech all prepared; it was a sincere speech in which he confessed his sinfulness. But his father isn't really concerned with his speech. He has already run out to meet his child, and he throws his arms around him and kisses him even before the boy makes his confession. The new rite beautifully reflects Jesus' parable. It was formerly the penitent who began the encounter in confession—"Bless me, Father, for I have sinned"—very much as the prodigal son planned it. Now it is the confessor who takes the initiative, welcoming the penitent and creating an atmosphere of acceptance and love before there is any confession of sin. The new rite thus places a substantial burden on the confessor and on his ability to establish an atmosphere which many Catholics have not experienced before in the confessional.

The change in atmosphere is capsulized in one remarkable sentence in the new rite: "Faithful Christians, as they experience and proclaim the mercy of God in their lives, celebrate with the priest the liturgy by which the church continually renews itself." That sentence is a description of what confession is supposed to be. It suggests that people come to the sacrament because they have experienced the mercy of God and now want to proclaim it in a sacramental act. They have come in response to God's love, so that confession is actually a celebration. Is that what confession has been for most Catholics? The question reveals the kind of challenge the new rite poses.

Confession is also a celebration *with* the priest. In the courtroom model of confession, the priest was seen as one who stands somewhere between (not with) the penitent and God. In the new rite, the encounter with the confessor is horizontal rather than vertical. It is an encounter in faith and prayer rather than an encounter in the spirit of law and judgment. Contrast the dark confessional box with the practice of some of the churches in the East, where the ritual of confession is celebrated with confessor and penitent standing together before an icon. This is precisely the "horizontal" atmosphere fostered by the new rite.

(2) *The sacramental moment of confession focuses on the love of God rather than on sin.* The story of the prodigal son is helpful again. The boy's father does not moralize on the wrong he did. There is no discussion of the boy's sinfulness; his father does not even exhort him to avoid wrongdoing in the future. Jesus' parable contains a profound truth about the dynamic of forgiveness which is often overlooked: there are many things that do not need to be analyzed or even verbalized in the act of forgiveness, once there has been a genuine affirmation of love.

The practice of confession has often been moralistic, characterized by an excessive preoccupation with right and wrong on the part of both priest and penitent. According to the new rite, confession is not primarily a time for the formation of conscience, moral instruction, or exhortations to sin no more. It is a liturgical act in which "the Church proclaims its faith and gives thanks to God for the freedom with which Christ has made us free." There is a challenge here for both penitents and confessors, their attitudes, their reasons for going to confession. Confession is not a time for extensive counseling, and it is not meant to be a forum for continuing spiritual direction.

Confessors might have to rethink the approach they take in helping penitents to begin their confession. The most spontaneous invitation penitents knew was probably along these lines: "Is there any problem you want to talk about, any major fault or sin that has been harming your relationship with God?" This kind of invitation is valid enough, but does it really fit the spirit of the new rite? It is a moralistic invitation, because it focuses more on sin than on the mercy of God. Might it not be more appropriate for the confessor to begin by asking: "Do you really feel that God loves you, and that He has called you here because of his love for you?"

Most Catholics would probably find such evangelical-sounding language, a bit strange in confession. But the spirit of the new rite seems

to call for that sort of approach, if the ritual itself is really to be a
"celebration" in which Christians "experience and proclaim the mercy
of God in their lives."

(3) *The new rite is addressed to the disease rather than the symptoms.*
Penitents are invited to "open their hearts" to the confessor, and the rite
avoids the legalistic approach of asking penitents to list their sins by name
and number. The rite takes account of the fact that sinfulness is not
always the same thing as sins. It encourages people to bring their
ambiguities and struggles to the sacrament, not just the clear wrongs they
have done. This has not always been an easy thing for Catholics to do,
because the grocery-list approach to confession never encouraged deep
spiritual discernment.

Everyone needs help in "opening their hearts" before the Lord, and
this again makes special demands on the confessor. As the new rite puts
it, he should "understand the disorders of souls" (the disease again) and
know how to help cure them. He should "acquire the knowledge and
prudence necessary for this task by serious study" and above all "by
fervent prayer to God." He should be an instrument in the discernment of
spirits. Discernment means "a deep knowledge of God's action in the
hearts of people," and this is a gift of the Spirit.

So the rite calls Catholics to something more than the prepared
speeches they brought to confession in the past. Bringing a list of sinful
acts (symptoms) is not necessarily the same thing as opening one's heart
(revealing a disease). Along the same lines, the qualities of the confessor
described in the rite suggests that hearing confessions is a particular
ministry, calling for special knowledge and gifts. Perhaps, as the new rite
takes hold, it will become clear that not every priest is gifted for this
ministry. Bishops may have to do some serious thinking about appointing
certain priests whose primary ministry would be hearing confessions,
because of their particular gifts and call.

(4) *The new rite clarifies the priest's role in the process of reconciliation.* The prayer of absolution completes or seals the change of heart
which the penitent has manifested to the confessor. This prayer is the
prayer of the church, and the new rite carefully makes clear that it is not
the priest who forgives sins. In fact, the priest is not even mentioned in
the discussion of the new rite about the meaning of absolution. This is no
accident. The authors of the rite were well aware of the many misunder-

standings about the priest's role that have existed in the past.

The priest's role problem can be put in terms of the classic statement: "Protestants go directly to God for forgiveness; Catholics go to a priest." The new rite makes it clear that this is a false distinction. It is only the Lord who forgives sin; the priest declares that forgiveness in the name of the Lord and his church. Throughout the rite, the confessor appears as a kind of "transparency," revealing to the penitent and leading him or her to see and proclaim the love of God. The ministry of the confessor is a ministry within and on behalf of the community of faith, not over it. This is another aspect of the "horizontal view" mentioned earlier.

(5) *Confession is a peak moment in a total process of conversion.* Contrition or change of heart is "the most important act of the penitent." Apart from an interior change of attitude, confession and absolution have no meaning and indeed no effect. People do not go to confession to "get" forgiveness. They go there to celebrate it sacramentally, which means that in the liturgy of confession they are proclaiming a process that is going on in their lives. What is this process? It is a "profound change of the whole person by which one begins to consider, judge, and arrange one's life according to the holiness and love of God." This is the definition of contrition or conversion given in the rite (the two terms are interchangeable), and the definition deserves much reflection.

First, it presupposes that there is something going on inside us, something special to proclaim and celebrate. The new rite locates confession within the church's larger ministry of reconciliation, which begins in Baptism and which continues in every celebration of the Eucharist. The Eucharist is our normal and ordinary sacrament of reconciliation, because it celebrates the "sacrifice which has made our peace with God." The sacrament of penance is clearly a special sacrament, something for special occasions, the fruit of a special experience. "How often should I go to confession?" One can no longer give a set answer to that question. The definition of contrition quoted above implies coming to the sacrament with some sense of a new beginning.

Priests used to preach the benefits of confession by putting the cart before the horse: "Go to confession often. It is an occasion of grace." The direction of the new rite is different: "Respond to the grace of a new beginning; then, go to confession and celebrate it."

A whole new style of preaching is called for here. In the past the church preached a discipline approach; confession was preached as one of the good and graced things Catholics should do. But an authentic sacramental approach demands that Catholics give serious attention to the experience of grace which they bring to the sacrament, an experience which is already operative before they come to confession. Confession is not in itself a new beginning. The new beginning has begun before they come to the sacrament, and before absolution is given.

The definition of conversion given in the rite suggests a whole new way of looking at sin. *Sin is something that prevents people from seeing and arranging their lives in response to God's love for them.* This is much more than arranging life in accord with rule-keeping. Here again is the importance of the confessor's invitation mentioned earlier. It is not just a moral sense of right and wrong that should bring people to an awareness of their sinfulness, but above all a sense of God's love for them. And confession of sinfulness, in a liturgical act, is most appropriately a response to the question. "Do I really believe the Lord loves me, no matter what wrong I have done?"

It is much easier to think of sin as the violation of a code than as a failure to arrange life in response to God's love. I am sure everyone has sought absolution as a means of "feeling clean" again.

A priest friend of mine who directs retreats, discourages people from beginning their retreats with confession. This is very much in the spirit of the new rite and its definition of contrition. Coming to judge one's life according to the love of God is not an instant process, and the new rite invites people to seek absolution for more profound reasons than "setting the record straight."

Absolution seals a deep interior process. It is an embrace, a fresh embrace from the Lord and his church. This is why the sign of absolution now includes not only words but also touch: the laying on of hands, which is the church's most ancient sign of healing and reconciliation.

The question of children's confessions is not dealt with in the new rite. Certainly the rite will force continued thinking about the appropriate age for a child's first experience of individual confession. If a child has no real sense of a new beginning, no sense of a "profound change by which one begins to arrange one's life in accord with the love of God," what can the sacrament possibly mean?

If "the most important act of the penitent is contrition," and if a child has not reached the sense of contrition which the rite calls for, the wisdom of a too early confession should be questioned.

Confession is not a sacrament of initiation into the Christian life, and it is not meant to be a training ground for a good Catholic life. Perhaps parents ought to experience the new rite themselves and reflect on that experience before they come to any decision about the right age for the first confession of their children.

Will the new rite be a pastoral success? I indicated the enormous challenge it poses to our past attitudes, our legalism, our moralism. It seems that the heaviest burden lies on priests, because it is the confessor's personal attitude and his ability to share prayer with the penitent which creates the whole atmosphere for the sacrament. Much will depend on how the sacrament is preached and that again is largely the burden of priests. The pastor who takes a legalistic approach to religion will not be able to communicate the spirit and direction of the new rite to his parish and the rite will simply not be implemented.

There is no evidence as yet that Catholics who have abandoned confession are returning to it in large numbers. The first task in any parish will be to provide a new experience—the experience described in the rite—for those who are still coming to confession. Others might return once they have heard from their fellow Catholics that confession really is a sacramental encounter.

The need to externalize what is going on inside is precisely the reason why Catholics celebrate sacraments. But some Catholics are not yet comfortable with active liturgy, with externalizing in a ritual manner.

Bad experiences of confession certainly need to be overcome. But insofar as some people are uncomfortable with ritual, with externalizing inner experiences of grace, they will remain uncomfortable with the ritual of confession and will keep coming up with arguments for "going directly to God." That is not the argument, because that is not what sacramental celebrations are about. The whole question is whether confession can really be a sacramental celebration.

With my head I can understand that God is loving and forgiving. In my heart I have to realize that God loves and forgives me, even me. The sacrament of confession is a liturgical act in which I express that realization, that grace. And the grace of the sacrament comes in and through the quality with which I celebrate it together with my confessor. "Faithful

Christians, as they experience and proclaim the mercy of God in their lives, celebrate with the priest the liturgy by which the Church continually renews itself.''

REFORM OF THE RITE OF PENANCE
Zoltán Alszeghy, S.J.

Community reaction is always a useful means of understanding any event in the life of the Church. In the case of the new *Ordo paenitentiae* the first reactions have differed. Some consider it dangerously progressive, others find it rigidly conservative. But the majority, especially those engaged in pastoral ministry, have experienced a certain confusion over the difficulties of putting the new rite into practice. This is not only a matter of instructing the faithful: More difficult is the fact that the new rite demands of both confessor and penitent a new attitude. They must both abandon fixed formulas and make room for personal initiative to meet the essential requirements of the sacrament. While the substance of the sacrament has remained and will remain unchanged, the reactions of the faithful prove that a profound change is taking place.

Great changes in the celebration of penance have always been characterized by a shift in emphasis from one aspect of this complex experience to another. To simplify somewhat, we may say that penance had two main structures.

For the Fathers penance was governed especially by the notion of *satisfaction*, that is, by the necessity of performing good works to expiate sins. The bishop did indeed have to know the penitent's sins and to impose his hands before the penitent could re-enter community life in the Eucharist, but uppermost was the thought of the elimination of the wrong committed (through prayer, fasting, and works of mercy).

From the Middle Ages down to our day the emphasis shifted to confession as a necessary condition for absolution. Confessor and penitent seemed intent above all on the integrity of confession according to number and species.

The "newness" of the revised rite consists not so much in new prescriptions, nor in the old prescriptions it omits (such as use of a confessional screen), but rather in structuring the whole penitential event around the central idea of reconciliation. This reconciliation is realized through conversion of the penitent to God in the Church, and the creative acceptance of the mercy of God realized in the ministry of the Church.

The first aspect of reconciliation is the conversion of the sinner to God. While conversion does in fact consist in disowning sin, it relates first of all not to sin, but to God. The *Ordo* explicitly cites the words of Paul VI in the Introduction: "Penance is a personal religious act whose goal is love of the Lord and trust in him" (*AAS* 50 (1966) 179). The whole rite is directed toward this concept of conversion which is the beginning of salvation, the fruit of the Lord's cross, but also participation in his resurrection.

Catholic theology has not been unaware that forgiveness of sins presupposes a sincere conversion of heart, and that this implies not only "sorrow and genuine detestation of sin committed with the purpose of not sinning again," but also trust in divine mercy which is the beginning of love. But in practice, while emphasis was put on the resolve to sin no more, it was not made equally clear that conversion consists not just in accepting a rule of conduct, but in acknowledging God as one's Lord, Savior, and Father. The prodigal son has to return to the father's house to receive mercy—preachers and confessors sometimes erroneously interpreted his return as the simple will to obtain in the sacrament a cancellation of merited punishment without a reform in the values which regulate personal conduct.

It is not just a humanly understandable exteriorization of a religious practice which accounts for such a development. History and apologetics have contributed their part. a principal concern has been to overcome the rigorist misunderstanding that made conversion a difficult and rare experience, almost impossible for a common Christian. As often happens, reaction to one extreme led to its opposite. A good number of the faithful went to confession hurriedly and without proper preparation, without true conversion. So it is fitting that the *Ordo* should react against the impoverishment of the sacrament without falling back into rigorism, either in theory or practice.

One conviction runs through the whole rite: Conversion is a gift of

God. It must be asked of God's mercy, as the preparatory prayer of the rite does. The conversion required is not just the decision to break with sin and obey the commandments. It is a constant and progressive orientation toward union with the Lord. The Introduction of the *Ordo* calls it "continuous penance" and the final prayer of the rite describes it as "walking in newness of life." Conversion implies therefore the will to persevere; it should become a fixed dimension of life, a growing in conformity to the image of the Son.

The rite more or less consciously presupposes a psychological model of change of heart instigated by God, initially in the penitential process, and tending to its growth and maturity, namely to realized conversion *sicut oportet* (as it ought to be; cf. Rm 8:26 and *Denz-Schön.* 396). While the liturgy does not side with particular opinions, it is our view that the experience expressed in the rite is best explained by the Thomistic concept *ex attrito fit contritus* (one passes from attrition to contrition). Conversion develops under the influence of grace not only "extensively" (the penitent accepts ever new demands upon his filial friendship with the Father), but also "intensively" (the motive of conversion is less one's own good and more the divine glory).

Not all the required manifestations of conversion are realized in the moment of the absolution; for example, to live in the unity of Christian brotherhood and to proclaim salvation to men. This fact answers the objection that since there is no psychological reaction in the moment of absolution, the sacrament produces no psychological change in the penitent. The causal connection between the human act (e.g., prayer, sacrament) and change of heart does not demand that they happen at the same moment.

In other words, the human act need not produce its saving effect in the same instant it is done. The death and resurrection of Christ had effect before being realized in time and continues to be effective after the first Easter. Sacramental grace remains active when the rite is concluded, as for example in an adult baptized but unrepentant of his sins. So there is no reason to deny that the effects of a sacrament or a good work in union with Christ should make themselves felt before they are realized—thus the sacraments "attract" those who approach them. The ultimate explanation of this lies in the universal mediation of the Church, Christ's primary sacrament of salvation.

The recovery of the ecclesial dimension of penance is an important development of modern theologians. As Xiberta, Poschmann, Rahner, and others have shown, the Fathers considered ecclesial penance a complex event: juridical, liturgical, and pastoral. Through it the Church readmitted the sinner to its living unity, lost by sin, so that the penitent found again in "the sphere of grace" of ecclesial unity his relation of son of God.

Above all, sin concerns not only God and the individual but the Church as well, whom "sinners wound by their sin" (*Lumen Gentium* n. 11). The lack of supernatural life in one member weakens the cooperation and mediation of salvation which the communion of saints requires.

Secondly, conversion, reconciliation with God, and re-entry into the life of the Spirit are obtained in virtue of the action of the Church "which by charity, example, and prayer seeks (sinners') conversion" (*LG* 11). The Council does not restrict the action of the Church to absolution, but includes a variety of elements. Some influence the penitent psychologically, providing motives capable of moving the heart of the sinner to conversion; others (such as prayer, especially liturgical) are means of grace to make the motivation really effective.

Finally, Vatican II teaches that the sinner achieves reconciliation with God not only through the influence of the Church, but through a new participation in the life of the Church. A son of God is a member of the Church not just in body but in his heart. So the sinner is brought to reconciliation not only *through* the Church, but also *in* the Church.

This teaching of the new rite is ever present. It underlines the social character of sin. Sin "divides and scatters;" in reconciliation "charity restores unity" (*Ordo* 99). Christian justice, the goal of on-going penance, encompasses reconciliation with one's neighbor, solidarity with all men of good will for peace and justice, and the insertion of the sinner in ecclesial unity (*Ordo* 5 and 3).

This last point is particularly interesting. The Introduction of the new rite carefully avoids the error of considering the Church as a community of the perfect over against the world, the community of sinners. The holiness of the Church does not exclude its need of purification; rather it consists in its capacity to effect the continual repentance of its members. Reconciliation is not an instantaneous change after which the penitent can stand fixed in the state of grace, but "the Church, embracing sinners in her bosom, is at the same time holy and always in need of being purified, and incessantly pursues the path of penance and renewal" (*LG* 8; *Ordo* 3).

The distinctive meaning of the rite is to effect the re-entry of the Christian into the coninuing process toward perfection. The penitent returning to the Father "sets out on the way of penance." That is an eloquent expression: It reinforces the dynamic concept of Christianity as a "way" toward a goal to be reached across a lifetime (Ac 9:2; 24:22).

The real innovation in ecclesial penance consists in bringing together all the aspects of the action by which the Church accomplishes the conversion of its members. The traditional administration of the sacrament presupposed the influence of the word, prayer, and sacrifice of the Church. It also presupposed an initial conversion of the penitent in the individual's preparation for the sacrament. Within the sacramental rite the priest's activity was principally judicial; his role was almost purely sacramental, directed to the infusion of grace.

This emphasis is avoided in the new rite. Naturally, central to the Church's saving action there remains "the absolution of the penitent through the ministry given by Christ to the apostles and their successors" (*Ordo* 8; cf. Mt 19:18; Jn 20:23). But this act is considered the culmination of a complex structure of saving acts performed by various ministers in a variety of ways.

Regarding ministers, the priest's absolution is integrated into the activity of the whole ecclesial community, so that "the whole Church as a priestly people exercises the work of reconciliation entrusted to it by God" (*Ordo* 8). This enhances the value of the works (merits, prayer) of all the faithful; hence the effort to structure the rite of reconciliation so that the whole community can participate.

Regarding ways or acts, the sacramental act is integrated into the complex of actions by which the Church, through its preaching of the word of God, *calls* the faithful to conversion, *testifies* to the forgiveness of their sins in the name of Christ, and *effects* their remission by the power of the Holy Spirit.

One probable reason for integrating these factors is the difficulty the faithful experience, when left to themselves in a world ruled by sin, of preparing themselves for the sacrament. By integrating the preparation into the sacramental rite itself, the communal unity of the assembly helps

the individual to approach conversion—and the whole process of preparation takes place in the sphere of sacramental grace.

But more decisive still was the new way of looking at the liturgy. The
psychological and pastoral effect of words and symbols is no longer
separated from the sacramental effect of the essential formulas. The
whole sacramental sign speaks to the heart of man. It provides motivation
at once understandable and moving. It also works in a supernatural way,
changing man's being and doing, producing in him a faith response. This
incarnational view of the liturgy requires the integration in the sacramental rite itself of all the aspects of ecclesial activity for the renewal of the
penitent.

This approach demands a change of style in the rite—or rather a
return to the older style (less juridical, predominantly pastoral) of the
Fathers. Along with clear and precise formulas, which express the effect
of the minister's role, this style uses a language rich in biblical images
and symbols which elicit an emotional response. A broad range of
choices is left to priests to adapt the material of the *Ordo* to the occasion.
This shows that the directives do not impose a rigid structure, but
constitute rather a directory whose purpose is to take a variety of pastoral
situations into account. The ultimate goal is the deepest possible
conversion.

The principal new feature of the new rite, which underlies all the
others, is its description of the role of the minister. Since the Middle Ages
the confessor has been considered above all as *judge*. He had to know
"the case" in order to pronounce "the sentence;" so his principal duty
consisted in asking questions that would insure the integrity of the
confession. The Introduction of the new rite, while it mentions the role of
judge and speaks of a sentence, puts the duty of *healing* first. The
minister should "diagnose the sickness of the soul and provide re-
medies," revealing the heart of the Father and the likeness of Christ the
Good Shepherd in his own bearing.

It is precisely this new accent on the healing function of the confessor
that explains the Church requirement that the penitent, in the case of
general absolution not preceded by individual confession, still must
confess his (already forgiven) sins after receiving general absolution—if
possible before receiving general absolution again, in any case within the
year (*Ordo* 34). One often hears the question: Are those sins forgiven or

not? If they are forgiven, why confess them again? Such a question, ignores the fact that not every true forgiveness cancels out all the bad effects of sin. So it is necessary to continue the work of purifying conversion even after forgiveness has been effectively granted. Especially does it fail to take into account the variety of ways the Church assists penitents. After absolution there is still need of that ministry by which the priest proclaims and witnesses God's mercy, authentically pronouncing what is required for a return to the Father's friendship in the case of each penitent. It must be remembered that this ministry— considered by Trent as part of the office of "binding" (*DS* 1692)— belongs to the sacrament and thus shares in the effect of the sacrament.

With the promulgation of the new rite it would appear that the reform of penance called for by Vatican II has been accomplished. Actually, not so. The various changes in the administration of penance have never been brought about by legislative acts alone. Even if today, thanks to a greater uniformity in church life, church authority can go beyond practice, showing the way to follow, still the legislative reform will have its full effect only when it is put into practice by the local churches.

Two temptations threaten the task of putting the reform into practice. The first is to continue to administer the rite as previously, only changing one or the other formula, and considering it pastorally impossible to follow the suggestions of the new rite. There is reason to fear that some priests, concerned about hearing the confessions of many faithful in a short time, will reject the new way of administering the sacrament. This attitude will only contribute to the diminishing number of penitents. More of the faithful will avoid a minimalist rite that lacks pastoral punch.

The second temptation is to use the new rite without absorbing its spirit, that is, to substitute for the individualistic "craftsmanship" of the confessional the "mass-production" of communal penance celebrations. This situation would result in a crowd impatient for a formula rather than a community in search of conversion.

The true reform intended by the recent directive must steer a course between these two obstacles by a serious but flexible use of forms which fit individual cases while remaining faithful to the norms laid down. These new forms should not be introduced suddenly and once for all. Like conversion itself, they should be continually improved through the experience of pastors and faithful.

Many of the faithful are accustomed to a certain fixity in liturgical and pastoral practices: They will be upset by this searching which now reaches the administration of penance. We must be convinced and convince others that all the forms the administration of penance has thus far taken originated in the same sort of concern. And finally, we will never put the desired reform into practice unless we courageously accept the burden and the risk of searching and experimenting.

LITURGICAL TRADITIONS OF CHRISTIAN ILLNESS: RITES OF THE SICK

Charles W. Gusmer

When the original draft of the Constitution on the Sacred Liturgy was presented to the bishops of the Second Vatican Council on October 22, 1962, the section on unction called for a change of name from extreme unction to anointing of the sick, declared that the sacrament was *per se* not a sacrament of the dying but of the grievously ill, and urged that the sacrament be administered at the beginning of a serious illness. The initial schema also provided for the repetition of the sacrament during the same illness.[1]

The definitive version of the Constitution promulgated on December 4, 1963, describes the name and nature of the sacrament in these terms: " 'Extreme unction,' which may also and more fittingly be called 'anointing of the sick,' is not a sacrament for those only who are at the point of death. Hence, as soon as any one of the faithful begins to be in danger of death from sickness or old age, the appropriate time for him to receive this sacrament has certainly already arrived." (art. 73).[2] No provision is made for a possible repeated administration of the sacrament within the same sickness.

We have before us the conflict of two theologies regarding the anointing of the sick: a sacrament of the dying (extreme unction) or a sacrament of the sick (anointing of the sick). Article 73 of the Liturgy Constitution represents a compromise between these two positions: the term "extreme unction" is retained, but the sacrament is better called anointing of the sick; the restrictive condition of a *periculum mortis* remains, but the sacrament should be administered at the beginning of a danger of death resulting from sickness or old age.

On the one hand the approach to anointing as a rite for the dying has received considerable impetus in this century from a thesis of Joseph Kern, which was a revival of the scholastic teaching on the sacrament. Granting the proper disposition on the part of the recipient, the sacrament of anointing has the power of canceling the total debt of punishment and thus preparing the soul for immediate entrance into heaven. This understanding of anointing as a sacrament of the dying and its corresponding purpose of an anointing into glory has been particularly influential among German systematic theologians.[3] The present discipline of the Code of Canon Law would also seem to support this interpretation.[4]

On the other hand, in recent years there has been a growing consensus that anointing is a sacrament of healing, a sacrament of the sick. The sacrament *per se* of the dying is viaticum. This approach finds itself on a firmer foundation exegetically (Jm 5:14-15); liturgically (texts for blessing the oil and the anointing itself); historically (experience of the first eight hundred years in the West); ecumenically (the practice of the Eastern and Anglican churches); and pastorally (fear and terror of the sacrament).[5]

The debate at the Second Vatican Council between two conflicting theologies of unction and the resulting compromise provides the necessary introductory background for this paper. We shall first of all trace the liturgical tradition of anointing of the sick. While our concentration will be on the tradition of the Western Church in a Roman Catholic perspective, we shall also consider the practice of the Eastern Church and the Anglican Communion. Secondly, we shall briefly outline the elements that should go into a theology of healing. It is not enough to simply state that unction is a sacrament for the sick: we must situate the liturgical rites for the sick—communion, penance, anointing and the laying on of hands—within the wider ministry of the church to sick people. Thirdly, we shall examine the Roman Catholic liturgical revision: the Rite of Anointing and Pastoral Care of the Sick.

I. The Liturgical Tradition of Anointing

Any treatment of the liturgical tradition of anointing should begin with the New Testament evidence for this rite. There are two such indications: the apostolic ministry of healing (Mk 6:13) and the presbyteral rite of healing (Jm 5:14-15).

The text in Mark reads: "So (the Twelve) set off to preach repentance; and they cast out many devils, and anointed many sick people with oil and cured them."[6] This action of anointing appears to have been a Palestinian custom of a medicinal-exorcistic nature taken over by the followers of Jesus. In this anointing with oil the church sees the prefigurement of the sacramental anointing of the sick.[7]

The more important New Testament evidence is found in the Epistle of James.[8] Beginning with 5:13, the unifying theme of prayer is applied to three existential situations of a Christian. The suffering Christian is to pray. The cheerful Christian is to praise God. "If one of you is ill, he should send for the elders of the church and they must anoint him with oil in the name of the Lord and pray over him. The prayer of faith will save the sick man and the Lord will raise him up again; and if he has committed any sins, he will be forgiven."

"If one of you is ill . . ." The Greek *asthenei* does not connote a grave illness. While the illness is perhaps a bodily affliction, its treatment in the Jewish mind would not be merely medicinal but exorcistic as well. James is unaware of the distinction between sin and sickness as we know it. He would also be unwilling to distinguish between body and soul. The subject of the anointing is a concrete sick person; the goal of anointing is restoration: both bodily and spiritual.

"He should send for the elders of the church . . ." The elders, the presbyters, are men of official authority in the local church. Hence their ministration is not a sheerly charismatic one.

"And they must anoint him with oil in the name of the Lord and pray over him." Here is an allusion to the liturgical action of the sacrament, the anointing with oil, and the liturgical word, the prayer of the presbyters. The fact that the anointing is done in the name of the Lord would seem to indicate more than a medicinal remedy. As in Mark 6:13, it symbolizes the healing presence and power of the risen Lord.

"The prayer of faith will save the sick man and the Lord will raise him up again." The prayer of faith: once again, not simply a medicinal remedy. The Greek verbs in the future tense, *sosei* (save) and *egerei* (raise up), should not be interpreted in an eschatological or spiritualistic sense, e.g., future resurrection of the dead, but rather the sick person will be "saved" from death and "raised up" to life and health.

"And if he has committed any sins, he will be forgiven." Is this a conditional effect of the sacrament or, as some commentators feel, does the forgiveness of sins have reference to a primitive penitential practice? In any case, we see once again the close interrelationship between bodily and spiritual sickness, almost as if anticipating the findings of psychosomatic medicine.

To sum up, the Epistle of James refers to an action to be performed by the ministers of the church (presbyters) for the benefit of sick Christians. The rite consists of the prayer of faith and the anointing with oil. The aim of this ministration is not simply eschatological or spiritual, for this does not correspond to the context—namely, a sick, not a dying Christian. Neither does James envision merely a bodily-medicinal result. Rather the effects of anointing touch the religious situation of the sick person: the threat to his salvation posed by religious powerlessness and weakness of soul, as well as the temptation and burden to his faith and trust. The sick person shall be raised up from this weakness and saved from the threat that sickness constitutes to his salvation.

How was the teaching of James observed in the early history of the church? Although our sources are meager, we have every reason to believe that for the first eight centuries anointing was practiced as a rite for sick people.

The most comprehensive study of the early history of anointing has been compiled by Antoine Chavasse. In a published dissertation not readily available, the French scholar treats the anointing of the sick in the Latin Church from the third century until the Carolingian Reform in the ninth. His sources are liturgical texts; the Fathers, most notably Pope Innocent I (†417), Caesarius of Arles (†543) and Venerable Bede (†735); and hagiographical accounts.[9]

Chavasse makes some rather startling conclusions. In the early history of anointing the important thing was that the oil for the sick be blessed. A primordial importance was attached to the epicletic blessing of the oil whereby the oil was imbued with a divine efficacy placing it in the category of a *sacramentum* (Innocent I). The application of the oil was secondary, simply providing an occasion to use the blessed oil already intrinsically efficacious by virtue of the blessing. While the blessing of the oil was strictly reserved to representatives of the sacerdotal hierarchy, usually bishops, the application of the oil could be made by presbyters and lay people alike.

If the use of fixed formulas in the Latin Church for blessing the oil is very ancient (Hippolytus, Gelasian and Gregorian sacramentaries), a different situation obtains as regards the application of the oil. Only the blessing of oil was liturgically organized before the middle of the eighth century. Diverse procedures were followed for the application of the oil: usually the oil was applied externally to an ailing member of the body (*ungere, tangere*); sometimes the oil was even taken internally (Roman formula *Emitte: gustanti, permanens in visceribus nostris*). Sometimes also the imposition of hands or a prayer accompanied the anointing.

The majority of texts stress the bodily effects of unction. Of the thirteen forms of blessing, for example, the five oldest mention no spiritual effect *per se*, three speak of a spiritual effect, the five most recent refer to the pardon of sins. But rather than speaking of bodily and spiritual effects, perhaps a sounder approach would be to say that the rite of anointing had to do with the wholeness of the total human person. Before the ninth century we have no indication of anointing ever having been a rite preparatory for death.

The oldest extant full ritual for the actual anointing of the sick is thought to be a Carolingian compilation from Roman, Gallican and Mozarabic sources dating from between 815-845.[10] A few brief observations on this ancient order for anointing will help re-enforce the understanding of unction as a sacrament of the sick during the first eight hundred years of its existence. The rite, which takes place in the sick person's home, envisions a community service: a number of presbyters, a choir to sing the antiphons, the family and friends. At one point the sick person is directed to kneel down, a prescription hardly possible if he were *in extremis*. The anointing may conveniently take place where the pain is most pronounced. The service, together with communion of the sick, is to be repeated for seven days.

But it was also during this very same Carolingian renaissance that we detect a development which, first in pastoral practice and later in theological reflection, will ultimately transform anointing from a rite for the sick into a sacrament for the dying. Reform councils held during this period stress both a revival of priestly ministry and the abandonment of the practice of lay anointing. Hence while lay anointing is being discontinued, priestly anointing begins to take on a more organized shape and is integrated liturgically with existing priestly functions, such as the administration of viaticum and the deathbed reconciliation of penitents.

Chavasse, in the second unpublished part of his thesis, outlines this development.[11] By the year 800, the practice of deathbed penance is widespread and of course administered only by presbyters. With the Carolingian emphasis on priestly ministry and the disappearance of lay anointing, the practice of anointing the sick exclusively by priests becomes liturgically organized. The presbyteral act of anointing now begins to be performed at the same time as the already established rites of deathbed penance. Thus the two key factors in the transition of the practice of anointing in the ninth century were the emergence of an organized ritual for anointing and the association of the anointing rite with deathbed reconciliation.

As a result of this change in pastoral practice, anointing in the middle ages came to be marked by the two characteristics which color the sacrament to this very day: a spiritualizing tendency, the remission of sins as a principal benefit (here the effects of deathbed penance and anointing have been confused); and a sacrament of the dying, a characteristic which evolved from the unfortunate association of the sacrament with deathbed penance and viaticum. By the twelfth century the original order of administration—penance, anointing, viaticum—had been altered to penance, viaticum, anointing.

It is easy to see how this gradual change in pastoral practice and liturgy beginning in the eighth and ninth centuries, led to a change in theological reflection on anointing during the scholastic period. The scholastic doctors are simply commenting on the practice of anointing in their age. The patristic and liturgical documents of the earlier period are largely neglected for they are seldom if ever cited. Although the early scholastic period preserved a tradition of anointing as a sacrament for the sick, the scholastic doctors of the thirteenth century view unction as a preparation for the glory of the beatific vision as a point of departure for determining the principal effect of the sacrament—be this the forgiveness of venial sins (Bonaventure, Scotus and the Franciscan school), or the remission of the remnants of sin (Albert the Great, Thomas Aquinas and the Dominican school).[12]

The deliberations of the scholastic doctors were especially influenced by the development of a systematic theology of the sacraments. How could a physical effect, the recovery of health, be an effect of a sacrament? Sacraments are means of grace, a supernatural perfection of man. Furthermore, if the sacraments always produce their effect *ex opere operato* in a disposed subject, how could the recovery of health—a result seldom realized—be the effect of anointing? These difficulties are resolved by concluding that remission of sins is the principal effect of anointing. Since the sacraments of baptism and penance already serve this purpose, it was logical to regard unction as destined for the removal of sin's last remnants, to delay its reception until the last moments of life, and to consider it as "extreme unction."

In view of the change in pastoral practice in the eighth and ninth centuries and the subsequent scholastic reflection upon anointing as a sacrament of the dying, it is noteworthy that the Council of Trent refused to canonize this approach. The council was primarily interested in reasserting the proper sacramentality of unction as one of the seven sacraments. We have at least three indications that the council fathers wished to avoid a definition of anointing as a sacrament exclusively for the dying. For example, the original draft on extreme unction stated that the sacrament is to be administered "only (*dumtaxat*) to those who are in their final struggle and have come to grips with death and are about to go forth to the Lord." The final wording was amended to read: "This anointing is to be used for the sick, but especially (*praesertim*) for those who are dangerously ill as to seem at the point of departing this life."[13] Furthermore, the canons of Trent say nothing specific about the function of anointing as a sacrament of the dying or the degree of sickness: three times the term *infirmi* is used to describe the subject of the anointing.[14] Finally, the benefits of anointing are described as the strengthening of the entire human person in time of sickness through the grace of the Holy Spirit with resulting spiritual, psychological and physical effects.[15]

What is the teaching and practice of the other Christian communities of the West as regards anointing? John Calvin in his *Institutes* rejected the sacrament as belonging to the charismatic gifts of healing of apostolic times and no longer applicable today.[16] While Martin Luther declined to sanction unction as a sacrament instituted by Christ, he nonetheless did not condemn the practice.[17] Today in both the Lutheran and Reformed Churches there is a movement in some circles advocating a restoration of anointing of the sick.[18]

The most remarkable development has taken place within the Anglican Communion.[19] The First Book of Common Prayer of 1549 retained an order for anointing in its office of visitation of the sick. Although the rite of anointing the sick was deleted in the 1552 Prayer Book, there have been reform movements of a high church persuasion in the eighteenth and nineteenth centuries advocating the revival of anointing. Today, under the auspices of an active healing ministry, anointing of the sick, together with the laying on of hands, is practiced in most of the member churches of the Anglican Communion. The new Book of Common Prayer for the American Episcopal Church provides a "Ministration to the Sick" consisting of three parts: Pt. I Ministry of the Word, Pt. II Laying on of Hands and Anointing, Pt. III Holy Communion. The order for anointing contains a form for blessing the oil by a bishop or priest. In case of necessity a deacon or lay person, using oil blessed by a bishop or priest, may perform the anointing.

Our survey of the liturgical history of anointing would be very incomplete if no mention were made of the tradition of the Eastern Church. The earliest extant liturgical source is the Egyptian Sacramentary of Serapion (c. 350), in which the two forms for the blessing of oil speak of a "healing medicine" and "medicine of complete soundness."[20] The Eastern tradition of anointing is most authoritatively expressed in the service for anointing in the Greek Euchologion.[21] The service is a public ceremony, when possible performed by seven priests, at least one deacon, together with a choir and a representative congregation. The oil is blessed by the ministering priests in the presence of the sick man. All persons seriously ill may be anointed; the danger of death need not be present. The rite may also be repeated. The service for anointing, called the "oil of prayer" (*euchelaion*), stresses physical and mental healing, but even more the spiritual benefits, especially the remission of sins. Besides serving as the ritual book for the Eastern Orthodox, the Euchologion has also been a model for the Armenian, Syrian and Coptic offices, although these today have largely fallen into desuetude.

II. Toward a Theology of Healing

We have seen that recent research into the liturgical tradition of anointing has uncovered its strong claim to be a sacrament for the sick, and not necessarily for the dying. There is, however, a notable dearth of serious scholarship on the theology of unction as a sacrament of the sick.[22] I would suggest that the problem is one of Christian anthropology, as well as the need for placing anointing within the context of the ministry of Jesus Christ to the sick as continued in his church. The confines of this paper will allow only a brief sketch of the possible approaches.

Let us begin with anthropological considerations. Christian thought still labors under an unconscious dualism: a kind of discarnate spiritualism. For example, we speak of bodily and spiritual effects of anointing, as if the human composite could be divided into two distinct parts. A far better approach would be to follow the lead of biblical thought in viewing the human person as an animated body, or as the contemporary anthropology of Karl Rahner would put it, a spirit in the world. If in the first eight hundred years of anointing physical healing was at times overplayed, and if the scholastic period could recognize only the spiritual effects of the sacrament, today we need a theology of healing which includes anointing and regards the sacrament as affecting the whole person.

A further anthropological reflection would be to explore the relationship between sin and sickness. As we saw, the Epistle of James seems to make no great distinction between human sickness and sin. Is this explainable from the primitive state of medicine, or is there a deeper insight we are unwilling to admit? The findings of psychosomatic medicine could be very helpful in this regard. In earlier days the English word ''health'' could be used to denote spiritual, physical or mental soundness, even salvation, e.g., Morning Prayer of Book of Common Prayer: ''We have left undone those things which we ought to have done, and there is no health in us.'' And while the newer theology of original sin is to be welcomed, perhaps we have become so antiseptic as to forget the ramifications of sin upon the total human person, an insight at least preserved in the exaggerated scholastic teaching of preternatural gifts, especially impassibility, freedom from suffering. The relationship between sin and sickness should not be misconstrued in the simplistic sense that personal sin causes illness or that sickness is a vindication of divine providence—a mistake sometimes made in the past. A proper understanding would be to recognize the human person as a historical whole who suffers sickness as a consequence of sin.

Against this background of the human race wounded by sin and in need of healing we can come to appreciate the ministry of Christ to the sick. The healing miracles are eschatological signs of the kingdom: the perfect reign of God which has yet to be fully revealed. The healing miracles, especially in the Gospel of John have a twofold meaning: the healing works are signs of the present offer of eternal life (the eschatological "already"); they are also signs of the ultimate transformation of man at the time of the resurrection of all flesh (the eschatological "not yet"). The paschal mystery of Jesus Christ—his passion, death, resurrection and ascension—confronts us with the curious paradox that the ultimate triumph over evil, sin and sickness is accomplished through suffering itself. The Apostle Paul expresses the Christian's participation in this paschal transformation: "All I want is to know Christ and the power of his resurrection and to share his sufferings by reproducing the pattern of his death. That is the way I can hope to take my place in the resurrection of the dead" (Ph 3:11-12).

We must also be able to identify how Jesus' ministry to the sick is continued in the church. The church's ministry to the sick takes place at three interrelated levels: charitable, charismatic and sacramental. The charitable ministry to the sick finds its model in the good samaritan: the compassion a Christian should have toward his suffering brother. Christ identifies himself with the sick: "I was sick and you visited me" (Mt 25:36). In our day this charitable ministry to the sick is continued by those who care for the sick in hospitals, at home or in the local parish.

There is also a charismatic ministry to the sick. Considerable evidence points to a flourishing charismatic ministry in the early church.[23] In our day this particular ministry is still manifested in the lives of saints, e.g., miracles in canonization proceedings, pilgrimage shrines of saints. Reports on the current healing activities of pentecostal groups enrich our understanding of this charismatic ministry.[24]

The sacramental ministry should be the liturgical expression of an overall concern of the church for the sick. This ministry is celebrated in the sacraments of the eucharist, penance, anointing of the sick and the action of the laying on of hands.

The eucharist as action is the representation of the healing power of the paschal mystery. The eucharist as sacrament, communion, is a healing sacrament, the pledge of the ultimate resurrection of the whole person: "Anyone who does eat my flesh and drink my blood has eternal life, and I shall raise him up on the last day" (Jn 6:54). The texts for communion in the eucharistic liturgy display a similar understanding: "Lord, Jesus Christ, with faith in your love and mercy I eat your body and drink your blood. Let it not bring me condemnation, but health in mind and body." "Lord, I am not worthy to receive you, but only say the word and I shall be healed." The restoration of the permanent diaconate and the institution of eucharistic ministers have greatly facilitated a more frequent and regular communion of the sick and elderly. It is good to recall, as do recent Roman documents, that the primary and original reason of eucharistic reservation is for purposes of viaticum and communicating the sick.

Since at times too great a penitential character has been assigned to anointing, it is good to reassert that penance is the healing sacrament directed toward the forgiveness of sins. We have seen before that there is some obscure relationship between sin and sickness, both of which are manifestations of evil in the world.

The sacrament of anointing will be considered further when we come to the provisional rites for the sick. In reflecting upon the sacramental ministry to the sick, however, some mention should be made of the gesture of the laying on of hands. The imposition of hands is the healing action par excellence in the New Testament. The laying on of hands is today performed at baptism, confirmation, penance and ordination. In ministering to the sick the laying on of hands may be done either formally within the context of a liturgical service, as foreseen by the Anglican and revised Roman rites, or informally, in the course of a pastoral visitation. This gesture should tangibly express the love and concern of a healing community.

We must especially recognize the important ecclesial dimension of all the sacraments for the sick. The eucharist is the sacrament of unity, hence the forceful significance of home masses with the family and friends, representatives of the local church, or communion brought to the sick from a parish mass. The sacrament of penance effects not only reconciliation with God, but also with the church. The Vatican Constitution on the Church teaches this reciprocal communal relationship of receiving and giving in the sacrament of anointing: "By the sacred anointing of the sick and the prayer of her priests, the whole Church commends those who are ill to the suffering and glorified Lord, asking that he may lighten their suffering and save them (Cf. Jm 5:14-16). She exhorts them, moreover, to contribute to the welfare of the whole People of God by associating themselves freely with the passion and death of Christ."[25]

All the sacraments for the sick are not only actions of Christ, but also acts of the church, the primordial or fundamental sacrament of the saving grace of Christ. The church is most church when it actively engages itself in the salvation of its members, in this case the sick and the afflicted.[26]

III. The Revised Rites for the Sick and the Dying[27]

The Latin text for the *Rite of Anointing and Pastoral Care of the Sick* was published by decree of the Congregation for Divine Worship, dated Dec. 7, 1972. This model ritual for the Latin Church is to be translated into the vernacular and adapted to local needs by the national episcopal conferences so as to be universally implemented by Jan. 1, 1974. The revision follows the terms of references given in the Vatican Council II *Constitution on the Sacred Liturgy* (73-75) with a resulting updated liturgy in the context of a treatise on the pastoral ministry to the sick.

Sacrament of the Sick. The title and order of chapters in the new *Rite* underscore anointing as a Sacrament of the sick. The misleading and ambiguous terms "extreme unction" and "last rites" have been avoided. The order of chapters reveals that the emphasis is on the normal ministry to the sick, beginning with the pastoral theological introduction, chapter 1 "Visitation and Communion of the Sick," and chapter 2 "Rite of Anointing a Sick Person." Later chapters treat of more urgent cases when the sick Christian may actually be dying: "Viaticum" (ch. 3), which now emerges more clearly as a Sacrament for the dying; "Rite of the Sacraments for Those near Death" (ch. 4), which includes the continuous rites of Penance, the apostolic blessing, anointing, and Viaticum. Two additions to the earlier provisional rites which had been briefly experimented with are "Confirmation of a Person in Danger of Death" (ch. 5) and the "Rites for the Commendation of the Dying" (ch. 6), which has been enriched by newer pastoral insights into ministering to the needs of dying patients. Chapter 7 consists of scriptural and other texts for use in ministering to the sick.

The most important single change is stated in the accompanying Apostolic Constitution, *Sacram Unctionem,* where Paul VI determines the essential rite of the Sacrament: the liturgical action (matter) and liturgical prayer (form). "The Sacrament of anointing of the sick is administered to those who are dangerously ill by anointing them on the forehead and hands with blessed olive oil or, according to the circumstances, with another plant oil and saying once only these words: 'Through this holy anointing may the Lord in his love and mercy help you with the grace of the Holy Spirit. R. Amen. May the Lord who frees you from sin save you and raise you up. R. Amen.' "

A major breakthrough is the omission of the danger of death as a condition for the reception of anointing. In accordance with the teaching of Jm 5:14-16, Christians seriously ill (*periculose aegrotans*) from sickness or old age are the proper recipients of the Sacrament (8). The anointing may be repeated in the course of the same illness as the sick person's condition becomes progressively more critical (9). When called to attend a sick person who is already dead, the priest is to pray for the dead person; he may administer the Sacrament conditionally only when doubtful if the sick person is actually dead (15).

Pastoral Ministry to the Sick. The opening paragraphs of the *Rite* speak of human sickness and its meaning in the mystery of salvation (1-4). We are urged to struggle against sickness and disease in the name of Christ, yet at the same time be mindful that the ultimate triumph over sickness and evil is achieved by our participation in the paschal mystery of the crucified and risen Lord.

The offices and ministries for the sick are placed in the widest possible perspective (32-37): all men and women who in any way serve the sick, all baptized Christians, the family and friends, and the priest who remains the proper minister of the Sacrament. The visitation of the sick is incumbent not only upon priests, but upon the entire Christian community (42-45). No fixed ritual for visiting the sick is provided; the reading of scripture and common prayer is encouraged.

The pastoral ministry to the sick, which is the ecclesial context for all of the sacramental ministrations on behalf of the sick, is further reflected in a movement away from the earlier normative private anointings to a communal service with a more proper liturgical setting involving the sick person's family and friends. There is also the possibility for communal celebrations in which several sick persons may be anointed at the same time. Such group anointings may be celebrated within Mass after the liturgy of the word, as a distinct rite, or in a Communion service.

Provision is also made for some measure of concelebration of the anointing by the priests in attendance (19).

Sacrament of Faith. "The celebration of this sacrament consists especially in the laying on of hands by the presbyters of the Church, their offering the prayer of faith, and the anointing of the sick with oil made holy by God's blessing. This rite signifies the grace of the sacrament and confers it" (5). This celebration in faith demands the earliest possible administration at the beginning of a serious illness. Priests are constantly to exhort the faithful, both publicly and privately, to request the Sacrament on their own initiative rather than to defer it. They are to explain the meaning of the Sacrament to the sick and their families so as to dispose and prepare them for its fruitful reception. This preparation normally includes some degree of liturgical planning, such as the selection of readings and prayers and, when feasiable, music. A massive catechetical effort is needed to dispel earlier misunderstandings about this Sacrament which brings strength and comfort to the sick.[28]

Footnotes

1. *Acta Synodalia S. Concilii: Oecumenici Vaticani II*, I, pars II (Vatican City: Typis Polyglottis Vaticanis 1970) 285.
2. *The Documents of Vatican II*, ed. Walter M. Abbott (New York: America Press 1966) 161. *See* also articles 74, 75.
3. Josephus Kern, *De sacramento extremae unctionis tractatus dogmaticus* (Regensburg 1907). Michael Schmaus, *Katholische Dogmatik* IV/I (Munich, 6th rev. ed. 1964) 695-725. A. Grillmeier, "Das Sakrament der Auferstehung. Versuch einer Sinndeutung der letzten Olung," in *Geist und Leben* 34 (1961) 326-336.
4. *Codex Juris Canonici*, Canons 937-947.
5. Bernard Botte, "L'onction des malades," in *La Maison Dieu* 15 (1948) 91-107. Paul F. Palmer, "The Purpose of Anointing the Sick: A Reappraisal," in *Theological Studies* 19 (1958) 309-344. The most recent monographs are Adolf Knauber, *Pastoral Theology of the Anointing of the Sick*, trans. by Matthew J. O'Connell from *Handbuch der Pastoraltheologie*, Bd. IV, Ch. 7. (Collegeville: Liturgical Press 1975). Mario Alberton, *Un sacrement pour les malades* dans le contexte actuel de la santé (Paris: Editions du Centurion, 1978). Claude Ortemann, *Le sacrement des malades* (Paris: Éditions du Chalet 1971). Bernard Sesboué, *L'onction des malades* (Lyon: Profac, 1972).
6. Scriptural passages cited are from *The Jerusalem Bible* (Garden City: Doubleday 1966).

7. Session XIV (1551) of the Council of Trent referred to the sacrament as "a Christo Domino institutum (cf. Mk 6:13) et a beato Jacobo Apostolo promulgatum (Jas 5:14)." *See* Denzinger-Schönmetzer (DS) 1716.

8. *See* Franz Mussner, *Der Jakobusbrief,* Herders Theologischer Kommentar zum Neuen Testament XIII/I (Freiburg: Herder 1964) 218-229. Kevin Condon, "The Sacrament of Healing," in *Scripture* 14 (1959) 33-42. Thomas W. Leahy, "The Epistle of James," in *The Jerome Biblical Commentary* (Englewood Cliffs: Prentice-Hall 1968) II, 376-377.

9. Antoine Chavasse, *Étude sur l'onction des infirmes dans l'église latine du IIIe au XIe siecle.* Vol I: *Au IIIe siecle a la reforme calolingienne* (Lyons 1942). The following are the author's conclusions found on pp. 163-202.

10. *See* Migne, *Patrologia Latina* 78, 231-236. This service has been researched by H.B. Porter, "The Origin of the Medieval Rite for Anointing the Sick or Dying," in *Journal of Theological Studies* 7 (1965) 211-225. Chavasse has further classified the medieval services for anointing into three types. The Carolingian service is an example of Type I. The present anointing rite in the Roman Ritual of 1614 is derived from Type III, a Benedictine version from Cluny, popularized by the Franciscans and introduced into the Roman Pontifical of the thirteenth century. *See* Antoine Chavasse, "Prieres pour les malades et onction sacramentelle," *L'Église en Priere,* ed. A.G. Martimort (Paris: Desclee, 3rd rev. ed. 1965) 596-612.

11. The insights of Chavasse's unpublished second volume are available to us through Placid Murray, "The Liturgical History of Extreme Unction," *The Furrow* II (1960) 572-593.

12. Palmer traces this development, 325-336.

13. André Duval, "L'Extreme-Onction au Concile de Trente. Sacrement des mourants ou sacrement des malades," in *La Maison-Dieu* 101 (1970) 127-172, esp. 171-172. *See* also DS 1698.

14. DS 1717, 1719.

15. DS 1696.

16. *Joannis Calvini Opera Selecta,* eds. Peter Barth and Wm. Niesel, V (Munich: Chr. Kaiser, 2nd rev. ed. 1962) 452-455.

17. *De captivitate Babylonica ecclesiae praeludium, D. Martin Luthers Werke, Kritische Gesamtausgabe* VI (Weimar 1888) 567-571.

18. For the Lutheran approach *see* Heinz Doebert, *Das Charisma der Krankenheilung, Eine biblisch-theologische Untersuchung über eine vergessene Grundfunktion der Kirche* (Hamburg: Furche Verlag 1960). The movement in the Reformed Church is described by Bernard Martin, *The Healing Ministry in the Church* (London: Lutterworth 1960).

19. Charles W. Gusmer, *The Ministry of Healing in the Church of England: An Ecumenical-liturgical Study* (London, Alcuin 1974). *Idem,* "Anointing of the Sick in the Church of England," *Worship* 45 (1971) 262-272.

20. F.X. Funk, ed., *Didascalia et Constitutiones apostolorum* (Paderborn: 1905; reprinted, Turin 1964) II, 180, 192.

21. Jacobus Goar, ed., *Euchologion sive Rituale Graecorum* (Venice, 2nd ed. 1730) 322-357. *See* also Theophilus Spacil, *Doctrina Theologiae orientis separati de sacra infirmorum unctione," in Orientalia Christiana* 24 (1931) 45-259.

22. Besides Knauber and the authors listed in note 5, the most recent serious attempt has been David Power, "Let the Sick Man Call," *The Heythrop Journal* 14, No. 3 (July 1978) 256-270. Good encyclopedia entries are M. Fraeymann, "Krankensalbung," in *Lexikon für Theologie und Kirche* VI (Freiburg: Herder 1961) 586-591; and J.P.

McClain, "Anointing of the Sick," *New Catholic Encyclopedia* I (New York: McGraw-Hill 1967) 468-577.

23. Evelyn Frost, *Christian Healing* (London: Mowbray 1954).

24. René Laurentin, *Catholic Pentecostalism*, trans. by Matthew J. O'Connell (New York: Doubleday 1977) 100-131 gives a superb account of healing experiences. The most comprehensive popular studies are by Francis MacNutt, *Healing* (Notre Dame: Ave Maria 1977) and *Idem., The Power to Heal* (Notre Dame: Ave Maria 1977). Charles W. Gusmer, "I Was Sick and You Visited Me: The Revised Rites for the Sick," *Worship* 48 (November 1974) 516-525. Much more serious scholarship is still needed in order to discern and distinguish this relationship.

25. *Lumen Gentium* II, Abbott, p. 28.

26. Karl Rahner, *The Church and the Sacraments*, tran. W. J. O'Hara (New York: Herder 1963).

27. The following is taken largely from C.W. Gusmer, "Anointing of the Sick, Liturgy of," *New Catholic Encyclopedia* vol. XVI, Good commentaries are also found in P.M. Gy, "Le Nouveau Rituel Romain des Malades," *Maison Dieu* 113 (1973) 29-49; *Ephemerides Liturgicae* vol. LXXXIX (1975) Fasc. V-VI; Manfred Probst and Klemens Richter (eds.), *Heilssorge für die Kranken* (Freiburg: Herder, 1975). *See also La Maladie et la Mort du Chretien dans la Liturgie*. Conferences Saint-Serge XXIe Semaine d'Etudes Liturgiques (Rome: Edizioni Liturgiche 1975). The writer of this article is at work on a volume on this subject for the series of Pueblo Publishing Co. entitled Studies in the Reformed Rites of the Catholic Church.

28. After the initial experience of the revised rites for the sick and dying in the provisional ("Green Book") stage, the International Commission on English in the Liturgy is moving towards a more definitive textual edition. It is expected that the finalized version will make a clearer distinction between the rites for those who are sick and rites for those who are dying. More attention will be paid to the hospital ministry. The rite will be enriched with pastoral introductions giving practical guidelines for good preparation and celebration of the sacraments as well as adaptation to special situations such as sick children and blessing the body of the deceased when anointing is no longer called for.

HEALING: SACRAMENT OR CHARISM?

Thomas Talley*

Number 6 of the Introduction to the new Roman Catholic draft revision of the Rites for the Sick, in speaking of the effects of the sacrament of anointing, sets before us the concern of this essay. "The proper grace of this sacrament gives strength to the sick person. This grace endows him with God-given peace of soul to bear his suffering. It also effects the forgiveness of his sins, if this is necessary. And, if God so wills, the sacramental anointing can even effect a total restoration of physical health."[1]

The last mentioned effect, "a total restoration of physical health," reflects a significant shift of nuance from the parallel statement of Trent. While the first schema of that council's decree on the sacrament of extreme unction would have limited the administration of the anointing "only to those who are in their final struggle and who have come to grips with death and who are about to go forth to the Lord"[2] chapter 2 of the final version says of the effects of the anointing:

"This reality is the grace of the Holy Spirit, whose anointing wipes away sins, provided there are still some to be expiated, as well as the remnants of sin, and comforts and strengthens the soul of the sick person, by arousing in him great confidence in the divine mercy; encouraged thereby, the sick person bears more easily the difficulties and trials of his illness, and resists more readily the temptations of the demon *who lies in wait for the heel* (Gn 3:15), and where it is expedient for the health of the

---

*(cf. editor's note on p. 251)

soul, he receives, at times, health and body.''[3] Here, the gift of bodily health is looked upon as ancillary to the good of the soul, while the more recent statement seems to suggest that the total restoration of physical health is a more ultimate good toward which the other effects of the sacrament tend.

In both statements, however, it is clear that physical healing remains a matter of some uncertainty. This may be forthcoming if God so wills it, but the sacrament itself gives no assurance that this will be the outcome. In such a case, then, one may well wonder in what sense physical healing can be considered an *effect* of the sacrament. If healing occurs, is such a restoration of bodily health a proper consequence of the sacrament, or has the will of God responded to some well-intentioned but nonsacramental prayer of the patient or the intercession of the church, or has God even willed the restoration of health without reference to any of these things? Or again, to consider all the possibilities, does the will of God at times operate within and through certain of the arcane procedures of the American Medical Association?

The point of all such haggling is not merely to play footsie with the Tridentine anathemas, but to pose the more serious question of the propriety of the cause/effect model in the theological articulation of the sacraments, a habit of medieval theological method which is thrown into high relief by this question, a habit which reduces the many-layered and richly textured liturgical experience of the church to a moment narrowly defined as the production of an effect in the recipient. This effect is usually cast up in terms which defy empirical verification, but the case before us first suggests it to be a verifiable effect and then seeks to weasel out on that by acknowledging that we are here before the incomprehensible mystery of the divine will, while continuing to assert that one of the possible outcomes, should it occur, will also be an effect of the sacrament. And what is left to one side is serious address to the liturgical phenomenon itself, to its sociological and psychological dimensions, its relation to the whole sacramental economy, to a theology of the liturgy in general, to ecclesiology, to soteriology, to eschatology, and to theology.

That such a diatribe as this is unfair does not amount to saying that it is whipping a dead horse. Probably no sacramental theology has ever been quite so narrow as the above critique would suggest, but it remains true that as consideration of the sacrament of anointing has sought to treat that rite as something more than a final perfection of penance *in extremis* there has come an increasing blurring of the distinction between the church's liturgical address to affliction and the charism of thaumaturgy, the effecting of miraculous cures, and with that blurring of distinction, a serious confusion regarding the whole nature of sacramental realities. Just as we have learned once again to discern the profound ecclesiological dimensions of baptism and eucharist, as we have passed beyond limiting baptism to removal of the guilt of original sin and can see eucharist as a bit more than a dole of divinity to a dissociated communicant, we seem, in the case of the anointing of the sick, to be driven further toward a preoccupation with the effect on the individual recipient, a preoccupation which is all the more problematic when emphasis falls on restoration of bodily health, for that brings to a situation already laden with anxiety a well-nigh inescapable tendency to administer the rite and then stand back and see if it is going to work.

Even allowing for wide variation in the quality of rites and the manner of their celebration, we need to remind ourselves that sacraments always "work," and that therefore what is claimed for them must be articulated within that certainty. That is to say, sacramental and liturgical realities are always and only that, and we do the theology of the liturgy no service by extravagant claims of extrinsic effects. Too many communities have already been brought to despair by the discovery that, having rearranged the furniture of the sanctuary and instituted an offertory procession, they still don't love one another. And, while one is ashamed to say it, there are those who have been told that sacraments and prayer in true faith would remove a malignant tumor, and so have learned from its continued growth the insufficiency of their faith, and have died in despair. And this because liturgy was confounded with charism.

The claims for healing in the Roman Catholic documents cited are mild indeed, but one can detect the beginning of a trend toward a preoccupation with physical healing such as has grown very rapidly in the Anglican Communion without the benefit of serious theological criticism, and has begun to assert that sickness and suffering are unqualifiedly contrary to the will of God. One does not need to go deeply into a Teilhardian view of the interrelation of life and death, of growth and decay, to suspect that such an oversimplification of the divine will as will set God always on the side of good health—that keystone of bourgeois beatitude—falls tragically short of an adequate understanding of the paschal mystery or perception of the strangeness of our salvation. The passion of Christ, his agony and death, was not a divine *lapsus* nor was it a defeat of his holy will. Rather, the holiness of his will, the utter otherness of his will, is revealed in that agony and bloody sweat, that cross and passion, that precious death and burial, as much as by his mighty resurrection and glorious ascension.

On the other hand, we must never lose sight of the mystery, indeed the miracle, of healing. The body's thrust to life, its struggle against disease and decay, is indeed an expression of the primacy of life and its ultimate victory over death, a victory archetypically achieved in the resurrection of the Lord. Thus all healing can be seen as an act of God, in that no therapeutic measure can have its effect apart from the dynamism of life itself. The practice of medicine is a dialogue with the life processes, not the simple manipulation of an inert material. And at the root of this life process there still resides the profound regenerative mystery which sustains the patient and the physician as well in humility and hope. There is no healing that is not an act of God.

Such a broad theological principle, however, does not speak really to the concern of those most interested in spiritual healing, in my experience. What is seen as important from the charismatic point of view is not merely the primary causality of God in every aspect of life or of existence, but the significant occasion in which healing seems totally out of proportion to the therapeutic measures undertaken or any reasonable hope for their success. Here there seems to be evidence of a special divine intervention at the level of secondary causality, a divine action not merely fundamental and prior to, but alongside and in addition to the natural recuperative powers of the body and the potency of the therapeutic processes employed.

It is presently irrelevant that such divine intervention is most evident to those possessed of faith or disposed to it, since the question before us is not an apologetic one. Nor is it to the point that Christians, including theologians, find themselves variously impressed (or unimpressed) by such phenomena. What is more to the point is that such intervention is not covenanted, nor is it patient of liturgical institutionalization. It is, by the nature of the case under consideration, the exception to every pattern, truly a wonder, a miracle. The perception of such intervention points to the radical contingency of human life and understanding before the transcendent freedom of God, and the phenomenon is for that reason various in its manifestation and in its attendant circumstances. So Calvin, writing against the sacrament of anointing, will argue that contrary to the claims made for biblical warrant, Christ himself heals in one instance by making clay of spittle and anointing the blind man, in another by a touch, in other instances by no action at all. He argues with equal vigor, though with considerably less force, that the age of such miracles is over, and that Christians should not presume to such apostolic power.[4]

The fact would seem to be that Christians have claimed to exercise such healing power in most ages of the church, though the fashion in such charisms has been inconstant. Still, there can be no question of the claim to the charism of healing well past the apostolic age. The thaumaturge is certainly no stranger to Christian hagiography. What is to the point, it would seem, is that he is a stranger to the liturgical tradition. While the Apostolic Tradition of Hippolytus, for example, does provide for the episcopal blessing of oil to be used by the faithful in illness, it further denies the appropriateness of ordination of those who claim the gift of healing, observing that their actions themselves will speak for them.[5] The distinction would seem an important one. In holy orders, as in baptism and confirmation, the church confers roles within the community of faith, stations within the liturgical assembly; and the authorities and prerogatives involved pertain in the first instance to that faith community and its sacramental structures, to its participation in and celebration of the paschal mystery. Charisms such as healing and prophecy, while they may be found in those who are ordained, cannot be restricted to them, nor (for good or ill) can it be shown that any rite of ordination confers them.

Yet, in that text from the Epistle of James (5:14-15) which has served as *grundschrift* for the sacrament of unction, it is precisely the presbyterate that is to be summoned when a Christian falls ill, to anoint him and pray, so that the Lord may raise him up and forgive him his sins. It should be noted that the early church seems to have received a different message from this text than did later generations. Its first use by any Christian writer is its quotation in a discussion of penance by Origen.[6] Oil seems to have been regularly blessed for use by the faithful, as were foodstuffs. Oil would have been the mainstay of the domestic pharmacopoeia, and was blessed as such. But to summon the presbyters of the church to administer it does not seem to have been a concern of the early church at all. Never has such a direct scriptural warrant been so extravagantly ignored, indeed. Our surprise at this might be mitigated somewhat by the observation that this text from James stands alone in suggesting a ritual, sacramental, liturgical role for the presbyterate in the first century. Otherwise, references to the presbyterate can suggest something much more like the administrative and adjudicatory role of the presbyterate in Jewish communities, a role which stood in some contrast to the liturgical roles of the *archesynagogos* and *hazzan* in the synagogue. Certainly, if the function of the presbyters at the sickbed was understood to be sacerdotal, it becomes difficult to understand the vast silence of eight to nine centuries on the subject apart from the questioned text itself.[7] What alternative understanding can be offered? Simply that the sickness or dying of a Christian needs above all to be held within the community, and that the presbyters are summoned as the constitutive representatives of the community, not as *thaumatourgoi* nor even as *sacerdotes*. Their function is not to heal nor is it yet to administer last rites, but to protect the sick member from dereliction and separation from the ecclesial body.

It is this which best takes account of the persistent association of the rite of anointing with penitential themes, it would seem. For sickness and sin go hand in hand as to modalities of disorder. Little has been so wrongheaded in pastoral theology as the reaction against the view that sickness is correlative to sin. When that meant that sickness was sent upon an individual in punishment for some specific wrongdoing on his own part, then certainly a severe reaction was needed. But the particular reaction we have offered, i.e., a simple denial of any connection between the two, amounts to little more than a secularization or profanation of sickness, a denial of its profound spiritual significance. The reason for this was, perhaps, laudable enough. Given our punitive attitude toward sin, it was indeed false and cruel to contribute further to the agonies of the sick. But that punitive attitude to sin was the last thing we were prepared to call into question, and that in turn because we could not see beyond an understanding of sin as the misdeed of an individual. We are learning better now, it would seem. We no longer suppose as glibly as we once did that disorder can be divided into guilty and innocent. Rather, we engage disorder as agents and as patients, and usually as both. In either case, the person in disorder is out of order. There is for him a *de facto* rupture of communion with his society and his cosmos. His place in the world is stripped of its grace, and the body (usually the very locus of creativity and communication) becomes inert and something of a prison. So it is that the sick man feels guilt. Whether at the naïve level of wondering what-have-I-done-to-deserve-this? or in terms of a more sophisticated and existential perspective which will insist that nothing happens without such intention on my part, that I am always an accomplice in my illness, guilty of my affliction, the separation from the world which sickness brings is real separation, real loss of community, and is, at the phenomenal level, a sort of excommunication.

Van den Berg, in *The Psychology of the Sickbed*, has described such an illness, an illness of no great seriousness or danger, which yet, in his description, brings out something of the similarity of the experience of illness and that of guilt. Having described the initial discovery of being sick upon awaking in the morning and determined to stay in bed, he says:

"Then, slowly, but irrevocably, a change, characteristic of the sickbed, establishes itself. I hear the day begin. From downstairs the sounds of household activities penetrate into the bedroom. . . . What I am hearing is the beginning of my daily existence, with this difference, though, that now I have no function in it. In a way I still belong completely to what happens downstairs; I take a share in the noises I hear, but at the same time everything passes me by, everything happens at a great distance. 'Is Daddy ill?' a voice calls out; even at this early moment, it has ceased to consider that I can hear it. 'Yes, Daddy is ill.' A moment later the door opens and they come to say goodbye. They remain just as remote. The distance I measured in the sounds from downstairs appears even greater, if possible, now that they are at my bedside, with their fresh clean faces and lively gestures. Everything about them indicates the normal healthy day, the day of work and play, of street and school. The day outside the house, in which 'outside' has acquired a new special meaning for me, a meaning emphasizing my exclusion. . . .

"The world has shrunk to the size of my bedroom, or rather my bed. For even if I set foot on the floor it seems as if I am entering a *terra incognita*. Going to the bathroom is an unfriendly, slightly unreal, excursion. With the feeling of coming home I pull the blankets over me. . . .

"The horizon in time too is narrowed. The plans of yesterday lose their meaning and their importance; they have hardly any real value. They seem more complicated, more exhausting, more foolish and ambitious than I saw them the day before. All that awaits me becomes tasteless, or even distasteful. The past seems saturated with trivialities. It appears to me that I hardly ever tackled my real tasks. Future and past lose their outlines; I withdraw from both and I live in the confined present of this bed which guards me against the things that were and those that will be.... The present, while always serving the future, and therefore often being an effect of the past, becomes saturated with itself. As a patient I live with a useless body in a disconnected present.''[8]

It is to such a sense of separation in the patient of disorder that the rite of anointing is addressed, just as the rite of penance is addressed to the like separation of the agent of disorder. And, as the object of the rite of penance is restoration to the body through a *metanoia* whose dynamic is baptismal and paschal, so the object of the rite of anointing can be understood as renewal of the baptismal anointing by which each of us is *christos* so that the suffering and separation of sickness become identified as participation in the *pascha Christi*. By such anointing, *anamnesis* is made of the passage of Christ through death to life and of the patient's consecration to that mystery. By such anointing, further, the suffering of the illness is oriented to a reopened future, a sense of movement in Christ through the present passion toward the kingdom. Sickness becomes a work, a work of learning in act that for those who are his, there is no suffering that is not his. Thus the separation and humiliation of suffering becomes invitation to a *conversio* from which one never returns to his ''former health''—the most regreattable phrase in the liturgies of anointing—but always moves into a deeper realization of life in the resurrection.

In the light of such an understanding of the anointing of affliction, it becomes considerably less important whether we see the sacrament as oriented toward healing or as oriented toward death. If we ask, ''will the patient live?'' the answer is a clear and triumphant ''yes.'' That was established on the day of resurrection, and just that is what it means to be an anointed one. But if we ask again, ''will the patient die?'' we must answer, still in accordance with the promise, ''unless the *parousia* comes first, yes.'' The meaning of every illness is dying, and every healing is resurrection.

The sacrament is more than a struggle against illness. It is the sign of the conquest of death. It seeks not to palliate, to lull, to console, but to reveal, in the light of the gospel, the meaning of sickness, and to consecrate it as sign. For sickness itself is already a sign, rich with ambiguity, revealing both our problems and our resources. As Jacques Sarano says, "Sickness is the sign of that which we are, but it is this in two ways. . . . The one *reduces* us to what we are (and nothing more); the other *calls* us to what we are (and nothing less)."[9]

As both retrospective and prospective, illness is always the passagepoint, the threshold, between a dying and a living. Situating me between the life I have lived and the life I am for, sickness is *liminal* in an unusually personal and bodily way. And it is just that liminality which calls forth the sacrament of anointing for the illumination of its ambiguity and the articulation of the transition it marks and demands. This may be transition to accustomed life patterns assumed with a renewed and deepened understanding of myself and my vocation, it may be transition to a radically transformed life, it may be transition to the glory of the kingdom. But a paschal valorization of the liminal condition need not and dare not limit the options. As symbolic structure, the liturgy of sickness has a broader scope than a mere ancillary therapeusis addressed to just this illness in just this patient. Sacramental and liturgical structures are more universal in their orientation. In the rites of affliction, indeed, we have neither a sacrament of the living nor a sacrament of the dead, but of the threshold between them. At this threshold, as in martyrdom, man finds himself at the very heart of the mystery of his being and of his being in Christ. And there he can cry, in agony and exultation, "I am crucified with Christ, and behold, I live; and the life which I now live in the flesh, I live by the grace of the Son of God who loved me and gave himself for me."

Here, both for the patient and for the community wounded by his separation from it, the outrage of disorder is subsumed to the very ground of their life, the salvation of the cross. Here the loss of everything becomes a new mode of possessing salvation. To proclaim this and to celebrate this is the purpose of the rites for the sick. Here as in all the tradition, the purpose of the rite is to reveal the presence of Christ.

But here we must return to a consideration of charismatic healing, for its end is the same. The difference between the sacrament of anointing and charismatic healing is not one of ultimate end. Both proclaim and reveal Christ and the power of his resurrection over all disorder. Both are instruments of God, and means of manifesting his glory. The covenant cultus, the sacramental economy, seeks to provide a Christian form for our living and dying. It must seek always to remain faithful both to the tradition and the tradition's dynamic of development. But it always aims at providing a continuity which can give the form of Christ to the wounds we sustain. Such a liturgical continuity manifests God, but does not contain him. Indeed, God is faithful to reveal his power in ways that are independent of this continuity, and which yet validate it by manifesting the power of him whom the tradition serves. On the other hand, it is life within the continuity, within the symbol complex, which enables us to recognize the source of the power of the charismatic, and thus the charismatic event.

What remains important is that sacramental continuity and charismatic discontinuity should vitalize each other in interaction, as the priests and the prophets of the Old Covenant, for without this the liturgy reverts to the law. Of the charism of healing there is, in fact, little to be said systematically, for it is not a systematic phenomenon. Our concern has been rather to show that it is God's sovereign power that is revealed in such phenomena, and not the unvarying content of his will for man. For most of us most of the time, it is the will of God that we should so live with ambiguity as to allow ourselves to trust in him and keep all options open to the power of his love. Illness, and not only serious illness, brings that ambiguity to a sharper focus than our living normally allows. To that ambiguity we can bring no more powerful sign than the renewal of the sign of our baptismal death and resurrection in the Anointed One. In that sign and in that assurance, we can know that the life God gives is the life to which he calls us, and that the death which is the way to it—whether the death of missing two days' wages with a stinking cold or the death that will be the last death—that death is no longer ours, but Christ's, and is the promise of his life.

Footnotes

*Editor's Note: This article, as its opening paragraph reveals, was written prior to the publication of the final text of the Rite of Anointing and Pastoral Care of the Sick *(Dec. 7, 1972), although the publication of the article corresponded closely to the time of the Apostolic Constitution* Sacram Unctionem infirmorum *(Nov. 30, 1972). A comparison of the final form of the rite with the quotation from the draft (paragraph 6 in each case) shows a closer correspondence with the Tridentine definition in the final text, a position more in line with the argument of this essay than was that of the draft. The author's argument seems as appropriate today as when first written.*

1. Rites for the Sick (Washington, D.C.: Committee on English in the Liturgy 1971) p. 2.
2. Cited by P. Palmer, *Sources of Christian Theology*, vol. 2: Sacraments and Forgiveness (Westminster, Md.: Newman Press 1960) 310.
3. Palmer, *op. cit.*, 311-312.
4. *Ibid.*, 307-308.
5. G. Dix, ed., *The Treatise on the Apostolic Tradition of St. Hippolytus of Rome* (London: S.P.C.K. 1968) pp. 10, 22.
6. Palmer, *op. cit.*, 278.
7. While reference to presbyteral anointing of the sick is found in the fifth century in Innocent I, Epistle 25 (Palmer, 283), it is clear from the same document that lay anointing continued as well. It seems the more common opinion that the use of the term *sacramentum* in this text refers not to the presbyteral anointing, but to the oil itself. For the liturgical institutionalization of the James text, one must wait for the Carolingian period.
8. J. H. van den Berg, *The Psychology of the Sickbed* (Pittsburgh: Duquesne University Press 1966) 24-25.
9. Jacques Sarano, *The Meaning of the Body* (Philadelphia: Westminster Press 1966) 158.

DEATH AS WORSHIP
Donald J. Keefe, S.J.

If death is not itself the greatest of mysteries, it is at least the moment
in which, for each of us, all other mystery is included and concluded, for
there the mystery of grace and the mystery of iniquity meet in the
intersection which is the cross, the paradigm of Christian worship. It is
the cross of Christ, the summation of his earthly life, which gives
meaning to our own ending, as it is the resurrection from death which
demands that we see our own dying as Christ saw his, as the deed by
which each of us gives himself over to the hands of the Father in a total act
of worship. And by this worship which is our death, our fallen humanity
enters fully into the redemptive mission of the Son: As this mission is
inseparable from the death of the Christ, so we cannot share in the new
creation over which the risen Christ is Lord unless we share in the mission
which culminates in the cross.

Briefly, the worship which is life in Christ requires that we die in
Christ.

This dying should not be glossed over, as though for Christians death
were merely a departure to a better world. Such an attitude trivializes
humanity, making illusion of all the grief and suffering which death
works in our lives and in the lives of those we love. Such a denial of the
reality of death makes little of Christ's death for us, reducing it to some
gnostic conjuring trick. When Paul, marvelling at the redemption worked
by Christ, cries out, ''Death, where is thy sting?'' he is speaking of the
release from the burden of sin, that release which is worked by the death
of Christ; he is not at all to be read as implying that death is a negligible
thing, little to be regarded or thought upon. From the first Epistle to the

Thessalonians, in Romans, and in the Second Epistle to the Corinthians, to the Pastoral Epistles, Paul's theology is a continual pondering on that existence in Christ which dies with him that it may rise with him. We have no business denying the loss and the bitterness of death, for in dying we share in the reality of the death of Christ, and we are too near to the scene and the liturgy of Good Friday to think that death a little or an easy thing. Christ's sacrifice makes our own death meaningful, and makes it possible for our death to be also our worship, our sacrifice; by no means does his cross remove our own: the opposite is true, for by entering into his death, our own dying has the value of worship, the worship of the cross.

In consequence, then, of the death of Christ, our life is given a focus, to become most powerful, most itself, at the point of its extinction in the negation and darkness of death. Here is more than paradox; it is the flat nonsense, at which the Sadducees and the Greeks on the Areopagus, mocked with a disdain as articulate in their day as it remains in our own. For no more than could Jesus, no more than could his Apostle, can we give convincing reasons, convincing, that is, to the unbeliever, for finding a positive significance in our dying; the faith that finds in death more and other than the final absurdity is too basic to have any argumentation underlying it. It rests upon the resurrection of our Lord. If he is not risen, St. Paul has told us, our faith is in vain. As his resurrection is not the annulment of his death on the cross but rather its validation, so our rising in him is not the nullification, the reduction to insignificance, of our own dying.

So then our death has value and meaning; so the Church of the martyrs has ever taught: Precious in the eyes of the Lord is the death of his saints, for in this do they most truly image him in whose image they are made. Such imaging of God is the very meaning of worship, and in seeking out this meaning we must remember that we do not know how to worship as we ought; there is no model of worship which we can construct by human inquiry and talent, by a misplaced reliance upon our own judgment of what is properly owing to God. That kind of worship is the domestication of God which Kierkegaard condemned in the last century, which Bonhoeffer has pilloried nearly in our own time, and which in the Book of the Apocalypse is castigated in unforgettable language as neither hot nor cold, a tepidity which nauseates the Christ who died for us. Rather, it is the self-donation of the martyr, the witness of the faith whose ultimate affirmation is his explicit entry into the death of Christ, that is the test-case of Christian worship, of Christian life. In our own day, this truth has been some little neglected by a new idiom, which prefers to speak, not of the Church militant, but rather of the pilgrim Church. This language, established in the Second Vatican Council, is intended to stress the viatory character of the Church and of the Church's institutions, an emphasis all too necessary for a generation which had come to suppose that the Latin language was constitutive for the Catholic faith. The viatory or pilgrim Church is not, however, in any tension with the Church militant: These understandings of the Church are both necessary, and neither need suppress the other. The pilgrim Church is the Church of martyrs for so long as her children shall wander in this desert which their sin has made of the world. In our own day, the notion of pilgrimage is devalued; we have heard too much of pilgrimages to this shrine or that to take seriously the hardships of the journey, and so the word conjures up a vision of pious jollity in a sedate and comfortable style. Applied to the Church, it can invoke precisely the mentality, too much at ease in our Father's house, which we have seen excoriated in the Apocalypse. To such a mentality, quite familiar to all of us, the equation of worship with death, the equation of Christian witness with martyrdom, comes as something of a shock. To the extent that we are shocked, we have forgotten that our journey toward the Kingdom is not through a green and pleasant land, but through a wilderness, even a howling wilderness, whose chaos and bitterness are as much within us as they are outside us; the desert is our very own, for we have made it out of the world which God made good.

This desert is so much our own that we can become accustomed to its climate; we can begin to find it possible to find here a full and pleasant life, and can learn to silence the conscience which tells us that such an ambition is fraudulent, that we have here no lasting city, that this night our lives may be required of us who have made ourselves so comfortable. These are the temptations of affluence, of a people who are not reminded by every feature of a harsh and painful existence that we are a fallen race, which shall find no rest until it rests in the City of God. It is hard for us, the rich to remember who we are; the poor know their world for what it is, and can find in their own destitution the apt symbol of the human condition. For we are all poor in that strict sense of being totally unable to help ourselves or those we love; we cannot, by taking thought, remove our death or theirs, and in the face of that full stop to our reality, all the blandishments of this world are ashes.

The fact of death is then that which summons us to recognize the desert for what it is; the only question which then remains is that of who we are, who must die. Does death reduce us to insignificance, as every paganism has thought? Does it place on one single level of futility the life-history of every human being who has ever existed? Does it cancel out the dignity of each of us, so that it is a matter of indifference what we do or think or say? Some philosophers, even some theologians of despair, have thought as much, but those whom men have held to be the wisest and the best have always refused the full implications of such nihilisms; the poets, the seers, the prophets have known better. On such hopes this dying race has been nourished for millennia before Christ; deprived of all assurance, men have never ceased to hope, in the very face of death. They have buried their dead with care and some approximation to reverence; such graves, such burial sites, are almost the first index of the humanity of their occupants, and this valuation of the dead is nearly the first indication of some kind of cultus, some sort of worship, among the earliest human beings. Death and worship are given together very early in human pre-history, and they remain together, for all the ability of men to prove their own insignificance.

We may affirm with some confidence then that it is death which calls us to worship, and this in a complex reaction: We are provoked by it to consider the possibility of our futility, and generally to reject this possibility, for all its surface plausibility, as finally untrue; secondly, we are driven by death to consider the human need for something like redemption, for death simply should not be, yet it is. And this turns us to God, the author of life, in a quest for that value, that worth, which is at once ours and not ours, which is lost and yet belongs to us. This quest is worship, the seeking for the vindication of the worth of our humanity at the hands of God, who is its author. This worship is inseparable from the value of our individual lives: Apart from the faith which fuels this quest, there is nothing in any of us which is worth being loved, and nothing capable of love. Nor without that faith is there anything in our world which is not blighted utterly. All positive valuation of it, in terms of truth and goodness and beauty, is reduced to illusion: supportable perhaps for a little time by those who can afford such luxuries, but without meaning in the end. For the poor man, the desert in which he wanders is absolute, apart from faith, and his destitution is without end, for without faith his world is loveless, valueless.

It is fortunate for us who are affluent and consequently forgetful of reality that we are all summoned to it, at least once in our lives, and more often, as our love for others may draw us closer to the poverty of our humanity. Death, ours or that of someone we love, is a destitution difficult to camouflage. If it is the death of someone whose life is intertwined with our own, so that the loss in some sense shakes our own foundations, we must either cease upon this dying to love the dead, or love them in a faith which then becomes more clear and explicit for being the correlate of love.

Those human bonds, forged of our baser metal, whether of family, of neighborhood, of race or nation, cannot resist the acid test of death. By it they are either brought to nothingness, or are transmuted into the agape, the love of which Paul wrote in 1 Corinthians 13. This transmutation of our all too human loves into the stuff that outlasts time and death is at the same time our baptism, our entry into the redemptive death of Christ, and thus into the Church which is his body. That body is risen, and is still with us, and our worship is the celebration of this truth, this reality which we are given in the pledge of the Eucharist, the sustaining manna in this desert through which we live, in which we are to share in the salvific work of Christ. It is in the circumstances of death that our dependence upon this risen life is brought home to us most clearly; this is obvious enough, and the familiar death-bed conversion accounts are eloquent testimony that then at least we are forced to acknowledge who we are, and how total is our dependence.

But even so, the proportion of instances in which one has an opportunity for such reflection is small, given the enormous range of human history and pre-history; even in our own century, the indiscriminate carnage of two major wars and half a hundred minor ones has littered the earth with tens of millions whose death looks remarkably unlike prayer; what have these to do with the thanksgiving which is Christian worship? What has the love of God to do with the slaughter of the battle of the Somme in 1916, with the shambles at Caporetto or Loos or the Argonne?

The story of the Angel of Mons stales somewhat at Verdun, where somewhere between a million and a half and three million men lost their lives over a year and a half—and these are only the battle casualties, in which notions of self-sacrifice and courage can lend some semblance of meaning to death. But what of such plagues as swept over Europe in the late Middle Ages, destroying whole towns, and wiping out a third of the entire population of Christendom? What of the mindless lottery that leaves some fifty thousand dead on our highways every year?—And so on, and so on. Death, on the average, has little concern for the niceties, with preparation and penitence: Now, as ever, we know not the day nor the hour. How then can death be worship? How, apart from pious imaginings, can it mean anything at all, even in the life of a saint? Augustine died in bed at 75; Robert Southwell was drawn and quartered some years short of 30; how can their deaths be compared in the single notion of worship? Some answer must be made if it is death as such which is worship and not simply the life, long or short, which preceded it.

Quite clearly, no human person's death, taken in itself, is a matter of any particular importance, as the individual himself is not. Nature intends what is permanent, so the Philosopher said, and individuals, being highly impermanent, have no significance which touches any cosmic concern. Life goes on whether or not we share in it and the teeming millions who are here today will be gone tomorrow without detriment to a world which indeed needs people, but not, so it appears, any particular people; all of us are eminently replaceable. But so to look upon the human situation is in fact to hate it; it is to wish the annulment of the human, to want to reduce the individual man to a thing, neither just nor sinner, but a mere cog in a vast and implacable machine.

We have seen that the redemptive work of Christ has revealed the falsity of such a nihilism; we are each significant and freed from cosmic necessities, free for the heights of sanctity as for the depths of malice by the freedom of the Spirit: by this Spirit, we are freed to love each other, or to hate each other, and this freedom was purchased at a great price. It is not possible, in this brief compass, to deal with the primal tragedy of the Fall of man: it is enough to say here that in the primordial moment of the creation of men in their freedom, a creation possible only by the presence of the Christ in his creation, the gift of freedom was refused, and the creation fell with the men upon whom it is focused to an unfree level of what we have called cosmic servitude; men became subject to the physical laws of the material universe instead of being free in that universe, and these cosmic laws are fundamentally inimical to life: The wage of sin is death.

The original sin of the refusal of freedom was not the undoing of creation, but it made the presence of Christ, in the world which is created in him, to be recreative of the fallen world, rather than simply creative of it. We have no justification for entering into speculation of what an unfallen world would have been like; what we do know is that the world is created in Christ and that this is also the creation of man in freedom. This freedom has been refused, but not wholly, for it is still offered by the presence of Christ in the world of men—but the offer by Christ of the Spirit which he was sent by the Father to give is also his redemptive life, and more especially, his redemptive death. By that death, his humanity is freed of this cosmos: Death has no more power over him, and since it is in him that we are created continually, so also death has no final power over us. This is true, as Karl Barth recently insisted, as Origen insisted 18 centuries ago, whether we like it or not; to be at all, is to be in Christ; the damned are no less dependent upon the Christ than the elect. Whatever our relation to God, whether it be that of a pilgrim in search of the Kingdom, that of the saint who has attained it, or the damned who has rejected it, we have that relation in Christ, without whom we are nothing at all. This relationship of ourselves to God is fundamentally our creation in Christ, a creation which is radically complete in the presence of Christ in our world: that is, in his life, his passion, his death, and in the eucharistic worship of the Church, by which he is present, in his risen humanity to the end of the world, for he has not left us orphans. He is risen, and still with us.

It is the intimate relation between the worship which is the Eucharist, and the worship which is our death, that we must begin to understand. Perhaps the best model or exemplar of what this relation is may be derived from the notion of the inseparability of Christ's presence in this world and his mission or "sending" by the Father, a notion which pervades the Epistle to the Hebrews. Christ's presence here, his reality, is to do the will of the Father; for this he was sent into the world. This is the meaning of his humanity, and consequently it is the meaning of all humanity, and it is this meaning, this humanity, this obedience to the will of the Father, which we celebrate in the worship, the eucharistic worship of the Church. That obedience led Christ to a criminal's death on a cross; in that death, he affirmed his own reality, his divinity and his humanity, to be that of the Son of God who is also the Son of Man, the First Adam and the last, the Alpha and the Omega. In his resurrection, that affirmation, made in the abandonment and the bitterness of his last hours, was vindicated, and the fall, which had hidden and brought to death the humanity which is created in him and which he handed over totally to the Father in his death, is overcome in his Resurrection by the Father as the final meaning, the full accomplishment, of his sending of the Son to do his will. It was necessary, as St. Luke records, that the Christ should die; if not, the mission of the Son by the Father, which is the full creation of the world and of humanity, is not fulfilled, and it must be fulfilled.

But it is not fulfilled by any overpowering by the omnipotence of God of our humanity, of our freedom; for our obedience must be in freedom, or it is not obedience, and our creation in the freedom of Christ, the freedom of the Sons of God, would be impossible. Further, the very purpose of the mission of the Son, which is to give the spirit of sonship, of obedience, of freedom, of life, would not be accomplished, but it is accomplished by the divine omnipotence which is not competitive with our freedom, but precisely is creative of it.

This Holy Spirit, by which we say "Abba, Father" is the gift to us of our humanity, our freedom, our sonship, our obedience: by this gift we are created, by it we live. And finally, by this gift we are enabled to understand the revelation of Christ; a hearing ear is given us, and we come to see who we are, what it is to be human, what it is to be free, and what is the worship which is the meaning of our life. Our freedom is understood, dimly, hesitantly, as in a glass darkly, to consist in that lifting up of our minds and hearts to God by which, over few years or many, we are unchained from our necessities to the point that in the encounter with the last necessity of death we are free indeed. And this is gift; it is not earned, not by an Augustine, not by a Southwell, not by any of the myriad millions who have inhabited the earth, not by any of the sons of Adam or the daughters of Eve. Nor is the gift to this one or that; it is to the Church. It is the creation of the body of Christ and of the history in which that body grows to the full maturity of the Christ, its head. This growth is hidden; we cannot judge or pass upon it. Rather, in it, our use of the gift is judged. This growth is universal; as Christ died for all men, so all men die in him. But this growth is not automatic, as some incautious ecumenists would suppose and as the several advocates of theories of predestination have believed, for it is worship, personal and free; it can be refused. Our human inability to judge the worship of others, to pass upon their sanctity, does not mean that there is no judgment; as we are created in Christ, so we are judged by him. This judgment is as much a part of his obedience to the Father as any other aspect of his mission. We, who can have no peace until we rest in him, can refuse that rest. His judgment is respectful of our choice, for it is left to each of us to reply on our own responsibility to the only important question, ''What think you of Christ?'' As we answer, so we are.

For those who die in the distraction of disease or war or the work of the world, who die suddenly in whatever way, death is still the ultimate dispossession of all the baggage which constitutes our poverty while masking it, and which all too often has played no part in our worship, so that it impedes rather than enriches our freedom. We are dispossessed as well of all the burden of age, illness, and the like; we stand, in short, outside the cosmic necessities which prevent all of us now from saying decisively, definitively, personally, and with a total assurance, precisely who we are. This standing outside the cosmos is the meaning of death. We are separated, not from bodiliness as such, but from the body which binds us to this fallen world. And in the freedom thus given us in death, we utter ourselves to God.

In that utterance, we know ourselves even as we are known. A life has prepared for this moment, whether the life be long or short, but the preparation is not the utterance, for only in death is one substantially accountable for oneself beyond all possibility of error, with a total clarity of decision which is decisive utterly. This decision is the moment of mystery: Only Christianity has dared assert so enormous a human freedom and dignity before the majesty of God. The decision is either a total unconditioned love of God in Christ, or a total aversion; no hesitation or compromise is possible. If our decision is worship, then our vision of the Christ seated at the right hand of the Father is our purgatory and our beatitude; if, as with Milton's fallen angel, we refuse that worship, we stand condemned before the Son of man, whose judgment of us is precisely the truth we have uttered of ourselves: as we know him, so we have him.

With these considerations, my treatment of this theme is ended; it is not of course complete, for the meaning of death raises questions which not even a lifetime of study can measure. What I have said, I have of course said as a private theologian, speaking responsibly, I trust, but with no more authority than attaches to the reasoning I have employed—which in a brief sketch cannot but be scanty. In concluding, let me read a few lines from the First Epistle to the Corinthians, which you have all heard many times, and which it is well to hear again:

> If there is no resurrection from the dead, Christ himself cannot have been raised, and if Christ has not been raised then our preaching is useless and your believing is useless; indeed, we are shown up as witnesses who have committed perjury before God, because we swore in evidence before God that he had raised Christ to life. For if the dead are not raised, Christ has not been raised, and if Christ has not been raised, you are still in your sins. And what is more serious, all who have died in Christ have perished. If our hope in Christ has been for this life only we are the most unfortunate of people.
> But Christ has in fact been raised from the dead, the first-fruits of all who have fallen asleep. Death came through one man and in the same way the resurrection of the dead has come through one man. Just as all men die in Adam, so all men will be brought to life in Christ, but all of them in their proper order: Christ, as first-fruits, and then, after the coming of Christ, those who belong to him. After that will come the end, when he hands over the kingdom to God the Father, having done away with every sovereignty, authority and power. For he must be king until he has put all his enemies under his feet, and the last of the enemies to be destroyed is death.

The eucharistic complement of this passage in 1 Corinthians is taken from the 6th chapter of the Gospel according to John:

> I am the bread of life. He who comes to me will never be hungry; he who believes in me will never thirst. But, as I have told you, you can see me and still you do not believe. All that the Father gives me will come to me, and whoever comes to me I shall not turn him

away; because I have come from heaven, not to do my own will, but to do the will of the one who sent me. Now the will of him who sent me is that I should lose nothing of all that he has given to me and that I should raise it up on the last day. Yes, it is my Father's will that whoever sees the Son and believes in him shall have eternal life, and that I shall raise him up on the last day.

Taken together, these lines from Paul and from the Johannine Gospel provide some basis for the assertion that our life and our death are inseparable from our eucharistic worship in the Church, and that only by entering into the mystery of his death can we enter into the fullness of his life.

EPILOG

"CHRIST, DYING AND LIVING STILL . . ."
Aidan Kavanagh, O.S.B.

There can be no doubt that Baptism and Eucharist are the two premier events in the Church's sacramental life. Not only do all the other sacraments flow from these two, but Baptism is the way the Eucharist begins, and Eucharist is the way Baptism is sustained in the life of the Church. This means that, far from being totally separate events, Baptism and the Eucharist work in the closest tandem. Their content is identical: Christ dying and rising still among the members of his Church, only the idiom of its realization differs. In one case the idiom involves bathing, while in the other the idiom involves dining together.

Over the past several centuries, Catholics have concentrated perhaps too much on the idiomatic differences that set Baptism and Eucharist apart from each other. The differences are obviously real. What is not so obvious is the equally real and crucially important identity of content shared by the two events. There is but one Christ, dying and rising, who pervades both the Church and all the Church's deeds. To be apart from him, in whatever degree, is, to that same degree, to be apart from the Church and its deeds. To be in him, in whatever degree, is, to that same degree, to be in his Church and involved in its deeds. As bands on a spectrum reflect one light, so into the convolutions of our lives the sacramental deeds of the Church refract one Christ, who is dying and rising still.

Yet of all the sacraments, Baptism and Eucharist assert this truth in the most emphatic way. I may live my own life in him without marriage or ordination, but I cannot survive without Baptism and Eucharist. Nor can the community of faith in which I live remain faithful without constant access to these two. A eucharistic group that is neither baptized nor baptizing may be many things, but it is not the Church. A baptized and baptizing group that never celebrates its death and life in Christ around the Lord's Table may be a sect of some vigor, but it is not the Church.

It can be argued that, while Catholics have rarely been tempted to this second course, we have perhaps come close to succumbing to the first. We may be the world's collective expert on the Mass, but we have had little to say or do about Baptism. This is an awkward position to be in if Baptism is the way Eucharist begins and Eucharist is the way Baptism is sustained in the Church.

For to know Christ only in terms of bread and wine can be to know him only in the dining room as guest and host. It is a valid enough knowledge. But it is inevitably partial and perhaps too civil—easily layered over with a brittle etiquette soon rendered obsolete when cultures change. It is a knowledge prone less to robustness than to niceness, reducing Eucharist to a sort of ecumenical high tea. The Lord as guest is readily sentimentalized. The Lord as host is readily transformed into an indulgent therapist of whatever lusts are momentarily ours. This produces arrogance in the young, depression among the old, and apostasy for the Church.

Two main forces have traditionally balanced this tendency and checked its spread. The first has been the attempt at keeping Eucharist as "banquet or meal" in tension with a perception of Eucharist as "sacrifice." The tension reminds one that, however elegant the knowledge of the dining room may be, it begins in the soil, in the barnyard and in the slaughterhouse—amidst strangled cries, congealing blood, and spitting fat in the pan. Table manners depend upon something's having been grabbed by the throat. A knowledge ignorant of these dark and murderous "gestures charged with soul" is sterile rather than elegant, science rather than wisdom, artifice rather than art. It is love without passion, the Church without a cross, a house with a dining room but no kitchen, a feast of frozen dinners, a heartless life. The pious (religious and secular) would have us dine on abstractions; but we are, in fact, carnivores—a bloody bunch.

Sacrifice may have many facets, but it always has a victim.

The second force that has traditionally balanced and checked the spread of a hypercivilized eucharistic knowledge of Christ has been baptismal. Here Christ is known not as he is in the dining room as guest, host, and food. Baptism's knowledge of Christ is that of the bathhouse. It is not a mannered knowledge, for manners, etiquette, and artifice fall away as one takes off one's clothes. It is a knowledge of appalling candor, robust and intimate. It is less mental than bodily, as when lovers are said to "know" each other. It is the inspired knowledge of the Song of Songs rather than that of the Epistle to the Romans, for God speaks not only in logic but also in smell and in the feel of oil and warm water on the skin. God says much in Romans about his union with humankind, but he says even more about the same mystery in the soft porn of the Song of Songs. There can be little doubt that more people have been willing to die for a lover than for a doctrine of regeneration.

This sort of knowledge is, of course, not awfully civil. It is rarely brittle and never rendered obsolete when cultures change. It abides. Profligates and great mystics share it: converts and lovers learn it quickly. Only the conventionally pious avoid it, rather for the same reasons, one suspects, that bourgeois society avoids having naked people to tea. A mannered situation cannot survive too much knowledge. Thus the noble aunt in Oscar Wilde's *The Importance of Being Earnest*, on being informed of her two grown nephews' approaching baptism, huffs that such a thing must be regarded as grotesque and irreligious.

That a bathhouse Christ leaves those grown accustomed only to a dining-room Christ uncomfortable is precisely what it should do. For the Great Civilizer was often uncivil, the Most Nice distinctly un-nice, the Cornerstone of all subsequent conventions quite unconventional, the Peacemaker sometimes unpeaceful. He was the Paradox Unequaled. Nothing less could have recreated the world.

To live in *this* knowledge, it is not enough to be a little mad. One has to be among the living dead—dead to all that is not, alive to all that is. For the sin we call original separates us not only from God but from all that is—his creation. It is an option that amounts to choosing ourselves instead of all else and then attempting to recreate all else in our own image. Our sorry state is the result of everything's intractable refusal to accept our tacky little providence as counterfeit for the Real Thing.

Feeling rejected and then frustrated, we savage both ourselves and everything that crosses our path, becoming alien in our own house. Death is the only exit. Which is why, when God came among us, even he had to go this way. Thus our Christian dinners are wakes, and our bathhouses are tombs—not for Christ but for ourselves. He sits at our table fragrant with the ointment of his own blood, and we dine not only with him but on him.

For the "unlively dead," such things are grotesque and irreligious indeed. But for the "living dead" they are eucharists and baptisms, births and banquets in which Life is celebrated as it was meant to be.

Having said all this, one would be less than candid if one did not admit that it suggests a vision which seems to be well-nigh irretrievable in our parishes today. This may be so because it has become difficult for us to take Baptism seriously anymore. Not only is it usually done rather hastily, upon sleeping infants, in private, with a minimum of symbolic robustness (teacups of water and dabs of oil), it has also been allowed to gloat free of the community's regular worship-life, especially at the Easter Vigil. And its normal finale—Confirmation and the reception of Holy Communion—has been separated into distinct parts often delayed for years or even decades. We are thus left with a pastel, truncated rite that looks more like a modest exorcism from sin or a rather dispensable social occasion. By its universal association with infancy, Baptism itself becomes a grotesque and irreligious thing to force on normal, healthy adults. This being the case, pastoral emphasis has shifted away from Baptism to the more crucial rites and ages such as Penance and First Communion for children and Confirmation for adolescents, with religious education and counseling programs to match. The shift encourages us to become fixated on youth, leaving baptized adults to shift for themselves, so far as the Gospel is concerned, and unbaptized adults unevangelized.

A Church such as this may not be apostate, but it is surely suffering from sclerosis. It will not hold its people for long if it moves into classrooms and office buildings, for it has nothing significant to say in these places that everyone else cannot say as well or better. To mutter to oneself is not the best way of proclaiming the Good News of Jesus dead and risen. To do this as it should be done, the Church will have to be found speaking from places that teachers and bureaucrats never frequent, but which keep a hold in terror and fascination upon the human spirit: tombs, barnyards, tubs, scaffolds, and smoking altars. The Church must tell about death and life from sites where the two meet and wrestle. And it must say these things not only in words but in "gestures charged with soul"—first of all to those who are old enough to be aware that they are, in fact, participants in the match rather than spectators at it.

It is a grim and serious business which must not be trivialized into mere ideology. It is not a situation comedy, nor is its peculiar knowledge reducible to some new therapeutic fad. Precisely because the match is grim and serious, its winning makes true celebration possible. Only those who have stared death in the face, seen their own reflection there, and thrown both to the ground in a bloody fight really know how to laugh. Having, like Dante, climbed down the shaggy sides of evil itself in their own conversion, these know an Easter morning whey they see one. Then the wake becomes a banquet, the tomb an oasis where the waters of creation sparkle up fresh beneath the Tree of Life.

It is so elemental an occurrence that it cannot be spoken of in mere prose. It requires snakes in the grass, bread and wine on the table, water and oil in the bath, and luminous lambs standing slain in courthouse squares. It cannot be put on a bumper sticker or in a missalette, for it is not a text. It is the recreation of the world.

If I really thought this occurrence and all that it implies were irretrievable, I would despair of the Church, for it is of this that Christ made his Church unique minister to the world. When he commanded the Church to go and teach, he did not mean physics or the social sciences or liturgical ceremonial. He meant that it should go out from itself, announcing the Good News that all is made new in Christ and forming men and women to live a wholly new life in a new creation. The point of complete entry into this is the burial-bath of Baptism into Christ himself. The Church is not a vague movement of gentle persons benignly disposed toward things in general. The Church is a blood-filled corps of those who have been plunged into Christ's death and who live his eerie resurrection-life around a sacrificial table. To these nothing human or divine is alien. They are the living battlefield where heaven and earth, life and death, spirit and flesh slam together and fuse. Baptism is nothing less than Christ's own passion, death, and resurrection thrown open to all: it is the Church's constant birth, fresh and new.

Baptism does not relieve the disease of original sin: it cures it, leaving its scars like trophies. Baptism does not offer a better set of therapies to soften death's inevitability: it destroys death itself. Baptism does not confirm bureaucracy and status quo: it dissolves the first and overturns the second. Baptism does not insulate us against reality: it throws back the covers and kicks us out to dance naked with the real in the light of the moon.

To know Christ baptismally is to know him in the awesome discovery of conversion. To live Christ baptismally is to know him in the subtle process of being formed by grace in heart and mind, body and soul, emotions and memory—through prayer and fasting and good works and contemplation. To be formed in Christ baptismally is to know him in water and oil, in bread and wine.

His power to do something *for* us is, as Thomas Jefferson said of the civil state, commensurate with his being able to do something *to* us. But unlike the state, what Christ does to us gives life and meaning only to what we have already, barrenly, done to him. We broke his body, and he feeds us upon it. We shed his blood, and he gives it to us as drink to rejoice our hearts. We buried him wrapped in rags in a borrowed tomb, and he submerges us in living water, anoints us with perfume. We turned him out, and he invites us in to dine with him beside the hearthfire of creation. We stilled his breathing, and he blows into us, screaming like the newborn, his own Spirit.

Yet even this is not enough, nor is it where the scandal lies. For to know him baptismally is to know him as we were first known when creation was new. Baptismal iconography has always imaged Baptism as cosmic rebirth, Eden restored. Early baptistries, decorated to resemble paradise, were filled with fertility, vines, sunlight, water, and a humid atmosphere. They were gloriously womb-like, for from them issued a new People whose purpose in life was to beget others by the Church, Christ's bride, in his power. Thus the ancient inscription in the baptistry of the Pope's cathedral in Rome reads:

Here is born
in Spirit-soaked fertility
a brood predestined
to Another City,

begotten by God's blowing
and borne upon this torrent
by the Church
   their Virgin Mother.
Reborn in these depths,
they reach for Heaven's Kingdom,
the born but once
   unrecognizable by felicity.
This pool is life
   that floods the world;
the wounds of Christ
   its awesome source.
Sinner sink beneath
   this sacred surf
that swallows age
   and spits up youth.
Sinner here scour sin away
   down to innocence,
for they know no enmity who are
by one Font, one Spirit,
and one Faith made one.
Sinner shudder not
   at sin's kinds and number:
for those born here are holy.

Here is the scandal. The knowledge of Baptism is not just knowing
what has been done to one as a passive receiver. The baptized also know
that, having been born into Christ, they have become cooperators in him
with respect to everyone and everything else. His broken body is my
broken body upon which others feed. His blood spilled is my blood shed
to rejoice the hearts of all. His tomb is mine, and in it others die to rise
again. I have become him, the Stranger, and through me he beats the
bushes, herding everyone in to dinner by creation's fireside. His unique
Spirit I breathe into each of my brothers and sisters. For he and I have
merged by grace into one being, and we abide together for the life of the
world.

Baptism enables me, when I look upon the host at Communion-time, to see not just bread and not only a Christ otherwise absent from my life, but to see myself in him, a living member of his Body, the Church. It is to this I say Amen before I receive what I have become. This is no longer just knowledge. It is wisdom.

Lest it be thought that I am trying to exalt Baptism at the expense of Eucharist, it must be remembered that Catholic teaching has always insisted that Baptism is the necessary condition for valid eucharistic activity. For this reason, the early Church dismissed the unbaptized from the assembly before the eucharistic prayer began, not because those not yet baptized were unworthy of the Eucharist, but because they were incapable of it. To celebrate Christ's Body, it is necessary to be a member of that Body, the Church.

The catechumenate, which was the formation program by which people were prepared for this membership, was a long-term process that emphasized less what we today would call religious education and more spiritual and moral formation. But the catechumenate was far more than just a formation program for non-Christians. It was regarded as an essential Church structure, an *order* not unlike the *orders* of ministry and the *order* of the baptized faithful. Catechumens were thus regarded not as pagans but as Christians who had already begun to believe in Christ but—rather like the apostles in the early days of their being called by the Lord to follow him—had not yet reached an initial maturity in faith that could bear the stress of full enfranchisement in the Body of Christ by being plunged into his death. Hearer of the Word and follower of Christ the catechumen had to be. And for this reason, the Church regarded him or her as an indispensable reminder of, and source of information about, its own nature as a community of continual conversion in Christ. The Church focused the whole of its most important time of the year, the Easter-preparatory time of Lent, upon the catechumens, viewing them almost as living "sacraments" of conversion who revealed its costs and glories. The Lenten readings thus were directed not only at the catechumen but at the whole Church, as both prepared to relive Christ's passage from death to life, from Good Friday through the Easter Vigil (when baptisms were regularly done). The great lessons of Lent—the story of the flood, of Jonah and the fish, of Susanna and the dirty old voyeurs, of the Exodus—sank so deep into the Christian consciousness as icons of turning from death to life that their scenes appear over and over again on early Christian baptistries, sarcophagi, mausoleums, catacombs, statuary, vessels, and even coins.

Such an intense climate of baptismal piety energized the Church to feats of evangelization and to pastoral, theological, and liturgical creativity hardly equaled since. The Church has always been at its most vigorous the closer it has stayed to cross and font.

In this light, several factors today give one cause for optimism, because all of them betray a growing awareness of the centrality of baptismal knowledge for Christian renewal. One such factor is the realization of how essential the spiritual formation of adults is to the Church. Charismatic groups are largely adult affairs, and their emphasis upon conversion, the quality of prayer, and communal support refurbishes elements that once were the core of the catechumenate as a structure within every local church.

Another factor is an increasing diversification of ministry within the Church. With this, it becomes less possible to sustain the fatal assumption that to be a bishop or priest is to be a "first-class citizen" in the Church, as opposed to everyone else, or that the aristocracy of ordained ministries at the top rests upon a proletariat of the baptized at the bottom. The assumption is fatal because of the warp it introduces into the nature of the Church and its sacraments. It is Baptism which is necessary for salvation, not Holy Orders. Mrs. Murphy is not baptized to serve her pastor: he was ordained to serve her.

A third factor is the baptismal reforms introduced since the Second Vatican Council, in particular the Rite of Christian Initiation of Adults (1972). This Rite not only restores the catechumenate and emphasizes the organic unity of the sacraments of Christian initiation (Baptism, Confirmation, and Eucharist, in that order), but it implies that baptism of adults should be the norm, thus putting a much needed premium on catechesis as conversion-therapy—rather than as classroom religious education. It also implies that, if there are to be sufficient adult candidates for its baptismal norm to become anything more than an embalmed ideal, evangelization of the unchurched must be placed much higher on the list of priorities than is presently the case in the Church. A Church in which infant baptisms outnumber those of adults is perhaps not evangelical enough.

A fourth and final factor is personal, and thus not wholly verifiable. It is my own intuition that we have begun to see through some of the recent totalitarianisms we absorbed as we leaped into relevance during the past decade. A colleague has referred to this as jettisoning some of the "wide load" we hauled out of the sixties into the present. In short, perhaps we are relearning (thanks at least to Vietnam, Richard Nixon, Charles Manson, and cold homes) the lesson St. Paul taught us in 2 Corinthians:

> For it is not ourselves that we are preaching, but Christ Jesus as the Lord and ourselves as your servants for Jesus' sake. It is the same God that said, 'Let light shine out of darkness,' who has shone in our hearts to radiate the knowledge of God's glory in the face of Christ. But we have this treasure in earthen vessels, to show that such overwhelming power comes from God and not from us. We are afflicted in every way, but never crushed; perplexed, but not driven to despair; persecuted, but not abandoned; struck down, but not slain; always bearing in our body Jesus' death, that his life may be seen in us.

Such is our mad good news, the meaning of our catechesis, the substance of our Lent and Easter, the content of our fonts, the food on our tables, the Life we live. It is the essence of the Church as it serves the world, judging it even as it holds it in its arms. It is the Ancient Wisdom we must continue to grasp firmly if we are to remain faithful to the present—shuttling back and forth between font and table, learning it whole and always anew. It is our old Naomi, we its loving Ruths.